# A Man of Faith

# A MAN of FAITH

The Spiritual Journey of George W. Bush

## DAVID AIKMAN

**W PUBLISHING GROUP**
A Division of Thomas Nelson Publishers
*Since 1798*

www.wpublishinggroup.com

A Man of Faith

© 2004 by David Aikman.

Published by W Publishing Group, a Division of Thomas Nelson, Inc., P. O. Box 141000, Nashville, Tennessee 37214.

All Scripture quotations, unless otherwise indicated, are taken from The New King James Version. Copyright © 1979, 1980, 1982, Thomas Nelson, Inc. Used by permission.

Scripture quotations marked NIV are taken from the Holy Bible, New International Version. Copyright © 1973, 1978, 1984, International Bible Society. Used by permission of Zondervan Bible Publishers.

Photographic research and acquisition provided by Creative Solutions, Atlington, Texas.

Interior design by Inside Out Design & Typesetting, Fort Worth, Texas.

*Library of Congress Cataloging-in-Publication Data*

Aikman, David, 1944–
    A man of faith : the spiritual journey of George W. Bush / David Aikman.
        p. cm.
    Includes bibliographical references.
    ISBN 0-8499-1811-1
1. Church and state—United States.   2. Bush, George W. (George Walker), 1946—
Religion.   3. United States—Religion.
I.   Bush, George W. (George Walker), 1946–      II. Title.
    BR516.A45   2004
    973.931' 092—dc22
2004002069                                                                                          CIP

*Printed in the United States of America*
04 05 06 07 08 BVG 5 4 3 2 1

*This book is dedicated*

*to all who love the United States*

*and who pray for the nation*

*and its leadership.*

# CONTENTS

# Acknowledgments

Many people have made this book possible. I would like, first, to thank President George W. Bush for agreeing to allow me to speak with some of his close Christian friends, family members, and associates. These include Secretary of Commerce Don Evans, Senior Political Advisor Karl Rove, former White House communications director Karen Hughes, Pastor Mark Craig of Highland Park Presbyterian Church in Dallas, Texas, Pastor Jim Mayfield of Tarrytown Methodist Church in Austin, Texas, Barbara Bush, and Michael W. Smith. Karl Rove acted as intermediary for my conversations or meetings with the above.

In Houston, Texas, Pastor Ed Young was hospitable, helpful and insightful. I much appreciate the patient willingness of B. J. Goergen in Karl Rove's office to pass messages back and forth during sometimes very busy periods in the White House.

In Midland, Texas, I owe a great debt to the generous assistance of Don Poage and Jim Sales.

At W Publishing Group, I deeply appreciate the friendly support and interest throughout the project of David Moberg and Greg Daniel.

My primary research assistant from the outset of the venture, Diane

Bryhn, gathered material of invaluable usefulness from many different directions and was a constant source of good suggestions and helpful contacts. During the writing phase a good friend in Beijing, Charlene Fu, did sterling and very fast work editing the material and making it far more palatable than it would otherwise have been. Needless to say, all factual mistakes and stylistic solecisms are entirely my responsibility.

I am very grateful to Deal Hudson, editor of *Crisis* magaazine, and Ambassador Mercer Reynolds, for their kind assistance in putting this book together.

I would like to thank David Sutherland, resident of Hong Kong, for generously inviting me to the Philippines to participate in a seminar called "Vacation with a Purpose," and for tolerating my spending long hours there completing the book.

I would like to thank my family: my wife Nonie, my two daughters Abbie and Amanda, and our dog Chip for putting up with me as I beavered away for unreasonable hours in my office at home.

# 1

## A POLITICAL BOMBSHELL

*When you turn your heart and your life over to Christ, when you
accept Christ as the Savior, it changes your heart.
It changes your life. And that's what happened to me.*

—GEORGE W. BUSH

THE GREATER DES MOINES CIVIC CENTER — a large, crisply modern, concrete structure on Walnut Street—has a capacity of close to three thousand people, but on the evening of December 13, 1999, it was by most estimates only half-full. The tickets for the event were free, and about twenty-four hundred had been handed out by Iowa Republican Party activists to likely, or at least possible, audience members. Obviously, some of the recipients decided to stay home.

The weather in this city in the very heart of the United States had turned chilly, and local weathermen were forecasting the imminent arrival of the first of the winter storms that can sweep over the Plains states from late November onward. But the mood in the civic center was upbeat, even festive. After all, this was the first debate in Iowa among the Republican Party's six presidential hopefuls. Several partisans of the six candidates had shown up wearing T-shirts supporting their heroes: Gary Bauer, Governor George W. Bush, Steve Forbes, Senator Orrin Hatch, Alan Keyes, and Senator John McCain.

The event was jointly hosted by NBC and the local Des Moines affiliate on WHO-TV, Channel 13. The cohosts were Tom Brokaw and WHO's talented and sharp local anchor John Bachman. The Iowan had flown to New York to discuss with Brokaw how the debate should be handled.

"Let's open it up and have it more freewheeling," Brokaw had suggested, and Bachman readily agreed.

The Iowa caucuses were still six weeks away, and all the candidates had also been stomping through New Hampshire preparing for the primary scheduled February 1, 2000. Tonight would be the best opportunity for a national television audience to see the six presidential hopefuls up-close, sparring among themselves.

A dark-blue stage background provided a minimalist setting for the candidates, who were seated onstage, side by side on the kind of chairs often found outside the human resources office of a Silicon Valley start-up. The candidates all wore dark-gray or dark-blue suits and simple red or blue ties; it was a uniform that made it clear that they all belonged to the same club. Indeed, in a way, they did—a Republican Party eager for political power after seven years of a Democratic White House.

The "freewheeling" rules of the debate allowed candidates to ask questions of each other and, if they felt the urge, to jump in with a comment on something any of the others had said. There were no bells or buzzers cramping this loose style. Still, for the first several minutes there were no pyrotechnics. The questions, first to Senator McCain, focused on the tragic Columbine High School shooting in 1999 and what might have caused such terrible behavior among American schoolchildren, on federal involvement in health insurance programs, on ethanol, on trade with China, on the Test Ban Treaty, and on tax cuts.

Then Bachman took the microphone from Brokaw and announced that he had a question for the candidates from "the good folks of Iowa," meaning that he had winnowed it out from a collection of questions submitted in advance by viewers.

"What political philosopher, Mr. Forbes," he asked, "do you most identify with and why?" Then he paused half-apologetically and added, "Which gives the remaining five time to think. I'm sorry." The audience chuckled loudly.

"John Locke," said Forbes, because he had "set the stage for what became a revolution."

Next Bachman turned to Alan Keyes, who said he thought that "the founders of this country" had had a profound effect on his own thinking. Playing the role of club radical, Keyes said America ought to "get back to their thinking" and even abolish income tax, funding the government through "tariffs, duties, and excise taxes" so that people could get back control of their money, "instead of having to depend on nice politicians like Mr. Bush or bad politicians like Bill Clinton." The partisan Republican audience of about fifteen hundred applauded.

Then Bush jumped in. "At least he called me nice," he said, drawing broad laughter from the audience.

"Governor Bush," Bachman resumed, "a philosopher-thinker, and why."

"Christ," said Bush without hesitation, "because he changed my heart."

There was a moment of almost shocked silence. Bachman, realizing that there needed to be a follow-up, turned back to Bush. "I think the viewers would like to know more on how he's changed your heart," he added.

"Well, if you don't know," Bush rejoined, "it's going to be hard to explain." His face took on an expression close to a smirk when he said this, irritating some observers who didn't like the remark in the first place.

But Bachman later said he had not interpreted this as a "you-dummy" response: "I was still caught unprepared because it [the answer] was so brief," Bachman explained.

In his follow-up, Bush elaborated, "When you turn your heart and your life over to Christ, when you accept Christ as the Savior, it changes your heart. It changes your life. And that's what happened to me."

Once again, there was a brief, almost stunned silence in the auditorium. "People were surprised and perhaps a little bit shocked," recalled Karen Hughes, who was Bush's communications director during the campaign and who attended almost every major appearance of candidate Bush. But then the audience erupted in a cascade of applause, despite the fact that Brokaw and Bachman earlier on had sternly instructed the audience not to display partisan applause at any point during the debate.

"Senator Hatch, Senator Hatch?" Bachman asked insistently, trying to move past the noisy audience response and get the debate back on track. "I agree with that," Hatch replied, "but I think it goes without saying—no question in my mind." Presumably, he meant Christ.

When it came to Senator McCain, the reply was Theodore Roosevelt. But Gary Bauer came back to Christ, starting off his response by quoting Christ from Matthew 25:35: "'I was hungry, and you fed me. I was thirsty, and you gave me drink. I was a stranger and you welcomed me.' Christ, with these words, taught all of us about our obligations to each other, to the unborn child, to those living in poverty, the need for us to be together regardless of the color of our skin. There is no figure in human history who, through his life, his death, and his resurrection has changed the world for millions, billions, countless [sic] of people. If America's in trouble in the next century, it will be because [we ignored] what he taught us, Tom."

Now there was more loud applause. Brokaw, who had now taken over from Bachman, paused briefly to let it subside before moving the questioning back to more familiar, political ground.

But the deed was done. The political bombshell had exploded. Nothing later in the evening matched the terse, almost awkward moment that followed Bush's utterance of the name Christ. Nothing aroused the attention of analysts or the wrath of critics quite as much either. Watching the debate on TV in Washington, D.C., was Kristi Hamrick, a conservative political consultant at the time and still today a keen evangelical churchgoer. "It was an astounding moment," she said. "It was absolutely exhilarating to see someone at that level be unafraid. I was taken aback by the fearlessness of the remark. I felt at that moment that Bush would be the president."

———————————————

PERHAPS MORE THAN ONE of Bush's Republican fellow aspirants that evening wished he had made the Christ comment first. Gary Bauer, later, was gracious enough to admit this. "My first immediate disappointment was that he had beaten me to the punch, that he was going first," he said. "I knew immediately, particularly for him, that it was the right thing to do. I knew it would also generate some howls from the secular elites, which I thought would be to his advantage."

As for Bachman, who had, before becoming an anchor, spent a year in Lutheran seminary and then another year at Mansfield College, Oxford, a theology college, both the audience's resonance with Bush's answer and the response from his own superiors were gratifying. WHO-TV is owned by the *New York Times*, and Bachman received a personal e-mail from the chairman of the board of The New York Times Company, Arthur O. Sulzberger, congratulating him for WHO-TV's handling of the debate and in particular for the Christ-philosopher portion of the show.

But the howls predicted by Bauer were soon audible. Some of the other secular elites jumped on Bush for his Christ comment within hours of the debate's conclusion. Not only did many people think Bush had blundered badly by introducing religious convictions in a political debate, but others thought that he had demonstrated a calculated political cynicism. A third group considered him crassly ill-bred. Merely by introducing his personal religious views in a political setting, they argued, he had demonstrated unconscionable political ill-manners, like a teenager belching at his grandma's funeral.

Hosting his own often feisty talk-show program *Hardball* at 11:00 p.m., MSNBC's Chris Matthews took advantage of the opportunity to comment directly on the debate. He sniffed, "I thought they should have had that performance tonight in a tent. That was an evangelical meeting. It was a . . . a . . . a . . . it was a revival meeting. I thought it had no place in politics, but hey, everybody has their [sic] own taste in this business of politics."

But NBC reporter Norah O'Donnell, a guest on the show that evening, said she thought Bush had delivered "a strong performance" in the debate and that his Christ comment "really stole the house."

Interestingly, asked about the debate nearly four years later, Matthews seemed to have modified his initial, rather glib "revival meeting" characterization of the debate. "I thought it was a rather gifted response," he said in November 2003. "[Bush] is very much like me, his Jesus is very anthropomorphic. I don't think he tries to communicate with some vast unspeakable entity."

The day following the debate, December 14, Bush came under sustained fire on the Fox TV show *Hannity and Colmes* from Democratic Party consultant Bob Beckel. "I mean, I think it's the dumbest possible thing I've heard," Beckel griped. This edition of the popular show later became difficult for viewers to comprehend as an on-camera argument developed between Hannity, the politically conservative one, and his guest Ron Barrier, of the organization American Atheists.

"The whole idea's ridiculous," Barrier asserted, not making it clear whether belief in God itself or the espousal in public of such a belief by a political candidate was ridiculous.

"Is your ego so big that you can't accept somebody greater than you?" Hannity snapped back.

"No, no," Barrier retorted. "My ego's not big enough to say that I know [whether or not God exists]."

Later in the show, Representative Charles Rangel (NY-D) complained that Bush's religious confession "knocks out Jews and Muslims."

The following day, Chris Matthews invited on *Hardball* the author of the first full-length and detailed biography of George W. Bush, *First Son: George W. Bush and the Bush Family Dynasty*. Bill Minutaglio, whose book has been widely praised as insightful, well researched, and well written, seemed oddly perplexed by what had happened in Iowa the night before. The Christ remark, he confessed, "grabbed me at the time as an odd thing to say," even though he acknowledged that it had resonated broadly among Americans who thought of themselves as strongly committed Christians.

But like a basset hound worrying over a tasty but hard-to-negotiate bone, Matthews wouldn't let the subject go. Two days later, he returned to the subject on *Hardball*, and this time his guest was political conservative Bill Kristol, publisher and editor of the *Weekly Standard*, a conservative Washington weekly owned by Rupert Murdoch. Kristol, who is of Jewish background, said he thought Bush's Christ comment had been "deeply revealing."

"Of what?" Matthews shot back.

"It's revealing [of] a kind of narcissism," Kristol explained. "I don't deny for a minute the sincerity of it, and I don't deny for a minute the importance of it for Governor Bush. But it is inappropriate, in a way, as a matter of public philosophy to appeal to a private religious experience." Kristol went on to characterize Bush's comment as "unnerving," because it was so much about himself. "In that respect," he added, "Bush is like Clinton. It's all—'I feel your pain.'"

Interestingly, four years later Kristol seemed to have changed his view from that of the first few days after the debate. "It was politically very skillful," he said in the fall of 2003. "It totally destroyed the conservative attack on Bush." Kristol, presumably, had in mind the efforts of the other primary contenders, notably Gary Bauer, Alan Keyes, and Steve Forbes, to characterize Bush as wishy-washy on important American conservative moral issues such as abortion.

The print media's reaction was as stridently critical of Bush's Christ remark as Bauer had anticipated. Sandy Grady, columnist for the *Philadelphia Daily News*, wrote at the end of December 1999 that Bush had been indulging in "cynical showboating." Then Grady went for the jugular. "Never mind," he noted, "that Bush's self-proclaimed Christianity didn't stop him from executing Karla Faye Tucker, whose heart was also changed by Jesus. Or dozens of others on death row." Grady went on, "I'm not a theologian, but pols who bandy his name might be reminded that Jesus was arguably a left-wing radical." Yes, there would be a lot of argument about that assertion, reinforcing Grady's own admission that he didn't know much about theology.

In the *San Diego Union-Tribune*, James O. Goldsborough was even more vociferous, writing flatly, "Jesus has no place in politics." He added, "To inject religion into the political debate is to polarize and harden politics, one of the reasons this Congress, with its roots in the Moral Majority and the Christian Coalition, has made a mess of things." Well, no prizes for guessing where Mr. Goldsborough's political sympathies lay, though what he thought about Jesus Christ was not clear.

---

ONE OF THE CURIOSITIES in the anticipated salvo of objections to Bush's Christ comment was that several of the commentators who objected most angrily to Bush's bringing up the subject of his faith then proceeded to pick him apart because of their own interpretation of different parts of the New Testament. David Corn, for example, Washington editor of the left-wing *Nation* magazine, declared that Bush's answer to the philosopher question in the debate had been "smug," but then he went on to attack Bush's record as governor of Texas at a time when that state executed more felons than any other state in the union. "What would Bush's personal Savior, who himself was executed, make of this?" Corn asked.

Corn, in his website article, noted that the United Methodist Church, of which Bush has been a member since his marriage to Laura Welch in 1977, passed a resolution condemning capital punishment in 1980. Despite his apparent annoyance with Bush's own public religious affiliation, Corn then cited the New Testament verse Matthew 5:21 ("You have heard that it was said to the people long ago, 'Do not murder, and anyone who murders will be subject to judgment.'") as scriptural grounds for opposing capital punishment. It's important to note, of course, that sincere Christians do indeed differ on the validity of the death penalty, but very few of those opposing it would use Matthew 5:21 as part of the argument. Most Scripture commentators would interpret this text as referring to the crime of murder, not to the role of the state in executing criminals.

Maureen Dowd, whose columns in the *New York Times* are often very witty but can be sulfurous when people in the public sphere irritate her, dipped deep into her acid jar of sarcasm in late December 1999. She opined, "George W. Bush finally scored some debate points on Monday night by supporting the holy trinity of ethanol, Jesus, and soft money. (Didn't Jesus throw those soft-money changers out of the temple?)" She went on, "When you take something deeply personal and parade it for political gain, you are guilty either of cynicism or exhibitionism. . . . Genuinely religious people are humbled by religion and are guided by it on the inside. They don't need to wear Jesus on the outside as a designer label."

Dowd, interestingly, cited President John F. Kennedy's run for the White House in 1960 as demonstrating what she considered the correct relationship of faith and public policy: total separation. She cited Kennedy as saying, "I believe in a president whose views on religion are his own private affair."

PBS aired a rather thoughtful TV symposium on the Christ-philosopher controversy on *The Newshour with Jim Lehrer* on December 24, 1999. Presiding over the segment of the show that dealt with the issue was Terence Smith, who also quoted Kennedy's private-affair view of religion in a president. The nation's first—and so far only—Catholic president had said, as Smith correctly quoted him, "I am the Democratic Party's candidate for president who happens to be a Catholic."

On the program, Cynthia Tucker of the *Atlanta Journal-Constitution* acknowledged that she had been uncomfortable with Bush's Christ comment, but the *Daily Oklahoman's* Pat McGuigan disagreed. "In fact, I think voters are interested in this kind of thing; a person's faith, the way they [sic] deal with their spiritual life, with their friends, neighbors and family, is a vital aspect of their character. . . . Faith is a vital component of human existence. Our rights, millions of us believe, our rights are natural. They are given to us by God, not by the state."

A fellow participant in the TV discussion was Robert Kittle of the *San Diego Union-Tribune*, whose columnist James Goldsborough was quoted earlier. "I don't think there's anything to be alarmed about here," he said. "I think, in general, it flows in line with the history of this nation. After all, the first settlers on these shores were motivated by religion to come here."

---

OF COURSE, neither the remarks in support of Bush by TV commentators, nor the appreciative newspaper comments did anything to dilute the continuing attacks upon Bush for his Iowa debate remarks. In a particularly bizarre twist, Bush was denounced on one website (www.counterpunch.org) by Wayne Madsen, who claimed that "many devout Catholic leaders"—he didn't name any—viewed Bush as "bearing the hallmarks of the anti-Christ." Madsen's comment served notice that, while there is indeed a phenomenon in the United States that might be categorized as the Religious Right, there also is one that ought to be called the Religious Left.

More thoughtfully, the popular evangelical monthly *Christianity Today* on its website took issue with those critics of Bush who complained that Jesus Christ wasn't actually a philosopher. Douglas Groothuis, associate professor of philosophy at Denver Seminary, wrote, "Being a philosopher requires a certain orientation to knowledge, a willingness to argue and debate logically, and to do so with some proficiency. On this account, Jesus was a philosopher. . . . For these reasons (and many more) I believe George W. Bush's show-stopping assertion [in Des Moines] was correct. Jesus was a philosopher and a great one."

On another website (www.hometown.aol.com), Gregory J. Rummo joined what seemed to be becoming a counterattack on Bush's early critics after the Christ comment. Rummo coined the term "theophobia" to excoriate what he claimed were double standards in the media on criticism of religious expression by political figures. Rummo pointed out that, a few days after the Iowa debate, President Bill Clinton, in an interview with anchor Peter Jennings of ABC's *World News Tonight* had worked the word "God" into the interview. (Maureen Dowd, in fairness, had complained in her piece attacking Bush that then candidate Al Gore had declared himself on the CBS program *60 Minutes* to be "a born-again Christian." This, she said in exasperation, proved that Gore had "sunk to the same level on religion" as Bush.)

But Rummo's case was that, by and large, American liberal political commentators kept pretty quiet when their own favorite politicians brought God into the equation. In that respect, Rummo was accurate. There was little public complaint by prominent liberal political commentators when, during his presidential campaign, then vice president Al Gore and his nominee for vice president, Senator Joseph Lieberman, frequently referred to the deity in public speeches. Rummo complained, "Liberals are not serious when they talk about God. Conservatives are, and that is what sends fear into the hearts of the Irreligious Left."

Rummo, of course, was making a generalization that was surely unfair to many liberals who take their faith—whether Christian, Jewish, or Muslim— very seriously. But he was certainly not alone in claiming that there was a double standard of judgment at work: former president Bill Clinton, for example, was not criticized by any liberal media for using church pulpits in the special California election of October 2003 to lend his support to the beleaguered incumbent, Democratic governor Gray Davis.

---

THE QUESTION REMAINS: was Bush in the Iowa debate making a calculated political move to cut into potential evangelical Christian support for Gary Bauer and Alan Keyes? Or was he quite spontaneously expressing a conviction of faith that was a central component of his personality? After all, it would surely be unfair to assume—as a *New York Times* reader pointed out in a response to the Maureen Dowd column—"that all politicians who express religious faith are either insincere or out of line." And might a politician whose policies were so unpopular with many voters still be quite sincere in his or her own faith expressions? To quote a witty comment attributed to former secretary of state Dr. Henry Kissinger, "Just because I am paranoid doesn't mean that I am not being followed." That is, even if Bush was aware during the Iowa debate of his need to bolster political support among America's Christian conservatives, is it a certainty that when he almost blurted out "Christ" in response to the question, he was following a carefully programmed, not to say cynically crafted, political script?

One member of Bush's campaign team who would certainly have known was Karen Hughes, later to be White House communications director. Of course, Hughes could be expected to be loyal to Bush if attacks against his Christ remark were based on the assumption that it was a political calculation. But since the consensus of political observers is that the Christ comment eventually turned to Bush's political advantage in the presidential election of November 2000, it is surely likely that Hughes would have acknowledged some advance role in its planning. American political advisors, after all, are notoriously prone to claiming credit for any statements by their political bosses that are regarded sooner or later as good statements. But Hughes, speaking in November 2003, said that no one in the campaign had any inkling that the philosopher question was going to come up in the Des Moines debate. "We had not anticipated that question," she said. "I never knew he was going to say that. But I remember being very proud of him for saying it. To me, that was the only answer he could have given."

Hughes describes herself as a committed Christian, "a follower of Christ," and can thus be expected to agree with the Christ remark. Let us, for the moment, give her the benefit of the doubt. After all, Bush's religious orientation was not a state secret at the end of 1999. Virtually everyone in Texas knew that he identified strongly with the Christian faith. Indeed, as we shall see, in 1993, while still governor, Bush ran into a hailstorm of criticism by reaffirming the classic evangelical position that a person has to believe personally in Christ in order to get to heaven.

What the 1999 Iowa debate demonstrated, though, was that, for better or for worse, George W. Bush was a political leader whose faith seemed more integrally linked with the rest of his life, and certainly with his political views, than was the case in almost all of the twentieth-century aspirants for the White House. Honest—and indeed dishonest—Americans can argue loudly about whether his policies have been good or bad for themselves, for America, and for the world. To do so is simply the normal business of political discourse in a political democracy. But there was something different about Bush's faith. It doesn't seem to be something he takes off when he leaves the Oval Office to return to the private quarters of the White House. From the accounts of many people, George W.'s faith has lent a certain modesty to some of his ways of doing things and it has rendered him unusually solicitous of the "little people" he has bumped into from time to time: baby-sitters, and former teachers and friends of his wife, Laura. Some have even said it has given him a certain humility, an understanding that, without the approval of the Almighty, he could easily be whisked out of the White House and sent back to his ranch in Crawford, Texas—a retreat in the heart of West Texas scrubland where he seems to be most at ease with himself and the world.

Would Bush be disappointed if he were not reelected in 2004? Of course he would; he would hardly be human if it were otherwise. But would he be devastated, as some political losers in past presidential races have been? Almost certainly not. That apparent equanimity, of course, has a great deal to do with the nature of his faith, a Christian faith. As we shall see, George W.'s faith didn't grow up in him in a vacuum, nor did it transform him overnight.

# 2

## Basic Training

*As my life has become more complicated, I treasure the basics:*
*faith, family, and my friends.*

—George W. Bush

George W. Bush's Christ-philosopher remark may not have been the result of any Machiavellian political calculation—in fact, almost certainly it wasn't—but it was not some half-baked afterthought either. As even many who disliked his Iowa debate response admitted at the time, it seemed to come from some core of personal belief deep within Bush's psyche. But how had that core come into being? Had Bush been zapped in some Damascus Road spiritual experience? Had he marched down the steps of a football stadium during a Billy Graham crusade? Graham, to be sure, played a major role in a crucial turnaround in Bush's life, but Bush, even though he later attended some of Graham's crusades, had not "come forward" at any of them as someone who wanted to receive the salvation message. Nor had he been channel-surfing and been suddenly sideswiped in his life by the mellifluous perorations of some televangelist. Bush's faith journey was a long one, with many important landmarks. But its primary source was very simple: his own family.

Many Americans are not comfortable with the notion of a family legacy. In fact, Americans often prefer the concept of personal reinvention:

15

creating a new *you* scraped clean of the emotional and psychological barnacles that have fastened themselves to you during a painful upbringing. Americans also tend to admire self-made success more than the seemingly undeserved outworking in a person's life of a previous generation's combination of good genes and good fortune. But insofar as the combination of good genes, wise choices, and a carefully nurtured sense of personal and social obligation can result in good "breeding" over several generations, the Bush family story demonstrates it in spades. The Bushes—George W. and Laura, and his parents George Herbert Walker and Barbara—have always disliked the term *dynasty*, as in "the Kennedy dynasty" or "the Bush dynasty." The very word seems to smack of old-world privilege, stuffiness, and pretension. What they would surely embrace, though, is a more benign formula expressed within the Bush family back through several generations: faith, family, and friends.

In March 2002, in the uncertain months between the end of major combat in Afghanistan and the unleashing of war upon Iraq a year later, President Bush received a heartwarming greeting from his former basketball buddies from Midland, Texas. "The old Central YMCA lunch-hour basketball crew thought that a little nostalgia and reminiscing might bring brightness to your day (Lord knows you can probably use it right now)," wrote Bob Landreth and eleven of his and Bush's former noon-time, pickup basketball teammates. "Some of us," he added, "have renewed a commitment to pray for you, and for God's direction in your leadership in this new year." Accompanying the letter was a photo of the twelve friends, in casual basketball attire, grinning happily at the camera.

Bush's handwritten reply came within three weeks. "I miss my friends from Midland and fondly remember our days playing noon ball," he wrote. He added, "As my life has become more complicated, I treasure the basics: faith, family, and my friends."[1]

"The basics." The Bush family had enjoyed these basics across several generations, reaching back into the early nineteenth century. In August 2001, in fact, George W. Bush's father, the forty-first president (henceforth to be referred to as "Bush Senior" for his full given name: George

Herbert Walker Bush) had written George W. Bush a letter with considerable detail about the Bush family ancestors. With impeccably correct protocol, Bush Senior had addressed his son:

> Dear Mr. President, I thought you might like to know more about your heritage, thus this little story about your great-great-great grandfather, who was the father of Samuel Prescott Bush, my dad's dad. Devotedly, Dad.[2]

Bush Senior was referring to an attachment to the letter, a privately printed memoir by a Bush family friend, William Barrett, that had been published in 1907. The memoir starts with the story of Obadiah Bush, who anticipated a generations-long family tradition of serving his nation in the military by helping garrison a fort in Buffalo, New York, during the War of 1812. A schoolmaster after the war, Obadiah settled in Rochester, New York, and fathered seven children. Heading West to California after the gold rush of 1849 started, Obadiah did well enough to settle on the West Coast. First, he chose to return to the East Coast by sea to wrap up his affairs, taking the notoriously stormy route around Cape Horn.

Tragically, Obadiah Bush died en route in 1851. It was his second son, James Smith Bush, born in 1825, who established what became a Bush family tradition by entering Yale College (as it was then called) at the age of sixteen. As Texas author Mickey Herskowitz notes in his admirable story of James Bush's grandson, Prescott Bush (Bush Senior's father), *Duty, Honor, Country: The Life and Legacy of Prescott Bush*, James Bush was described by his contemporaries as "tall and slender in person, rather grave of mien . . . ever kind and considerate and always a gentleman . . . fond of athletics [an oarsman and a high jumper]."[3]

A man of obvious spiritual inclination, James Bush at first wanted to be a Presbyterian minister. But with his father away from home panning for gold, James decided that he needed to support his mother and siblings, so he studied law. He married the following year, after his father's death at sea, but his beautiful wife died eighteen months after the wedding of a brain "fever" (probably a hemorrhage in today's terms). The sudden and terrible loss turned James's thoughts back to spiritual things once more. He now abandoned law to study to be a priest in the Episcopal Church. Rather than serving as a curate (or assistant rector) for several years, James took charge of a parish in Orange, New Jersey, immediately after his ordination and served there for ten years. He remarried, and his bride had distinguished antecedents in the Revolutionary War. Her maiden name was Prescott, and she was a descendant of the Samuel Prescott who rode with Paul Revere from Boston to Lexington in 1775 to warn that the British were coming.

In 1865, James Bush became acting chaplain and secretary to Commodore George Rogers (who had served under Admiral Farragut during the important Civil War naval battle at Mobile, Alabama) on a U.S. Navy trip to several South American countries. The small flotilla sailed through the Caribbean then down the Atlantic coast of South America before rounding the Horn and arriving in San Francisco. There he was entertained by Governor Henry Haight, a Yale classmate. Deciding to stay, he served as rector of Grace Church from 1866 to 1871, when he moved back East to the Church of the Ascension on Staten Island, New York.

It was while in New York that James Bush developed friendships that were to prove, ultimately, to undermine some of the convictions of the Christian faith that had initially propelled him into the Episcopal Church. One of his friends was The Reverend Doctor R. Heber Newton, a fellow-Episcopalian who scandalized the hierarchy of his church by making comments highly critical of traditional Christian and, indeed, Episcopal Christian doctrine. Newton was so critical of his own church's tradition that his sermons were approvingly quoted by a prominent atheist of the day, Robert Green Ingersoll (1833–1899). Citing a sermon by Newton entitled "A New Religion," Ingersoll made these favorable comments:

The Episcopal creed is a few ages behind the thought of the world. For many years the foremost members and clergymen in that church have been giving some new meanings to the old words and phrases. Words are no more exempt from change than other things in nature. . . . Mr. Newton, moreover, clearly sees that people are losing confidence in the morality of the gospel; that its foundation lacks common sense; that the doctrine of forgiveness is unscientific, and that it is impossible to feel that the innocent can rightfully suffer for the guilty, or that the suffering of innocence can in any way justify the crimes of the wicked.[4]

Newton, however, didn't rest his case on a modernist disenchantment with traditional Christian doctrine as expressed by the Episcopal Church of that day. He moved off into the newest philosophical and religious trends of the day—Divine Science and New Thought—eventually becoming an officer in The International Metaphysical League. The League's goals, as noted at the time, were, among other things, "to establish unity and cooperation of thought and action among individuals and organizations throughout the world devoted to the Science of Mind and of Being," and

to teach the universal Fatherhood and Motherhood of God and the all-inclusive Brotherhood of Man; that One Life is immanent in the universe, and is both Centre and Circumference of all things visible and invisible, and that the Intelligence is above all and in all; and that from this Infinite Life and Intelligence proceed all Light, Love and Truth.[5]

Newton, in effect, absorbed many of the doctrines of Theosophy, a mystical philosophical-religious movement deeply imbued by occultism and spiritualism (channeling of spirits), which was formally introduced into the United States in 1875 by Helena Petrovna Blavatsky, a Russian immigrant and by her longtime associate, Col. Henry Steel Olcott.

How much these ideas influenced James Bush in his departure from the Episcopal Church is unclear. The book he wrote in 1883, *More Words about the Bible*, does not read like a heretical tract. Yet one statement in the book that would certainly have sounded alarm bells among traditional

Episcopal readers was this: "Revealed truth, at the best, as it comes to us in the Gospel of Christ, is not absolute, but relative."[6] The following year, James Bush resigned his rectorate and lived in Concord, Massachusetts, until his death in 1889.

Another of James Bush's close friends and later admirers was author and journalist George William Curtis (1824–1892). Without realizing it at the time, Curtis appears to have helped nudge Bush down the road to his eventual break with Episcopal Christianity. He showed James Bush a poem by Ralph Waldo Emerson, "The Problem," which stunned the clergyman by articulating ideas with which he himself had come to agree. Emerson was a central character in the Transcendental Movement in New England, a literary and philosophical interest group that included such other eminent American literary names as Henry Wadsworth Longfellow, Nathaniel Hawthorne, and Henry David Thoreau. Emerson held that nature transcended all human and religious truths, and his poem "The Problem" is one of the most biting expressions of that viewpoint.

It is thus not surprising that, after resigning from his position as Episcopal priest, James Smith Bush moved to Concord, the location of Henry David Thoreau's celebrated book *Walden: Or, Life in the Woods.* When it came time for his youngest son to enter Cornell University, he moved the family once more, this time to Ithaca, New York, to be close to the university. But notwithstanding his departure from Christian orthodoxy, James Bush seemed to have retained a serene and warm disposition, endearing himself to all who encountered him.[7]

William Barrett, the amateur chronicler of the Bush family previously cited by Mickey Herskowitz had these interesting comments on James Bush:

He had a fine, strong, handsome face, with a kindly smile and charming grace of manner. His chief characteristics, it seems to me, were a nature free from guile and a gentle cordiality of manner refreshing to see. Pure and unspotted from the world, he was in the truest sense a spiritually minded man.[8]

James Bush died in 1889, leaving four children, of whom it was the second son, Samuel Prescott Bush, who laid the groundwork for the phenomenal careers of Bush Senior's father (Prescott Bush), Bush Senior himself, and George W. Bush. Samuel Prescott Bush graduated from Thaddeus Stevens College of Technology in Lancaster, Pennsylvania. After college, Samuel Bush moved to Ohio to work for the Pennsylvania Railroad, where he not only became a successful corporate executive but a powerful figure in state politics in the Democratic Party. He was surely the last man in the Bush presidential line to be a Democrat. During World War I, Samuel worked in Washington, D.C., for the War Industries Board.

But it was his son Prescott, George W. Bush's grandfather, who set the Bush family on a pathway where faith, family, and friends were constant major landmarks. Though born in Ohio when his father Samuel was working there, Prescott Bush started the family tradition of being packed off to a prep school on the East Coast, in his case to St. George's, an Episcopal school in Rhode Island. Influenced by a perhaps more orthodox brand of Episcopalianism at St. George's than his grandfather had been comfortable with, Prescott, while still at school, initially considered going into the Episcopal ministry. Instead, he became the first of three consecutive generations of Bushes to attend Yale.

Prescott was tall, good-looking, an excellent athlete (first baseman and captain of the Yale baseball team), a good debater, and had an outstanding singing voice. He joined the Whiffenpoofs, originally a quartet from the Yale Glee Club but later a group of male voices famous for close harmony singing. Prescott's voice was so good that he was voted by later generations of Yalies an "all-time" Whiffenpoof member. Prescott set the precedent for three generations of Bush men to be "tapped" for Skull and Bones—an elite campus secret society founded in 1832 that has acquired over the decades a lurid reputation among global conspiracy theorists in the United States—a subject that will be explored later.

But it was not Yale secret societies that preoccupied the graduating seniors in 1917; it was the prospect of American military involvement in the war in Europe. President Woodrow Wilson declared war on Germany on April 6, 1917, after a combination of a vicious German U-boat campaign against neutral vessels (including American ships) and the notorious German "Zimmerman note" encouraging Mexico and Japan to make war upon the United States (The note was intercepted and decoded by the British.)

At the time of graduation, Prescott Bush had been voted by classmates as "most versatile" (he was on the varsity golf and baseball teams) and came in third in the "most admired" category. But almost immediately after graduation, he joined the U.S. Army, commissioned as a captain in field artillery. He and his regiment landed in France in June 1918, and he saw action soon after as United States forces stopped, and then finally pushed back, the last great German offensive of the war, not far from Verdun.[9]

After the German military collapse and the armistice of November 1917, Prescott remained first in France and later Germany for much of 1919 as part of the American army of occupation. When he returned to the United States in the fall of 1919, he took a job in St. Louis as a management trainee for the Simmons Hardware Company. Though he remained there only a few months, Prescott fell in love with a woman who was to have a profound influence on him and two subsequent generations of Bushes: Dorothy Walker, the second daughter of George Herbert "Bert" Walker, founder of the G. H. Walker Investment Company.

Bert was a rebel, the son of a Scottish Catholic family who had defied his parents by marrying a Protestant. Dorothy had inherited much of her father's feistiness and had wanted to attend Vassar, the women's college in Cambridge, Massachusetts. But Bert didn't believe in college educations for women and sent Dorothy, instead, to Miss Porter's Finishing School in Farmington, Connecticut. Founded in 1843 to produce "resourceful, informed, responsible, and ethical young women," Miss Porter's today remains one of the top independent all-women's boarding schools in the United States, according to *US News & World Report*. It isn't clear what impact the school had on Dorothy, but it surely reinforced intensely strong competitive instincts in the athletically inclined teenager, and it may well have helped form in her what became a life-long Christian piety within the Episcopal Church tradition.

Dorothy Walker, even before her engagement and marriage to Prescott Bush, was one of the top-ranked women tennis players in the country, placing second in a national women's tournament in 1918. She also enjoyed challenging friends to a one-mile swim in the frigid waters of the Atlantic off Kennebunkport, the family's summer retreat in Maine. Barbara Bush, mother of President George W. Bush, has described her as "the most competitive living human,"[10] and stories of Dorothy urging children and grandchildren on to games of everything from tennis to tiddlywinks are legion. Miss Porter's School in the year 2003 had a tennis cup award named after Dorothy Walker. Prescott and Dorothy Walker were married in Kennebunkport, her birthplace, in the Episcopal Church of St. Anne's-by-the-Sea on August 6, 1921. The church was to be the site of many subsequent Bush family baptisms and weddings.

Dorothy Walker's influence on the Bush family went well beyond instilling in them intense competitiveness, as Prescott also liked to do. As her son Bush Senior wrote of her in a family testimonial presented to her on Mother's Day 1985, Dorothy demanded total honesty from her family and those around her, and she made it clear she expected her offspring and their descendants to be concerned for the welfare of others. Bush Senior wrote of her movingly:

> Her goodness, her kindness, her propensity to forgive, her love, all stem directly from her following the Bible and from her faith in God. Mother is a Christian. Her light really does shine.
>
> When Dad [Prescott] died of lung cancer [in 1972]—and, oh, how she loved him—she said to Nancy and to her daughters-in-law, "Wear bright colors for the funeral. Your dad is in heaven. There is lots to be joyful about."

In the same testimonial, he quotes Barbara Bush saying that Dorothy was "the most remarkable woman I have ever known."[11] George W. Bush, speaking of his grandmother in the late 1980s, while she was still alive, described her as "a pretty righteous lady. Her values are well set." His younger brother Marvin said during the same interview, "She is one of the most spiritual people I have ever met. She's also very comfortable with people. . . . When you sit down and talk with my grandmother, you come away feeling better about yourself."[12]

Dorothy and Prescott shared a deep mutual faith, saying grace over family meals, attending church, and praying together on a daily basis—another tradition that three generations of Bushes have upheld. "My husband and I used to read together in the morning and then again in the evening," Dorothy recalled in the last decade of her life. She also referred to such daily devotionals as John Baillie's *Diary of Private Prayers* and John Stott's *Focus on Christ*.[13]

Prescott was a man whose formality could be truly intimidating, especially to his grandchildren. He insisted that George W. and other grandchildren address him in his own home as "Senator" after he was elected to represent Connecticut in the U.S. Senate (1952–1962) and that they wear jacket and tie for every evening meal in the family home. But he was also a man of impeccable moral decency at a time when great currents of change and controversy were swirling through the nation. He was instrumental in turning back the zeal of Senator Joseph McCarthy in unearthing Communists in the United States by voting for the Senate censure of McCarthy in 1954. Yet when McCarthy was dying of cancer in the spring of 1957, Prescott Bush wrote him a warm personal note—visitors were not permitted in the patient's hospital room at the time—wishing him a recovery and return to the Senate.[14]

As for Dorothy, she seems to have been a constant fount of grace and good cheer to the entire family, drawing not only upon her own natural gifts but the strength she obviously derived from her own faith. She said this of her family in the late 1980s:

I taught them love. I taught them to love everybody, no matter what their background, and I taught them to be unselfish.

24

One of my favorite verses in the Bible is First Corinthians, Chapter 13: "Though I have the tongues of men and of angels and have not love, I am nothing." And of course, the twenty-third Psalm ['The Lord is my shepherd . . .']"

I taught my children to be kind and I taught them the golden rule: "Do unto others as you would have them do unto you." There are so many favorite Bible verses. They are all beautiful.[15]

Dorothy Walker Bush's kindness was not limited to her own family. She went out of her way to reach out to anyone she felt needed encouragement. When Anne Morrow Lindbergh, widow of the aviator, wrote a book called *Gifts from the Sea* in 1955, Dorothy Walker Bush wrote her a warmly complimentary note in which she said, "Life gets so hectic that I just feel I am constantly in a jet plane, whirling through space. I am more determined than ever to let nothing interfere with our quiet little time for reading and prayer together each morning before Pres [Prescott] goes to the Senate."[16] She also said that she had learned from her own mother that "prayer was an important part of one's daily life. I think that helped me greatly."[17]

Dorothy Bush was an active member of a woman's Bible study group in Connecticut. But as she approached her end in 1992, her eyes began to fail, and it became hard for her to read. At one Bible study meeting, when it was her turn to read the designated passage from the Psalms, she instead quoted it from memory. According to Beth, wife of Prescott Bush Jr., Bush Senior's youngest sibling, who was at that Bible study meeting, Dorothy recited the Twenty-third Psalm, which she knew by heart, in a clear voice. "Those who heard her say, gently, 'The Lord is my Shepherd,' knew then that he truly was."[18]

---

IT WAS INTO THIS CLIMATE of fierce family loyalty, keen competitiveness, insistence on personal modesty, and quiet but unmistakable

Christian pietism, that George Herbert Walker Bush was born. The fourth of five children (and the third son) came into the world on June 12, 1924, in Milton, Massachusetts, when his father, Prescott Bush, was working briefly for Stedman Products, a manufacturer of rubber flooring for hospitals, banks, and other major buildings.[19] Though well paid, Prescott was not happy in the job and gladly accepted other positions, first with U.S. Rubber, and then with an investment firm established by E. H. Harriman (from whom the distinguished United States diplomat Averill Harriman is descended) that later became known as Brown Brothers, Harriman. Dorothy's father, G. H. Walker, had been brought in by railroad magnate E. H. Harriman[20] to run the company and hired his son-in-law to be part of the corporate management. Prescott moved his family to an upscale home in Greenwich, Connecticut, about a seventy-five-minute commute from Manhattan—in the 1920s and the twenty-first century. "People say I was a man of privilege and by that they mean money," Bush Senior has said. "But I was privileged in the question of values—a mother and father who were determined to help their kids be good people."[21]

Bush Senior has often used the term "good people," surely passing the notion on to his children. But with the ever-competitive, quietly pious, and devoted matriarchal mother Dorothy Walker Bush running the household, Bush Senior was indoctrinated early on into the primary value of family loyalty too. At the age of fourteen, he was packed off to the all-boys' boarding school of Phillips Academy in Andover, Massachusetts, even then one of the premier private boarding schools in the country. In fact, Phillips Academy is the oldest incorporated boarding school in the United States (founded in 1778) and boasts famous alumni and great historical moments in America's past. Its rolls, even before Bush Senior arrived, included such American notables as Oliver Wendell Holmes, Dr. Benjamin Spock, Humphrey Bogart, inventor Samuel Morse, and Secretary of War Henry Stimson. The patriotic song "My Country, 'Tis of Thee" was composed there in 1832 by Samuel Francis Smith. The five-hundred-acre campus and meticulously designed quadrangles ensured that Andover would be for generations one of the most beautiful boarding school settings anywhere in the world.[22]

Bush Senior excelled in multiple areas at Andover: president of the senior class, captain of the baseball team, and captain of the soccer team. For all of these achievements and more, he was named "Best All-Around Fellow," and portraits of him hung in the school buildings for several decades after he left it, including into the 1960s when George W. was a student there. But Bush Senior's real fame at Andover, which was also to become almost legendary long after he left, rose from a single act immediately upon graduation in 1942, when the nation was at war. Secretary of war and Andover alumnus Henry Stimson had advised all the graduating seniors to complete their education before signing up for the military. Legend—or the truth, be it known—had it that Bush Senior had approached Stimson immediately after the secretary of war's commencement address and said, "I don't wanna go to Yale right now; I wanna fight for my country."[23]

Bush Senior's father, Prescott, attending the commencement, made no effort to dissuade him. Mickey Herskowitz reports a conversation between father and son just after the Stimson speech. Had the secretary of war changed the son's mind? he asked. "No sir," said Bush Senior. "I'm going in."[24]

Years later, Bush Senior reflected on that moment of decision as he prepared for another great test of a different kind, running for the U.S. presidency in 1988. He told Doug Wead, author of the 1988 campaign biography *George Bush: Man of Integrity*, "I wanted to go right into the navy when the war broke out. But my parents and relatives were upset; they felt that the thing for me to do was go on to college. Yet I was shaken by what had happened at Pearl Harbor; and I was patriotic and wanted to do something about it. So I dug in my heels and pulled it off."[25]

That almost Victorian statement of duty was no empty bravado. One week later, Bush Senior was on his way to Boston to enroll as a trainee pilot officer in the U.S. Navy Air Force. At eighteen, he received his pilot's wings and became the youngest pilot in the entire U.S. Navy. In a well-reported incident, his Avenger dive bomber in 1944 was shot down during a bombing run on a radio station on the Pacific island of Chichi Jima, and Bush Senior bailed out. His two fellow crewmen were not as fortunate and died as the plane went down. The wind and current were pushing his frail rubber dinghy back toward the shore of the Japanese-occupied island. Had the *U.S.S. Finback* submarine not been patrolling nearby and spotted the lone American in a vulnerable location there would certainly have been no Bush Senior presidency. As crewmen photographed the scene, the young pilot was pulled aboard. He stayed with the submarine for several weeks until it returned to base in Hawaii.

This Nathan Hale patriotism was not the only aspect of Bush Senior's early life that would later make a huge impact upon his children, including George W. His mother, Dorothy, remembered Bush Senior as an unusually kind person from an early age:

> The most consistent characteristic in his life, the characteristic I could see in him as a young child and that has stayed with him over the years, is his kindness to others. He has always worried about the other person. He wanted everyone to have a fair chance, and he was always looking out for the underdog.[26]

While still at Andover, during the Christmas holidays of 1941, Bush Senior met Barbara Pierce, direct descendant of America's fourteenth president Franklin Pierce, at a dance at Round Hill Country Club in Greenwich, Connecticut. She was only sixteen, and Bush Senior was eighteen. After just a few more meetings, they had fallen in love and kissed, the first kiss for each. In a romance that seems almost medievally chaste by twenty-first-century standards, they wrote each other almost daily and were able to see each other in person only on the rare occasions when Bush Senior was on leave. They became engaged at Kennebunkport in June 1943 during one of those leaves. Bush named his Avenger aircraft aboard the *U.S.S. San Jacinto* "Bar # 2" (Barbara) and continued to write to her as frequently as his duties permitted. They were married during another of his leaves, in January 1945. Barbara has often described her romance with Bush Senior this way: "I married the first man I ever kissed. When I tell this to my children, they just about throw up."[27]

———————————————

WHEN THE WAR ENDED in August 1945, the couple were at their base in Virginia Beach, Virginia, awaiting orders for another carrier assignment in what everyone assumed would be the bloody, final invasion of Japan. Bush Senior and Barbara went to church to give thanks for the end of the war and then joined friends in major festivities. A month later, Bush Senior was able to leave the navy and begin his long-postponed studies at Yale University. Enrolled in a two-and-one-half year accelerated program for military veterans, he graduated in 1947, once again a standout success. He was first baseman on the Yale baseball team and in his junior year was tapped for the senior-year secret society Skull and Bones, just as his father had been.

But in what was to become something of a family tradition, Bush Senior had no desire to establish a career in the comfortable family environment of New England. After the adventures of air combat against Japan, he decided to embark on an unfamiliar course by heading far away from New England to find fame and fortune in the American southwest. Just a week after his graduation, he set off in a red 1947 Studebaker, a present from his father, with three thousand dollars he had saved from his navy pay. He arrived in Midland, Texas, where he had been offered a job at the International Derrick and Equipment Company, a subsidiary of Dresser Industries. Barbara, then just twenty-one, followed by plane a week later with the couple's first child, George W. Bush, born July 12, 1946.

———————————————

THE STORY of Bush Senior's life is a well-traveled tale of hard work at the bottom of the corporate ladder, entrepreneurial risktaking, and finally political success—achievement in important branches of the U.S. government before attainment of the greatest pinnacle of all, presidency of the United States. It is certainly not a rags-to-riches tale, because Bush Senior grew up amid affluence and privilege, and his father's connections undoubtedly played a role in the early opportunities that came his way. But it is a story of remarkable moral consistency at a time when the country was undergoing an unprecedented change in national mores. True, many of those changes were long overdue and desperately needed if the United States as to remain true to the stated ideals of its founding fathers:

- civil rights and honorable national respect for African Americans;
- legal, professional, and social recognition of women;
- a diminution in the shrillness of public criticism of those who did not conform to long-held social standards of marital conduct.

Yet many of the other social and cultural changes in American life that came with advances in civil rights for African Americans and enhanced opportunities for women may not have been as socially desirable. For example, the radical change in acceptable sexual mores helped hasten the collapse of the American tradition of respect for sexual restraint, family loyalty, and the sanctity of marriage that began in the 1950s. By the year 2003, one-third of all children born in the United States were born out of wedlock, and nearly half of all marriages of 2003 would statistically end in divorce. It is a striking testimony to his example of family loyalty, faith, and mutual support that, more than four decades after getting married, all of Prescott's five children were still married to the mates they had wed in their youth.

---

IN TEXAS, Bush Senior and Barbara found themselves daily confronting the rougher side of life in Odessa by sharing the bathroom of their first apartment, a one-bedroom duplex at 1519 East Seventh Street, with a mother-daughter prostitution team. By 1949, the Bushes had moved into a new, one-story home on East Maple Street in Midland, a far more genteel, upscale town than raucous Odessa. George W., often called "Georgie" by the family but never "George Junior," was an energetic handful for his parents. Bush Senior described the young boy, then just thirteen months old, in an August 1947 letter to a friend: "Whenever I come home he greets me and talks a blue streak, sentences disjointed, of course, by enthusiasm and spirit boundless." Bush Senior wrote this, unwittingly looking forward to a time when his son's mispronunciations and occasionally mangled syntax would be a source of humor. Bush Senior went on, "He is a real blond and pot-bellied. He tries to say everything and the results are often hilarious."[28]

This idyllic existence of a young family entertained by the antics of their firstborn seemed to be crowned with a cherry when the second child and first daughter, Robin, was born in December 1949. A year later, Bush Senior wrote in another letter, to his father, about his wonderful family: "Robin is now walking around, and Georgie has grown to be a near-man, talks dirty once in a while and occasionally swears, aged four and a half. He lives in his cowboy clothes."[29]

Robin was adorable: pretty, charming with grown-ups, and very close to George W. despite the boy's rambunctious habits. But the idyll of joyful children was brutally interrupted. Not long after Barbara gave birth to another child, the boy who was to become known as Jeb, in February 1953, Robin was found to have leukemia, a cancer-related illness about which little was then known. Despite her parents' valiant efforts to take her for consultations with every medical expert in the country, Robin's health slowly declined. Blood transfusions and other radical medical procedures failed to save her, and she died in October 1953 at the Memorial Sloan-Kettering Cancer Center in New York City. As Robin got worse, her anguished parents experienced a profound deepening of their faith. At 6:30 every morning, Bush Senior went to the Presbyterian church in Midland they attended to pray privately for Robin's recovery.

When the pastor learned of this daily visit, he began coming as well, saying nothing, simply joining in prayer.

When Robin passed away in her mother's arms, Barbara too seemed to turn more intensely than ever before to her childhood faith. "For one last time I combed her hair," she wrote in her memoirs, "and we held our precious little girl. I never felt the presence of God more strongly than at that moment."[30] She told a *USA Today* reporter in 1988, "First of all, I know there's a God, and secondly, I know Robin left. We both had that feeling that she wasn't there. We combed her hair and she wasn't there."[31]

The pain of this loss was so intense that both parents complained about physical pains as they struggled to cope with the grief. But Bush Senior's own faith seemed to have found new depths through the experience. He told an interviewer later, "Actually, the pain of that experience taught us just how dependent on God we really are, and how important our faith is. In a moment like that, all you have is God."[32]

Robin's illness also seemed to have awakened in young George W. an awareness of the deep and troubling aspects of life. When his parents drove to Midland's Sam Houston Elementary School to inform him of his sister's death, George W., seeing their car coming up the gravel drive, assumed that they had brought his sister for another of her infrequent visits between breaks in her treatment.

But it wasn't so, and George W. learned to his unspeakable grief that his sister had died. His parents had never told him that she was as desperately ill as that. He later described the moment as "the starkest memory of my childhood, a sharp pain in the midst of an otherwise happy blur."[33] Within days, he began to realize how profoundly deep was the pain of his mother's grief. He sought, even at the age of seven, to assume a protective presence near her when his father was away from home. One day, Barbara heard George W. telling a boyhood friend that he couldn't come and play with him because his mother needed him.[34] But George W. also showed at this stage of his life a tendency that was to remain with him throughout his life—a desire to lighten the mood with jokes if he thought people were acting too gloomy. When his father took him and some family friends to a football game, everyone froze in awkward embarrassment when George W. said he wished at this moment that he were Robin. What did he mean? someone gently asked. George W. replied, "I bet she can see the game better from up there than we can here." He meant, of course, that she was looking down on things from heaven. Barbara later wrote of this uneasy period of recovering from grief: "He made it okay for our friends to mention her, and that helped us a great deal."[35]

The Bush family at this time were regulars at First Presbyterian Church in Midland. George W. grew up with parents whose faith was palpably helping them cope with a major family loss and whose church attendance was as much a part of their lives as Bush Senior's coaching of George W.'s Little League team or having cookouts with friends on Saturday evenings. The youngster spent his spare time with other Sam Houston classmates playing pickup baseball games in the schoolyard or on any available open space near the family home.

It was a time, too, when George W. began to develop a phenomenal memory for names. While in junior high school, for example, George W. could name the starting lineup of every United States major league baseball team. This feat combined his lifelong passion for baseball with a skill that was to have formidable political usefulness to him later on. Meanwhile, with his father constantly traveling, it was his mother whom George W. resembled in personality more than his father, who became the family disciplinarian, breaking up sibling fights between George W. and Jeb and sternly reminding them that their father would be home soon and would be "disappointed"—the ultimate Bush Senior expression of rebuke. George W. would recall later, "Dad taught us about duty and service. Mother taught us about dealing with life on a personal basis, relating to other people."[36]

When he was twelve, George W. started attending San Jacinto Junior High School, where he showed incipient leadership skills by being elected class president in the seventh grade. His parents were experiencing changes, too, first moving from their modest ranch house to a larger, pool-equipped home on Sentinel Street, then moving from Midland to Houston a year later, in 1959. The Zapata Petroleum Corporation that

Bush Senior had founded in 1953 at the beginning of the Texas oil boom had divided into two parts, with Bush Senior taking charge of the off-shore component, headquartered in Houston. The Bushes lived in a large house on upscale Briar Drive and sent George W. to a private day school called Kinkaid. Here, George W., with his jokey social style and good looks, became popular among the 889 students. Already, he was beginning to develop his strong people skills, attending his father's Zapata parties and working the room with the name-recollection skills of an established pol.[37]

For all his Kinkaid popularity and adolescent people-skills precocity, though, George W. was finding a new source of spiritual inspiration: St. Martin's Episcopal Church, Sage Road, Houston. His parents, born and raised Episcopalian, had enjoyed First Presbyterian in Midland, but they decided to return to their ecclesiastical roots when they moved to Houston. George W. became an altar boy at the church and helped the priest prepare the communion service, including lighting the candles on the altar, carrying the candles in procession, and preparing wine and water for the sacrament of communion. The powerful ceremony of the service based on the ancient English *Book of Common Prayer*, the candles, the organ music, and the rich church vestments, made a strong impression on the teenager. "I loved the formality, the ritual, the candles, and there I felt the first stirrings of a faith that would be years in the making," George W. said in his 1999 campaign autobiography.[38]

But George W. had no opportunity to develop this incipient Episcopalian spirituality further. In 1961, his parents decided to put him on the same path that Bush Senior had taken back in the late 1930s: Phillips Andover. "Bush, what did you do wrong?" George W. jokingly says a friend in Houston asked him after learning that he was being sent to this stiffly formal preparatory school in cold New England. "In those days," according to George W., "Texas boys who got shipped off to school were usually in trouble with their parents."[39]

Andover meant rigid academic discipline and a school life measured in classroom periods and precise between-class breaks of seven minutes.

Coats and ties were worn for all classes and for the daily morning chapel session. For George W. and his fellow Texan friend Clay Johnson, the formality, the intense academic pressure, and the rigid schedules were at first intimidating. But George W. not only survived, he became prominent at Andover, not through athletic skills like his father, but through a talent for organizing fun. He started up an informal, intramural game of stickball and designated himself "stickball commissioner." George W.'s organizational and mobilizing skills involved entertaining fellow students even as he led them. A childhood friend from Midland who attended Andover recalled,

> He was a figurehead, well-suited to deal with a diverse group. He bridged and brought them together. Bush was slightly impulsive, it was hard for him to bite his tongue and keep from saying something that would get him in trouble. It was a completely different heritage from his father's. His dad was from an oligarchic background. GWB was a prankster, mischievous.[40]

It was at Andover that George W. began to develop what became a life-long habit of nicknaming people. Usually, these nicknames were funny and benign, but almost certainly there were some that were sarcastic and unflattering. But after he left Andover, George W. recalled his initiating the stickball program and naming himself Boss Tweed, after the notorious Tammany Hall political boss of the nineteenth century, as "a way of spreading joy, sharing humor, and lightening up what was otherwise a serious and studious environment."[41]

Andover, according to George W., "taught [me] how to think." He added, "I learned to read and write in a way I never had before." He also discovered the joys of history. Tom Lyons was a gifted teacher about whom George W. later wrote, "He taught me that history brings the past and its lessons to life, and those lessons can often help predict the future."[42]

Despite his academic progress, there was doubt, even on the part of George W. himself, about whether he would gain acceptance to Yale, the alma mater of both his father and his grandfather. In his 1999 autobiography, *A Charge to Keep*, George W. admitted that a school dean had suggested he choose some other colleges, in case Yale turned him down. He responded that the University of Texas at Austin was the only alternative to Yale with which he was comfortable.[43] During the spring break of his senior year, several friends heard him speak enthusiastically about the University of Texas and not at all about Yale, an indication that perhaps he himself didn't think he would make it to the elite, Ivy League institution.[44] But he did, of course.

By the time George W. graduated from Andover in 1964, he had imbibed the sometimes stern rectitude of his grandfather, Prescott, his grandmother's kindly and alert Episcopal pietism, his mother's quick tongue and hand, and his father's duty-oriented sense of propriety and justice. He had also embraced a fierce family mutual support system that from time to time was articulated by various family members. In *A Charge to Keep*, George W. remembered the inaugural prayer breakfast for his brother Jeb Bush after Jeb, on his second attempt, won the governorship of Florida in 1998. The incoming governor placed his hand on two Bibles, one of them used at Bush Senior's presidential inauguration in 1989. George W. says that Jeb "spoke eloquently of faith, and family, and friends. 'It is here that most of life's principles are forged,' he said, quoting Jeb. 'Loyalty, empathy, generosity, and caring are cords of a rope that bind us together into something far stronger than we can ever be individually.'"

"Faith, family, and friends," George W. continued in *A Charge to Keep*:

> The three joined together on that cold January day in 1999 just as they
> have joined together on most major occasions in my life. They guided my
> father during twelve years as President and Vice President; they are the
> ways by which, ultimately, I believe all our lives will be measured.[45]

Sometimes, Bush wrote, his parents didn't approve of their children's behavior. Certainly, George W. had felt their disapproval while at Andover and at times afterward. But, George W. said, "Our mother and dad would always love us. Always. Forever. Unwaveringly. Without question. They said it and they showed it."[46]

Even before George W. set off for Yale, his family had set in his mind certain guidelines—guidelines that were to play a decisive role in the friendships he was to develop over the years and the decisions that he would make. In his heart there were definite seeds of faith in God and an intuitive leaning toward its Christian expression. Those seeds would not take solid root until much later.

As the fall of 1964 approached, George W. was embarking on life as a young man with a privileged family background and considerable personal and social skills. But he also had an impulsive streak that would land him in trouble more than once before his path became, in early middle age, finally quite clear. Meanwhile, Yale beckoned.

# 3

## The Long Shadow

*I've got my daddy's eyes
and my mother's mouth.*

—George W. Bush

When I was young and irresponsible," George W. Bush famously said when he was running for the governorship of Texas in 1993, "I sometimes behaved young and irresponsibly."[1]

The statement was certainly true, but it implied more than he had wanted to imply and very probably more than reality warranted. The career of George W. between 1964, when he entered Yale as a freshman, and the summer of 1986, when his life decisively turned around and he gave up drinking alcohol, were years when millions of young American men indulged in drinking and womanizing. But those years were also marked by other, very positive elements in George W.'s life. In a way that may attract the attention of more psychologically minded biographers in future years, George W. seemed to carry within himself during this period two quite different personalities, sometimes overlapping, but seldom fully integrated: a snappy, irreverent, cocky prankster on the one hand, and a serious-minded, duty-oriented, disciplined achiever on the other.

Much of George W.'s first personality had its origins in the quick-mouthed iconoclast that his mother could sometimes be. The dutiful achiever was easily traceable to Bush Senior. George W. was well aware that people who knew him and his family well would often knowingly point out the parallels between mother and son. He often cashed in on that frequent association for the laughs it would draw. "I've got my daddy's eyes and my mother's mouth,"[2] he often quipped. It was Barbara who, during the 1984 Reagan presidential reelection campaign, wise-cracked infamously about Democratic vice-presidential candidate Geraldine Ferraro, who had derided the Bush family as being rich and out of touch with ordinary Americans. Barbara told a reporter toward the end of a tiring day of campaigning that Ferraro was "a four-million-dollar—I can't say it, but it rhymes with witch."[3] Barbara later apologized, and Ferraro accepted the apology, but her quick and sometimes very sharp lip was definitely inherited by George W.

---

BUSH'S ADMISSION to Yale, as we saw, had not been anticipated by some of Andover's faculty—with good reason. His SAT scores were mediocre by Yale standards in 1964: 566 (verbal) and 640 (math).[4] He had, of course, the advantage of being the scion of highly distinguished Yale alumni—his grandfather, Prescott Bush, and his father, Bush Senior, each of whom had not merely attended the famous Ivy League institution but had lent glory to its name both while there and after graduation.

Did George W.'s distinguished ancestry grease the skids of his admission to Yale? Quite possibly. Bush had, in fact, been right in the middle of Andover's graduating pack, ranking 114 in a class of 238.[5] As he was to recall much later, George W. had been profoundly impressed by his Andover history teacher, Tom Lyons, and had developed an interest in the subject that he was to pursue at Yale. But no one ever accused him, either at Andover or at Yale, of being a closet intellectual. In fact, just as had been the case at Andover, George W. seemed to pass through Yale deeply conscious of the long shadow cast upon that institution by his father and grandfather, and well aware that his own shadow while at this university was unlikely to stretch as long.

Yale changed enormously during 1964 and 1968, the years George W. was there. When he arrived in 1964, it was an elite institution known for a large annual intake of preppy boarding school graduates, just as Bush was. (At least thirty of his Andover classmates entered Yale the same year.) By the time George W. graduated in 1968, Yale had been ravaged by anguished campus debate about the Vietnam War, national tragedies such as the assassinations of Martin Luther King Jr. and Democratic presidential candidate Bobby Kennedy, and the explosion of rioting by African Americans in cities across the United States.

Strobe Talbott, the former Clinton administration deputy secretary of state and a contemporary of George W.'s at Yale—though Talbott does not recall ever meeting Bush—describes their undergraduate years there:

The [Vietnam] war issue was pretty pervasive, more in some parts of the student body than in others. For people like me editing the *Yale Daily News* it was very pervasive. It was a drumbeat. There were people off doing athletics and leading an active social life. There was no great divide or wall of hostility between them.

They were just off doing their thing. I was very close to the chaplain William Sloan Coffin. I was deacon in the chapel at Yale. It was largely thanks to him that I was that. The majority sentiment among undergraduates was anti-war, and Coffin was a very popular person.

We were grappling with the big questions of life. Many of these questions are spiritual in nature. We batted it around. I'm making a distinction between the intellectual and the spiritual. Secular humanism, it would have been true of me. One of the reasons for my viewpoint was my opposition to the war. I was raised an Episcopalian. I can't tell you anything about Bush.[6]

Talbott, who after Yale became a Rhodes scholar at Oxford University where he roomed with fellow Rhodes scholar Bill Clinton, was active as a campus journalist. He later rose through the ranks of *Time* magazine in the 1970s and 1980s to be editor-at-large and a foreign affairs columnist before joining the Clinton White House.

George W., in fact, was as turned off of organized religion by William Sloan Coffin as Talbott had been drawn to the chaplain's leadership at Yale by Coffin's strong antiwar sentiments. In an incident that seemed to burn itself sharply into Bush's memory for decades, he introduced himself to Coffin one morning late in 1964, after Bush Senior had been defeated in a run for a senate seat in Texas by Ralph Yarborough. Bush had been so deeply hurt by his father's loss that he had sat by himself, with his head facing the wall, so people wouldn't notice the tears in his eyes when the results were announced. But Coffin, pastor or not, had no words of consolation for the freshman son of a politically vanquished Yale alumnus when the met shortly afterward on campus.

"Oh yes, I know your father," Coffin said, according to Bush's recollection of the incident. "Frankly, he was beaten by the better man."

Years later, to his credit, Coffin apologized for this unkind comment. Barbara Bush, looking back on the incident, believes that Coffin's comment helped alienate George W. from church attendance at Yale. She recalled, "That [comment by Coffin] kept him away from church at Yale. We were just shattered. That was an enormous shock."[7]

But George W. even then seemed to have an interest in Christian things. He kept a copy of *The Living Bible* open by his bedside in his parents' home in Houston. Barbara remembers showing friends around the house when her son was about twenty and at Yale. One of the friends commented, "Oh, he'll outgrow it," as though Bible reading were some passing teenage phase, such as marijuana smoking or playing hooky from school. "I don't know why he said that," Barbara recalled with some indignation.[8]

Certainly, observers at Yale could be forgiven for not discerning much spiritual inclination in the way George W. conducted himself. His first two roommates in the freshman dorm known as the Old Campus were Andover schoolmates Clay Johnson (also from Texas) and Robert Dieter. Even then George W. was exhibiting a characteristic he was to display long into adult life: slovenliness in dress, an unfortunate habit that people noticed. Johnson recalled later that Bush paid scant attention to his laundry. "He would grab a T-shirt off the floor and put it on," Johnson said. "He'd wrap a tie around his neck, and technically he would wear a coat, but there might not be any arms on the shirt under it."[9]

However, George W. was also demonstrating a striking skill in an area that paid huge dividends later in life. He was astoundingly good at remembering people's names. One friend at the time, Roland W. Betts, said he thought that Bush was able to recall the names of half of the entire freshman class. He would approach people on campus he did not know, introduce himself, learn their names, and somehow fix them in his mind. This gift was demonstrated vividly in Bush's second year at Yale, when he pledged the Delta Kappa Epsilon fraternity, familiarly known as Deke. Johnson and Dieter joined Deke at the same time. During the pledge week rush, George W. stunned both Deke veterans and his fellow rushees by reciting perfectly, when asked to recall whom he had met that evening, the names of all fifty-four people in the room.[10]

Bush's gregariousness, his bonhomie, and his cocky humor won him many friends at Deke, which elected him fraternity president in his junior year. He was interested in sports—he attended basketball, baseball, and football games, and even a frat-house all-night poker game—in drinking (mostly beer), and of course, in girls. Terry Johnson, a sometime roommate at Deke, remembers him this way: "I think that people would say, objectively, that we were reasonably intelligent, but that we didn't spend a lot of time reading poetry in coffeehouses. George liked, more than anything, to be with people."[11]

Robert McCallum, a friend from another fraternity, said, "People didn't think of George as an intellectual policy wonk or anything. George spent a lot of time learning from other people. Those who were book-oriented would think he wasn't a serious student, but he was a serious student of other people."[12]

Of course, George W. was also seriously popular with the girls. At the age of twenty, in his junior year, he fell in love with Cathryn Wolfman, a gifted student at Rice University whom he had met during school breaks at home in Houston. During the Christmas vacation break of 1967, he announced their engagement.

Although it didn't endure, the engagement was a striking throwback to that of his father, who had become engaged also at the age of twenty while serving as a navy pilot during World War II. In fact, even as he enjoyed the fraternity drinking binges, the shadows of his father and grandfather were falling across him in another way.

---

IN HIS JUNIOR YEAR, George W. was "tapped" (invited by existing membership) for Skull and Bones, the well-known Yale senior-year secret society that was founded in 1832 and has been the focus of wild, indeed sometimes paranoid, conspiracy theories ever since. Skull and Bones is the most famous of the Yale societies, which admit a dozen or so juniors as lifetime members. Since the intake is so small, there are only around eight hundred Bonesmen (women were admitted for the first time in 1992) at any time, and Yale being already an elite institution, it is hardly surprising that Bonesmen have risen to be United States cabinet secretaries, Supreme Court justices, and even, on three occasions, presidents of the United States—most recently, Bush Senior and George W.

The prestige of Skull and Bones membership and the fear of its alleged power among many of the society's critics are products of the secrecy in which the society has operated from the outset and the unmistakable achievement of generation upon generation of Bonesmen. President and Supreme Court Justice Howard Taft, Ambassador W. Averill Harriman, Secretary of State Henry Stimson, Massachusetts senator and Democratic presidential aspirant John Kerry, conservative political commentator and author William F. Buckley, and of course Bush Senior's father, Prescott Bush, later himself a U. S. Senator, were all Bonesmen. But while the first century and more of the Skull and Bones tradition was heavily Waspish from the 1950s onward, both African Americans and foreigners were admitted.

Among those tapped along with George W. were an Orthodox Jew and a Jordanian Arab. Bonesmen traditionally are supposed to leave the room anytime a "barbarian" (i.e., non-Bonesman) even mentions the name of the society or the numeral by which it is also sometimes known, 322. In *A Charge to Keep*, George W. is dutifully reticent, writing, "My senior year I joined Skull and Bones, a secret society, so secret I can't say anything more. It was a chance to make fourteen new friends."[13]

The Skull and Bones initiation ritual—which appears never to have been fully and credibly penetrated by outsiders—does seem to involve some hocus-pocus ceremonials, but almost certainly not of any genuinely "spiritual" significance. It focuses on stripping initiates of any pretense or barriers of reserve about who they really are—a process that, in its turn, is likely to reinforce a sense of bonding among the fifteen "knights," as the newly tapped members are called, for the rest of their time at Yale and, for many Bonesmen, for the rest of their lives.

In his important 1951 book, *God and Man at Yale*, William F. Buckley, a Bonesman, denounced the socialist and atheistic leanings of much of the Yale faculty, even as several bonesmen from earlier classes vigorously defended the university against Buckley's attack. They included McGeorge Bundy and none other than William Sloan Coffin, later to be a thorn in the flesh of freshman George W.[14] In effect, if there had ever been some nefarious, anti-Christian plot cooked up within the "Tomb," as the Skull and Bones building is called, it does not seem to have made much imprint in the Bonesmen of the late twentieth century.

As for George W. Bush, Bonesmen reportedly never saw him return to the Tomb for reunions or dinners, unlike his father who was at a Bones Tomb celebration as recently as 1998. Though George W. certainly kept in touch with some of his fellow Bonesmen, he has affected an almost insouciant unawareness of the institution's recent or current activities. According to Alexandra Robbins in her informative history of Skull and Bones, George W. responded to a question about Bones by ABC News by saying: "Does it still exist? The thing is so secret that I'm not even sure it still exists."[15]

Bush's ambivalence about Skull and Bones probably is in part explained by the general suspicion of alleged East Coast supra-governmental conspiracies against American freedoms concocted by Ivy League elitists like Bonesmen, by members of the New York-based Council on Foreign Relations, or by the Trilateral Commission. When Bush Senior was running for the U.S. Senate from Texas in 1964, critics said that he seemed tarred with the brush of East Coast elitism. The same charge—hardly possible to disprove—was later to be used against George W. when he ran unsuccessfully for Congress in Texas in 1978.

There are two other possible explanations for Bush's seeming lack of interest in the secret society of his senior year at Yale. One is that his own Christian experience later in life, an experience replete with deep and lasting spiritual relationships over many years with close Christian friends, has eclipsed whatever friendship bonding occurred at Skull and Bones. The second is George W.'s apparently lifelong distaste for the pretensions of much of the predominantly liberal world-view of many of the students and faculty on Ivy League campuses.

"I always felt that people on the East Coast tended to feel guilty about what they were given," he told an interviewer years later. "Like, 'I'm rich; they're poor.' Or, 'I went to Andover and got a great education, and they didn't.' I was never one to feel guilty. I feel lucky. People who feel guilty react like guilty people."[16]

Some of that guilt, to be sure, was an outgrowth of the heightened social concerns of the 1960s, including exactly that preoccupation with Vietnam referred to by Strobe Talbott earlier. Fellow Bonesman Mohammed Saleh from Jordan had this to say of George W. at Yale in relation to the Vietnam issue:

> He was not obsessed by anything, or a cause. He didn't have an agenda, a timetable, a program. We were in the Vietnam era, it was a big subject, and the big thing about George is really that he was not doctrinaire about anything. You would think, coming from a political family, that he would take strong views.[17]

Mickey Herskowitz, a Texas journalist who is the biographer of Prescott Bush and has come to know the entire Bush family well, links a similar detachment from the Vietnam issue with George W.'s Christian interests while at Yale. Herskowitz says this:

> He wasn't ardently pro- or anti-war [at Yale]. I think he supported the war, but he wasn't passionate about it. I think he probably went to church with his family when he was with them at Kennebunkport. George W. Bush at Yale and before that at Andover probably was tolerably religious. The Bush family doesn't really argue politics or religion. Bush Sr. often used to say to me that they were not like the Kennedys who discussed politics at the dinner table.[18]

At Yale, in fact, Bush would have had little time for extended study of religion, beyond his private-time Bible reading. Appropriately enough for what was to happen to Bush later on, Yale, like many other New England colleges, was established to train ministers. America's most famous theologian and arguably the country's most brilliant Christian intellectual, Jonathan Edwards (1703–1758), was a Yale tutor from 1724 to 1726. For the first several decades of its existence, the college laws stated, "Every student shall consider the main end of his study to wit to know God in Jesus Christ and answerably lead a godly sober life." Between 1702 and 1739 no fewer than 46 percent of the graduates took up positions in full-time Christian ministry.[19] Indeed, chapel attendance was compulsory at Yale until 1926.

But though George W. throughout his Yale years may well have had godly inclinations, sobriety was not high on his list of priorities. In the 1966 Christmas season, he and other Yalies descended upon New Haven, surely well lubricated by some beers, and tried to grab a Christmas wreath from a storefront. Bush was questioned, briefly arrested, and later charged with disorderly conduct, though the charges were subsequently dismissed.

On another occasion, he and his Yale buddies tried to dismantle the goalposts at Princeton University during the annual Princeton-Yale game. They were ordered by police to leave the premises of Princeton forthwith. It was, of course, youthful high spirits, though his cousin Elsie Walker admitted that during his undergraduate years she and others had considered George W.'s behavior "outrageous." She went on: "Pop off, hilarious, imitate people, very, very broad. I mean, he got away with it because he was so funny, but if most people would try what he would try, they would fall flat."[20]

---

THERE WERE PLENTY OF UNFUNNY THINGS happening in the United States while Bush was at Yale too. The 1960s, after all, was one of the most socially tumultuous periods in American history. Despite George W.'s lack of deep engagement in the larger foreign policy and domestic political issues that were roiling Yale and scores of other campuses across the United States, by 1968 there were some events that not even an entirely apolitical student could ignore: the assassination of Martin Luther King Jr., for example, in April 1968. Bush wrote later that he had been "shocked" by that crime and then "stunned" by the violence in America's cities that followed King's murder. Despite his years of schooling in Texas, where racial prejudice certainly existed well beyond the 1960s, Bush's own parents had rigorously opposed any expression of racial intolerance within their own family. Bush says that his mother had once washed out his mouth with soap after hearing him repeat a racial slur he had picked up in school.[21] He also writes that even within his Deke fraternity there were good across-the-board relationships between him and African American fraternity brothers. But by 1968, with the United States involvement in Vietnam dramatized yet further by the intensity of the fighting following the Tet offensive in January 1968, the war was no longer a matter of academic debate for Yale undergraduates.

In fact, for many young men the options boiled down to two: to await the inevitable call of the draft and find themselves shipped out to a war zone in a conflict they probably opposed in totality, or to skip the country and wait the war out in Canada. Bush himself was to write later:

We discussed Vietnam, but we were more concerned with the decision each of us had to make: military service or not. I knew I would serve. Leaving the country to avoid the draft was not an option for me; I was too conservative and too traditional. My inclination was to support the government and the war until proven wrong, and that only came later, as I realized we could not explain the mission, had no exit strategy, and did not seem to be fighting to win.[22]

Bush had already registered for selective service with Texas Local Board No. 62. But he says that during the 1967 Christmas break, he learned from contemporaries in Houston of openings in the Texas Air National Guard. There has been speculation that Bush's family pulled strings to get him accepted by the Texas Air Guard, but biographer Minutaglio quotes military officials, who were familiar with both the procedure for applying at that time and with George W., as doubting that this was actually done.[23] In fact, it's highly unlikely that someone could be admitted to any flight training program in the United States military without meeting stringent skill standards determined through rigorous testing. Flying a supersonic jet that costs millions of dollars and whose crash also could cost several lives isn't something entrusted to the first person to come through the door with the right last name.

There is a simpler explanation for Bush joining the Texas Air National Guard: it was the closest he could come to replicating yet another aspect of his father's brilliant career. In fact, when asked by the Texas Air National Guard commander of 147th Fighter Group what the *real* reason was for his wanting to join the Texas Air National Guard, George W.'s response was quite simple: "I want to be a fighter pilot because my father was."[24]

THE AIR NATIONAL GUARD was not a slacker's alternative to being drafted by or volunteering for the regular United States military forces. It required fifty-five weeks of full-time flight training with regular U.S. Air

Force units. Bush began his training in November 1968 at Moody Air Force Base in Valdosta, Georgia, starting with single-engine propeller aircraft, then moving upward through higher and higher performance planes until, at his graduation in December 1969 one year later, he was qualified to fly the T-38 jet. He then transferred to Ellington Air Force Base in Houston for training on the already obsolete but still supersonic F-102 Delta Dagger fighter jet. This aircraft was first flown in 1953, and by the time it was pulled from service, some one thousand had been built and assigned to twenty-five Air Defense Command squadrons in the United States. When the U.S. Air Force transitioned to more modern fighters, the F-102s were assigned to the Air National Guard throughout the country.

It is easy to discern in George W.'s decision to learn to fly in the Air National Guard a desire not merely to emulate his father's sterling military career in some small way but to test his own mettle. Flying a high-performance aircraft is extremely demanding, requiring constant attention and considerable self-discipline. Bush wrote later:

Cockpits of fighter jets are tiny and close, and they force you to learn economy of motion. They also force you to master yourself, mentally, physically, and emotionally. You have to stay calm and think logically. One mistake and you could end up in a very expensive metal coffin.[25]

That was no mere theoretical bluster. Several Air National Guard pilots have died in training accidents over the years. But a contemporary Air Guardsman was complimentary about the young Yale graduate's performance, saying, "He was certainly competent. He didn't put on airs."[26]

Discipline, danger, and duty. These inclinations in George W.'s character were certainly being fed in the Texas Air National Guard. But there was plenty of time for off-duty carousing too. Bush joined fellow officers in well-lubricated, raucous sessions at the bar of the officers' mess. His outgoing, ebullient personality was suited to air force life. But Bush Senior's political life was never far from George W.'s mind. In 1970, while

Bush Senior was seeking President Nixon's strong backing for a run for a Senate seat in Texas, George W. was picked up at his base in Valdosta, Georgia, by a United States government aircraft and flown to Andrews Air Force Base in Maryland. The purpose? A dinner date with the older of Nixon's two daughters, Tricia. Bush has never discussed what took place that evening. But though his fellow officers mercilessly ribbed him about it, the date, which in theory could have led to a major political dynastic alliance of President Nixon and the Bush family, never developed into a romance.

George W. completed his full-time flight training on the F-102 Delta Dagger in June 1970, when Bush Senior was well into a serious Senate campaign in Texas. Once back in Houston, he rented an apartment in a landmark community of Houston singles, the Chateaux Dijon, and started an entry-level job with a former employee of his father's. He was garrulous, sometimes funny, popular with the girls, and always ready to party. He also frequently drank heavily—not to the point of passed-out drunkenness, but to the point of no longer being funny and sometimes quite rude. It isn't clear whether George W. was still reading his Bible regularly at this time, but he did attend church when with his family at Kennebunkport in the summer, or in Houston, and later in New York. (Bush Senior, after failing to win a Texas Senate seat in 1970, was awarded the cabinet-level post of ambassador to the United Nations in 1971.) One weekend each month, Bush would show up for national guard duty at Houston's Ellington Air Force Base.

The following year, in 1972, Bush changed his reserve duty base to Montgomery, Alabama, when he decided to work for a few months on the political campaign of Winton M. "Red" Blount, who was running for the U.S. Senate seat then held by John Sparkman.

During early 2004, there was controversy over Bush's national guard service in Alabama, with Democrats questioning whether he had even shown up. In response the White House released Bush's military records, including his pay stubs and dental records, to prove that Bush had indeed done his duty in Alabama.

By midsummer of 1972, the Watergate scandal had broken with the initial Washington, D.C., break-in. In November 1972, George W.'s candidate, Winton Blount, was soundly defeated in Alabama. Meanwhile, after the 1972 election, Bush Senior was being wooed by Nixon away from his job at the United Nations to run the Republican National Committee.

All five of the Bush children returned to their parents' house in Washington, D.C., for the Christmas vacation. George W. spoke revealingly of the great attractiveness of the family environment of love and acceptance created by Bush Senior and Barbara:

> One reason we came home was the atmosphere was comfortable and warm. Another reason we came home is the way we were raised. I've never heard George and Barbara Bush utter a harsh or ugly word to each other; never heard either of them characterize each other in an ugly way. They set the tone. The final reason we came home was unconditional love. They loved each other and there was no question they loved us children.[27]

But this vacation time was marred by another landmark incident that reflected George W.'s fondness for the bottle. Driving home with his brother Marvin, then fifteen, one evening after probably several drinks, George W., banged the car into a neighborhood garbage can, which then attached itself to the car wheel and made a terrible clattering noise as the car headed into the family driveway. Bush Senior was at home and demanded that George W. see him immediately in the den. In a confrontation that has been described many times, George W. engaged in bluster: "I hear you're looking for me. You wanna go *mano a mano* [hand to hand] right here?"[28]

It was a tense moment, fraught with the risk of a really ugly confrontation, and was defused only when Jeb announced the unexpected news that George W. had been accepted by Harvard Business School's prestigious M.B.A. program. Bush had toyed with the idea of going to law school but had been rejected several months earlier by the most prominent university of his home state, the University of Texas at Austin.

Some observers have speculated that application to Harvard was a sort of thought-I-couldn't-do-it-eh? ploy by a young man who appeared to be somewhat flailing around in his life. He was obviously intelligent, albeit no intellectual. He loved being with people, he had a phenomenal memory for names, he enjoyed spending time with the ladies—and the sentiment seemed to be amply reciprocated—and he seemed to have a mind acutely tuned to political issues. He had also sowed something of a young man's adventurous oats by learning to fly high-performance aircraft with other talented fighter pilots. But at the age when his father had won medals for gallantry as a World War II pilot and had set off to start his own oil company in Texas, George W. didn't yet have an especially impressive résumé. It is more than probable that the "achiever" component of his personality came to the fore at this stage. He decided to accept the Harvard admission. There is no record of how his family responded to this decision, but it may well have been with relief.

---

GEORGE W. COULD HAVE FILLED the nine months between Christmas 1972 and entering Harvard in the fall in any number of ways, some of them perhaps reasonably lucrative. Instead, at the suggestion of Bush Senior, he went to work in Houston's inner-city impoverished Fifth Ward with an organization called PULL (Professional United Leadership League). PULL had been organized by two former professional football players as a way to introduce the tough and often alienated youngsters of Houston's inner city to successful athletes, a few of whom had themselves started amid considerable social disadvantages. Bush worked with other PULL staffers to raise money for the program. His comfortable familiarity with prominent and successful people impressed his PULL colleagues.

George W. also demonstrated something that was little noticed before. He seemed to connect with many of the inner-city kids who flocked to PULL. One tough youngster named Jimmy in particular seemed to bond with Bush, who helped buy clothes and shoes when the boy needed them.

More significantly, though, Bush seemed willing to spend time just hanging out with the boy. Years later, in the summer of 2003, when President George W. Bush was visiting the Power Center, an outreach program of the Windsor Village United Methodist Church in Houston, the African American pastor, Rev. Kirbyjon Caldwell, told an interesting story. Caldwell said he had been approached by a young African American just a few months earlier who had said, "Let me tell you something about the president. When the president was a younger man, he spent an entire summer with me, and I am the person I am today because President George W. Bush spent personal time with me some years ago during the summer."[29] That man was Jimmy.

What is striking about this episode in Bush's life, confirmed by an African American pastor decades later, is that, for all of his prankish exuberance, George W. was not only deeply touched by the needs of kids with obvious disadvantages in life but willing to spend the time and the emotional capital necessary to respond to them. All of this preceded the spiritual encounters that were to change his life ten years later. But at PULL, Bush showed a streak of genuine compassion that wouldn't necessarily have shown up on any political résumé.

By the time George W. arrived at Harvard in the fall of 1973, his earlier suspicions of what he considered East Coast intellectual snobbery were well in place. But he also sensed that Harvard might teach him some useful things—not just business knowledge but an understanding of how to come to terms with a career itself. He was to write later, "When I saw the Harvard application I was intrigued. Completing it required taking stock of your life. It forced me to think about what I had accomplished and what I hoped to achieve. I had learned to fly jets and acquired a good education; I had not yet settled on a path in life."[30]

Nat Butler, a Harvard classmate who had known George W. years earlier when they were cheerleaders for their rival schools—George W. for Andover and Butler for Exter—learned soon after the two met up again that Bush wasn't on the big corporate track that the majority of Harvard M.B.A. students seemed to be following. Butler said, "Some people at that school wanted him to be the head of Citicorp, but he didn't have a specific focus like that." Bush wrote later, "I hadn't gone to business school to work my way up a corporate ladder. . . . I wanted to be my own boss." Harvard, he wrote, was to provide him with "the tools and the confidence to do so."[31] He called it "a turning point" in his life.[32]

Nevertheless, he appeared to resent not just the East Coast elitist snobbery of the university but the strikingly liberal political attitude of most of the undergraduates and even many of the M.B.A. students. The Watergate crisis was approaching its apogee in late 1973 to 1974, and George W. was no supporter of Nixon after it became apparent that he had not been open for months about how much he had known about the break-in. At the same time, however, something in him resented the smugness of much of the political liberalism of that day. Perhaps in reaction to that, George W. would often wear his national guard flight jacket around the Harvard campus and would chew tobacco and then spit it out into a paper cup. He became health conscious, eating raw carrots and pursuing with zealous discipline what was to be a lifelong passion that consumed his spare time until he became president: running.

As Watergate wound its way inexorably to the political demise of Nixon, Bush Senior had his hands full trying to keep the Republican Party together. In July he wrote a long letter to his four sons recounting his own disgust with the Watergate coverup and the seediness of some of the characters involved in it. (One of the Nixon White House players was Chuck Colson who, a few years later, became a well known Christian convert. In the letter, Bush Senior described Colson at that time as having "no judgment, a mean and vicious streak—so insidious and ugly." Later, after the transformations in each of their lives, George W. and Colson came to be on very good terms.[33] "I expect it has not been easy for you to have your dad be head of the RNC at this time," Bush Senior wrote his sons, noting that it had been "a tough eighteen months" for him as chairman of the Republican National Committee, leaving him "battered and disillusioned." But then came what George W. called "gratuitous advice": "Listen to your conscience. Don't be afraid not to join the mob—if you feel inside it's wrong."[34] It was characteristic of Bush Senior's almost nineteenth-century sense of duty and loyalty that he stayed publicly faithful to the Nixon White House, even as he analyzed privately with his family his own disgust with what was happening within it.

On August 8, 1974, Nixon announced his resignation, effective the next day, which resulted in a job change for Bush Senior that was to impact his son. The incoming president, Gerald Ford, grateful for Bush Senior's faithful but thankless task of running the Republican Party throughout Watergate, agreed to appoint him chief of the U.S. liaison office in China—in effect, United States ambassador to China—at a time when the two countries had no formal diplomatic relations.

Bush Senior and Barbara brought vigor and surprising informality to the small and close-knit American residents in Beijing as the 1966–76 cultural revolution was winding down. They rode around the city on Chinese "Flying Pigeon" brand bicycles, much to the amazement of ordinary Chinese. But to the Chinese officials who kept the Bushes under careful watch, the American couple did something even more striking: they attended weekly Protestant English-language church services in a makeshift church in Rice Market Street. With every building of religious worship shut down sinde the beginning of the cultural revolution, the Chinese authorities permitted the English-language service for foreigners only. "Four Chinese oldsters," Bush wrote in another letter to his children (this time including Doro) "singing forth in Chinese as we fourteen petitioners, equally divided between African and European diplomats, sang in English. Mum and I were both choked up—here we were worshipping in a land where this kind of worship is all but forbidden."[35]

The significance of this hesitant contact of an American Christian diplomat and Chinese Protestant believers was to become clear a year later, in the summer of 1975. After graduating from Harvard, George W. and all his siblings except Jeb flew in June to visit their parents in China. The occasion was not just the annual family reunion—Beijing instead of Kennebunkport—but a baptismal service in the Rice Market Street church for sister Doro. This was almost certainly the first baptism of a foreigner in any Chinese church since 1966, and one of just a handful since 1949, when Communist rule began. After the baptism on June 29, 1975, Bush Senior wrote in his journal that the ministers had been "extremely happy and smiling." In fact, Bush Senior became very friendly with the senior Chinese pastor, Rev. Kan Xueging, who later visited the Bush family in the United States. Rev. Xueging to this day remembers the baptism and George W. Bush. "He looked just like the typical American college student," Xueging said, "wearing a T-shirt and tattered sneakers. That's even what he wore to the baptismal service."[36]

During his six-week stay—a long visit to China by any standards and exceptionally long in 1975, when few foreigners of any kind visited as tourists—George W. ran almost every day—an indication of his continuing preoccupation with health and fitness. But something of Bush's Harvard business education had clearly rubbed off on him. "My visit underscored my belief in the power and promise of the marketplace," he wrote later, "and deepened my belief that by introducing capitalism and the marketplace, China will free her people to dream and to risk. I was also reminded of how lucky I was to be an American, and I was looking forward to Midland and the promises it offered."[37]

---

AFTER HIS RETURN FROM CHINA, George W. followed yet another of the pathways pioneered by his father decades earlier. He piled into his blue 1970 Oldsmobile Cutlass (his father had driven a red Studebaker back in 1947) and drove cross-country to Odessa-Midland in West Texas. Funded by a twenty-thousand-dollar start-up grant from the Bush-Walker trust fund in his name, he earned a salary of one hundred dollars a day from work as a "landman"—someone who researches the records in town courthouses to determine who owned the mineral rights beneath any piece of land. He lived very basically in a small apartment that was as cluttered and messy as his undergraduate room at Yale. His sartorial style continued to be eclectic sloppy: sometimes mismatched socks, cotton slip-on shoes purchased in China, hand-me-down shirts, loafers held together with adhesive tape. But he was attentive to what he was learning as he hung around big-time oilmen at a time when prices per barrel were rising fast in Texas. He founded Arbusto (Spanish for "Bush"), a company that went through various permutations over the next few years before becoming subsumed into larger corporate groupings that were content to use George W.'s various talents and his useful name.

George W. also fit himself into the civic scene around Midland. This involved, among other things, teaching Sunday school at First Presbyterian Church, which the Bush Senior family had attended during George W.'s boyhood. He cracked jokes endlessly, greeted everyone with great boister-ousness, often drank quite a lot—but only in the evenings—dated around whenever the occasion arose, and, according to one observer, "cursed harder than a grease-stained roustabout."[38]

In 1976, George W. was thirty, hadn't accomplished very much, and obviously needed to settle down in some important ways. That began to happen in 1977 with a fateful meeting with a librarian from Austin, Texas, named Laura Welch. Laura was a close, longtime friend of Jan O'Neill, the wife of one of George W.'s boyhood friends, Joe O'Neill. The two men had been grade school classmates, and O'Neill had returned to the city of their childhood, Midland, after years in different parts of the country. Laura was even born in the same year as George W., 1946, but on November 4, four months after George W.'s July 12 birth date. The two met at a cookout the O'Neills arranged for Laura during one of her trips back to her family home in Midland from Austin. George W. was smitten. Instead of leaving the O'Neills early, a common practice for George W., who prided himself on both punctuality and early nights, he stayed late, talking exuberantly to Laura. She seemed to pay close attention.

Within days, the two were dating regularly, and when George W. departed for Kennebunkport for the 1977 summer family vacation there, he called her constantly in Austin. In his 1999 campaign autobiography, *A Charge to Keep*, George W. devotes an entire chapter on his romance and marriage to Laura, entitling it "The Best Decision I Ever Made." He is also unusually candid about how this marriage seems, on a purely emotional level, to have matched two completely opposite personalities:

> Laura is calm; I am energetic. She is restful; I am restless. She is patient; I am impatient. But our differing styles exaggerate our differences. We share the same basic values. We share a West Texas upbringing that taught us that each individual is equal and equally important, but also that each individual has a responsibility to be a good neighbor and a good citizen. We both love to read, we both love spending time with our friends, and we both, very quickly, fell in love with each other.[39]

Very quickly indeed. Just three months after their first meeting on November 7, 1977, George W. and Laura were married at the First United Methodist Church in Midland, where Laura and her family had worshiped for years. George W., despite having been a diligent Presbyterian Church member, quickly adapted to the United Methodist Church. He formally joined Laura's church, and their twins were baptized there in 1981, a few months after they were born.

If George W. had been asked at the moment of his marriage whether he were a Christian, he probably would have indignantly replied, "Of course I am." He had been a Sunday school teacher and was on the finance committee of Midland's First Presbyterian Church. He read the Bible frequently, and he knew that his parents were both churchgoers and people who prayed daily. Although unfastidious in dress, he was not a bad person. He was charming, generous with those he liked or admired, and genuinely interested in the underdog. But if he had been asked, "What is God's purpose in your life?" he probably would not have had a ready answer.

This was true in 1977 when he and Laura embarked on George W.'s first run for political office—for the Texas 19th Congressional District of the U.S. House of Representatives. George W. had announced his plan to contest this position even before he and Laura had begun to fall in love. The possibility that a Republican might take over the recently vacated seat of a longtime Democratic incumbent was enticing. Even though the conservative governor of California, Ronald Reagan, supported George W.'s Republican primary opponent, the young Bush won his party's nomination and went on to fight the Congressional election of November 1978.

But Bush lost. One reason was that his canny opponent, State Senator Kent Hance, succeeded in portraying George W. as an out-of-towner, an East Coast preppy who really didn't know very much about real life in Texas. Hance also accomplished something that would never happen again in George W.'s political career: he succeeded in mobilizing Christian conservatives against Bush. A Bush campaign staffer had unwisely advertised free beer at a "Bush Bash." Hance sent out campaign letters to known antialcohol church members accusing Bush, in effect, of corrupting the youth of Texas by offering them free beer. "Dear Fellow Christians," the letter from Hance's camp began, and the rest was predictable. A journalist much later wrote this about the incident: "Long before the Christian Coalition was a force to be reckoned with, Bush received a baptism by fire into the world of fundamentalist politics and learned firsthand the perils of running afoul of religious zeal."[40] "Frankly," Bush confided later, "getting whipped was probably a pretty good thing for me."[41]

But if George W. had been "whipped" in his first contest for electoral office, the Bush family as a whole didn't have much time for licking their wounds. Bush Senior had, with encouragement from several highly placed Republican leaders, decided to throw his hat into the ring for the GOP nomination in the 1980 election. When Reagan swept the Republican field, Bush Senior at first disdained to be available for the vice presidential slot on the ticket, even though George W. considered this to be a very advantageous position for a later run by his father, perhaps in 1984 or 1988.[42] But when the call came through to Bush Senior's suite in Detroit's Hotel Ponchartrain, the patriarch was willing to accept it.

---

AFTER REAGAN'S INAUGURATION in January 1981, the entire Bush family got used to going "home" to join Bush Senior and Barbara at the official vice presidential residence at the Naval Observatory in Washington, a roomier dwelling than the White House and with greater privacy. When George W. visited, he enjoyed comfortable runs within the large and well-protected grounds.

But George W., after his own initial political defeat, turned his energies to his family and to trying to make something of his still-uncertain entry into the world of oil exploration. Meanwhile, Laura was pregnant. Her pregnancy with twins in 1981 became dangerously complicated by the onset of toxemia, an ailment of pregnant women in their third trimester. Though the birth was successful, it was an anxious time for George W.

Bush's oil business wasn't proceeding particularly well either. In 1983, Bush Exploration ranked a low 993 among ongoing Texas oil production companies. In 1984 he merged with Spectrum 7, an oil investment fund. But still the world oil prices continued to fall. Bush took a brief leave from his Spectrum 7 responsibilities to campaign for the Reagan-Bush re-election bid. It was then that he met a political consultant who was to play a major role later in his father's presidential bid, Lee Atwater. George W.'s feisty, in-your-face attitude found a connection in Atwater, a fellow-Southerner who was used to near-physical confrontations in arguments. The two men hit it off.

George W.'s friends in Midland had become worried, though. Despite his apparently good marriage to Laura, his work-hard-and-play-hard philosophy was causing heads to shake. Though he remained disciplined in his daily runs, often taken in the middle of the day, his personal style was conspicuous for its rough edges. The Midland Country Club created the George W. Bush award for the worst-dressed golfer. Both he and Laura smoked, and George W. maintained an old habit of spitting chewing tobacco into a Styrofoam cup.

But worse was his drinking. Though he was devoted to his family, there were evenings when he'd come home clearly worse for the wear and stumble around the house. Over the Labor Day weekend in 1976, he had been pulled over while driving near Kennebunkport and charged with "driving under the influence" of alcohol. He paid a fine of one hundred and fifty dollars and his license was suspended for a month. The story never surfaced publicly until a Democratic Party sympathizer released the information just days before the 2000 presidential election, obviously hoping to cause the maximum damage to Bush's election hopes.

Bush's secretary, named Dyches, was frightened by the way George W. was continuing to "curse like a sailor." He was doing so, in fact, while also teaching Sunday school, coaching Little League, helping the United Way program, and playing a significant role on the church's finance committee. It would be quite wrong to say that George W., in the early 1980s, was "conflicted," to use psychological jargon. However, the two coexisting personalities were certainly not effectively integrated: the backslapping, joking carouser on the one hand and the disciplined, focused, dutiful achiever on the other.

Bush often expressed exasperation during his run for the governorship of Texas in 1993 with journalists who wanted a chapter-and-verse account of all of his youthful actions that he had in mind when he said he had been "young and irresponsible." Many wanted to know then—as they did when he was running for president in 1999—whether George W. had ever smoked marijuana or snorted cocaine. Marijuana, in fact, wouldn't have been such a damaging admission, if it had indeed happened. Even President Clinton had admitted to that, while claiming he never actually inhaled while he was smoking.

But a Midland resident who knew George W. quite well in the 1970s and 1980s and who was, by his own admission, both an alcoholic and a sometime cocaine user at that time, strongly doubted that Bush had gone the drug route at all. "Listen," said Don Poage, now a recovering alcoholic and a social service counselor in Midland, "I'd be sitting at the bar snorting cocaine. If Bush had ever done that in Midland, I would have known about it."[43]

Of course, it's possible that Bush tried marijuana either at Yale in the 1960s or a few years later at Harvard. But there are some compelling reasons why he probably didn't. One is the distaste he has so often voiced for the psychedelic turn of music in the late 1960s—even the Beatles—a characteristic of people deeply into hallucinogenic substances. Another was his own almost obsessive desire to stay healthy: the long workout runs (and eventually a completed marathon), the carrot diets, the refusal to drink alcohol in the mornings. Bush's friends from that era are adamant that, thoroughly enlivened by alcohol though he could be, there was a part of him that just would not let things get totally away from him.

Mercer Reynolds, a business colleague who has known Bush from 1980 on and who spent a lot of time working, working out, and partying with George W., is unwavering in describing the future president as someone who hated to lose control of things. Reynolds said, "He never did anything that I think was embarrassing or out of control. I was never with him when he was totally inebriated. He had a great sense of loyalty and duty." Of course, a friend and supporter of the president, he would be expected to defend George W. against allegations of crazy behavior.

So many others, though, have said almost identical things—the picture of George W. Bush before the reemergence of his Christian faith is pretty much as it has been portrayed by all of the existing public stories. Bush, to put it simply, was a young man of talent, intuition, hard work, and discipline, who was also humorous, feisty, backslapping and exuberant to a fault. But he was without a consistent framework for either his behavior or his longterm goals. As he approached forty, George W. would have struck many people as funny and fun to be around, but he almost certainly would not have impressed anyone as a person capable of reaching for, much less attaining, the highest elected office in the United States.

Then something remarkable happened to George W. that entirely changed his life.

# 4

## COMING TO THE CROSSROADS

*As I studied and learned, Scripture took on greater meaning,
and I gained confidence and understanding in my faith.*

—GEORGE W. BUSH

ABOUT A MILE OUTSIDE MIDLAND, on the right-hand side of Texas
Route 20 as you head for Odessa, looms a large white billboard with black
letters: "Dear Permian Basin, if my people will pray and seek my face and
turn from their wicked ways, then I will forgive their sin and heal their
land." The billboard is paid for by Cornerstone Christian Church, but the
words carry no copyright. They are a paraphrase of one of the most
frequently quoted passages from the Bible, 2 Chronicles 7:14: "If my
people, who are called by my name, will humble themselves and pray, and
seek my face, and turn from their wicked ways, then will I hear from
heaven and will forgive their sin and heal their land" (NIV).

These are the words that God said to Solomon after the Jewish king
finished constructing the temple in Jerusalem and wanted to dedicate it.
The text has frequently been invoked when Christian communities have
sought to reform themselves or to pray for revival, cleansing, or renewal,
often during times of fasting. President Ronald Reagan used this scripture
during both of his presidential inaugurations.

The billboard's location just outside Midland says a lot about the city, but it doesn't fully convey Midland's nature as a community of churches and steady-minded Christians who have weathered the wild swings of the economic climate and somehow not lost touch with the tough soil of West Texas. Tumbleweed and wild grass grow spreadeagle across the dry, flat panorama on either side of the road—residents of this hardscrabble environment long before humans came and set down roots here.

The slow and steady emergence of George W. Bush's faith cannot be explained without understanding Midland. George W. wasn't born there, but he spent the formative years of his childhood there, and like so many of his close friends, he came to love the place, both for being the place of important childhood experiences and as the place where he came to spiritual maturity and began the long walk that led eventually to the White House. He has often said he wants to be buried in Midland. In fact, Midlanders already seem to anticipate their city becoming famous because of its association with a United States president. Steps have already been taken to preserve the home of Bush Senior and Barbara on Ohio Street, where George W. spent part of his childhood while attending Sam Houston Elementary School and San Jacinto Junior High School. A large sign on the lot says, "Childhood home of George W. Bush Incorporated." Midland's website (www.ci.midland.tx.us/gwb.htm) proudly declares that the community, home to some ninety-five thousand people has been ranked for more than a decade among the top one hundred and fifty cities in the United States in which to live.

Midland is the embodiment of West Texas in many ways. It is the administrative center of the petroleum-producing region called the Permian Basin, which holds some 20 percent of all of America's oil and gas reserves. Midland's slogan is "The Sky's the Limit," which George W. invoked during the 2000 Republican National Convention. People have waxed both eloquent and cynical about Midland as the apotheosis of American middle-class boosterism. "The values Midland holds dear to its heart are the same ones I hold near to my heart," Bush told the convention. "It's a town of risktakers . . . a town that knows the value of hard work and having an optimistic vision."[1] Musing on the president's hometown and its impact on George W.'s character, Karl Rove, his senior political advisor and a close friend of many years, says this:

> I know Midland. I didn't grow up in Midland but I grew up in towns like Midland. Midland is the West. The guys living next to you today could be up tomorrow and down the day after. You could just as easily be living next door to the Mexican tool-pusher as you could be living next door to the oil millionaire who's got a high-school education and struck it rich by gumption. It's that kind of place. Dream it, you can do it, and realize you may be up one day and down tomorrow and what really matters is not what you got but who you are, the content of your character. So you take Midland, and you infuse it with Methodism—I've always viewed Methodism as sort of the working man egalitarian: Everybody's worthy of respect, we're Methodist because the Anglicans think we're too good for them, you know, that kind of thing. And I really do think this belief that every person is worthy of dignity and respect, it comes in part from his egalitarian roots, and in part from his faith. And it informs his thinking and his way of speaking naturally because it's there. That's who he is.[2]

Midland had a thriving evangelical Christian community when George W. was living there. That community continues to be active today and has become influential in international politics. The Midland *Yellow Pages* list more than three hundred "churches" (including two mosques under the "churches" category), divided into thirty-eight Christian denominations. Some two hundred Midland churches today comprise the Midland Ministerial Alliance, a remarkable core of activist congregations whose campaigning on behalf of religious freedom from Sudan to North Korea resonates in Washington itself. The cover story in the December 2003/January 2004 issue of the *American Spectator* magazine reported how the alliance has come to play a major role as go-between in talks of the warring parties in the Sudanese civil war. Midland has played host to prominent Sudanese Christians, including well-known Roman Catholic bishops from Southern Sudan. The ministerial alliance has sent large delegations to Washington to meet with State Department officials and with the Sudanese ambassador. Rather quaintly, the ambassador and Sudan's foreign minister refer to Midland as "President Bush's village."[3]

Bush Senior was part of the first generation of East Coast risktakers to settle in the Permian Basin and achieve major success in Midland. In fact, Midland experienced two major oil rushes, the first in the 1950s and the second one in the 1970s. George W. returned to Midland right in the middle of the second oil rush. From 1973 to 1981 the price of oil rose 800 percent, creating a thick crust of Midland millionaires. George W. was not part of that group, not only because his own firm, Arbusto, was a startup in the mid-1970s but also because, as his friend Joe O'Neill put it, "We were raising kids."[4]

In fact, George W.'s own entrepreneurial efforts, though risktaking, energetic, and diligent, were notably lacking in the kind of gusher success that had fallen on an earlier generation. Not only was he a generation late in enjoying millionaire success, but by the early 1980s, the oil boom had become an oil drought in Midland. Very quickly, it began to hurt to be in the oil business at all. Secretary of Commerce Don Evans, a Midland native who has known George W. since the mid-1970s, recalls those times:

> When we showed up there in 1975, everything was easy. I mean, the economy was booming, you know, showing that you're making progress and showing that you're continuing to build something more material than anything else. In fact, all the material signs made things look pretty easy. And then in the early 1980s, in 1981, it started getting a little tougher. And then, in 1982 and 1983, it got a whole lot tougher. And we saw—we had friends that were going bankrupt. We saw people lose their marriages. We saw companies going bankrupt. We experienced the pain of telling somebody they didn't have a job, which is a terribly painful thing to do. And the industry really collapsed in 1986.[5]

IT WAS INTO THIS GLOOMY ENVIRONMENT that an eccentric, even controversial evangelist showed up in April 1984. Arthur Blessitt, age sixty-three in 2004, is an oddball, though deeply sincere evangelist, whose website (www.arthurblessitt.com) boasts that he is in the *Guinness Book of World Records* for having undertaken the world's longest walk ever, at thirty-six thousand miles (as the website proclaims: "Now 300 Nations, 36,067 Miles [58,042 KM] 33 Years and Still Walking!") Blessitt's "walking," however, isn't the typical Sunday stroll through the park. It involves carrying a twelve-foot cross that weighs sometimes as much as seventy pounds (depending on the wood used) and has a small rubber wheel on the bottom so the wood is not worn away as Blessitt drags it behind him, resting on his back.

Blessitt has been carrying the cross around the world since 1969, which is when he says that God first told him to carry it across the United States. Midland's First Baptist Church invited him in 1982 to speak about this odd mission, but that first visit made little impact on the city. Two years later, though, he was invited back for a seven-day evangelism crusade in the Chaparral Center, a popular venue for sports events and concerts. Local radio stations carried his sermons, and George W. heard Blessitt's preaching while driving around town and was intrigued. He knew that a fellow Midland oil landman he had known for several years, Jim Sale, had been instrumental in arranging Blessit's visit; so George contacted him. (Sale later accompanied Blessitt on one of his walks with the cross through part of India. He said that "thousands" of Indians were converted when Blessitt stopped and preached the gospel to them.) During "Decision '84" evangelism week, Sale made his Midland home available for Blessitt to meet and pray with the numerous visitors who sought him out at the end of each evening's preaching.

But George W. didn't want to be part of any throng and asked Sale to arrange a private, daytime meeting. Sale was present when George W. and Blessitt sat down at a table in the Holidome of a local Holiday Inn. It was midafternoon, Tuesday, April 3, 1984.

George W. got straight to the point, according to Sale. He told

Blessitt, "I want to talk to you about how to know Jesus Christ and how to follow him." In the account of the meeting on his website, Blessitt describes himself as "quite shocked at his direct and sincere approach. Few people just bring up that topic themselves and especially within only two or three minutes of our meeting," he explains.[6]

Blessitt continues in his Internet account:

> Now I whispered a silent prayer, "Oh Jesus, put your words in my mouth and lead him to understand and be saved."
>
> I slowly leaned forward and lifted the Bible that was in my hand and began to speak.
>
> "What is your relationship with Jesus?" I said.
>
> He replied, "I'm not sure."
>
> "Let me ask you this question: If you died this moment, do you have the assurance you would go to heaven?"
>
> "No," he replied.
>
> "Then let me explain to you how you can have that assurance and know for sure that you are saved."
>
> He replied, "I'd like that."[7]

Blessitt goes on to describe proceeding through the scriptural basis of personal salvation through faith in Christ, beginning with the classic statement of the sinful nature of mankind. He started with Romans 3:23, "All have sinned and come short of the glory of God." Then he went to Romans 6:23, "The wages of sin is death but the gift of God is eternal life through Jesus Christ our Lord" and several other verses.[8] Then, in the empty hotel restaurant, Blessit, Sale, and George W. held hands and prayed together. The prayer that Blessitt led George W. in was essentially "The Sinner's Prayer," which is a confession before God of the need for salvation through Jesus Christ and a request for forgiveness and acceptance of that salvation.[9] In the fall of 2003, looking back on his conversation with George W., Blessitt said, "I have to fully believe that he meant it as much as anyone I've been around."[10]

The three men sat quietly for a few minutes before George W. got up to go to another appointment, according to Sale. Before leaving, he tried to make a financial contribution to Blessitt, but the preacher firmly asked him not to, which made a strong favorable impression on George W. Blessitt says that he wrote to the future president a few times over the next year or two, but there was no real contact in the following years, mainly due to Blessitt's demanding schedule of walks with the cross in several different countries. Then, in June 1999, when George W. had already embarked on his run for president, Blessit attended a thousand-dollar-per-plate fund-raising breakfast in Fort Myers, Florida, paying his own way. When George W. saw Blessit, as he moved among the guests, the candidate immediately recognized the preacher and the two hugged. A photo of the two shaking hands captures the meeting.

For many evangelical Christians, that moment in Midland in 1984, witnessed by a third party, written about by the evangelist Blessitt, and certainly never denied by the White House, marks the entry point of George W. into the born-again Christian experience. Perhaps, in a theological sense, that is indeed what happened. Yet the president never mentioned this meeting to any of his close political acquaintances and failed to report it in his book, *A Charge to Keep*. Rove says that when he learned about the website material a year or so into George W.'s presidency, he asked the president about it. The president, he said, remembered the meeting clearly and recalled Blessitt with genuine warmth. But others who were, or had been, close to George W., including his longtime Midland friend and then secretary of commerce Don Evans, as well as Karen Hughes, his longtime political aide, also had no recollection of ever hearing from George W. about the encounter with Blessitt.

The reason they didn't, it seems clear to them as well as to Sale, who claims no credit for George W.'s prayer encounter with Blessitt, is that the meeting was only one in a series of developments in George W.'s spiritual journey—a journey that eventually led to major lifestyle changes in the future president.

Certainly none of his Midland friends noticed any life changes after

George W.'s meeting with Blessitt. He continued to play noontime pick-up basketball at the YMCA, continued to enjoy convivial evenings of conversation and alcohol with his business and social friends, even as he also remained faithful in his conduct of business in the First United Methodist Church, which he and Laura attended regularly. In contrast, the city of Midland was changed by Blessitt's visit. Many Midland citizens were converted during the weeklong meetings. One was Don Poage, today a social service counselor in Midland but at that time a businessman with connections to various parts of the Midland oil business. Poage had watched George W. playing Little League in Midland back in the 1950s but had come to know him as an adult only after George W. returned from Harvard in the late 1970s. When George W. ran for Congress unsuccessfully, Poage and his wife organized a coffee meeting for mutual friends.

Poage had been an alcoholic for many years but had sobered up in April 1983, just a year before Blessitt's week-long evangelistic meetings. After his afternoon prayer with Blessitt, George W. went to Poage's house to watch the final game of the NCAA basketball tournament with friends. Between plays, the conversation turned to Blessitt, and George W. said he had prayed with him and had been very impressed with Blessitt's refusal to take a donation from him. Poage then decided that, the next night, he too would meet with Blessitt. Unlike George W., though, Poage went to Sale's home after the evening meeting. It was late and Blessitt was curious about what Poage wanted. "He asked me what was going on. His eyes were so penetrating and full of love. He asked me, 'Don, if you died tonight, do you know where you'd go?'" As Poage floundered around for an answer, Blessitt got up to leave. But Poage asked him to stay and pray for him, which the evangelist did. As Blessitt anointed him with oil (Mazola, as it happened, because Blessitt didn't have any olive oil with him and there was none in Sale's kitchen), Poage recalled, "I had my eyes shut and my head down and I was on my knees. I felt big lightning bolts, big shafts of light."[11]

THIS APPARENT RICH HARVEST of new souls in West Texas was just the beginning. Shortly after, men in Midland's Christian community began meeting to study the Bible in a program developed by a nationwide organization called Community Bible Study (CBS). CBS was started in 1975 by a group of women in a prominent Washington, D.C.-area church, Fourth Presbyterian in Bethesda, Maryland. Their idea was to establish Bible study groups that would operate in conjunction with existing community churches, but not as part of any particular church organization. Originally for women only, by the 1980s CBS had branched out into Bible study for men and teenagers as well.

In Midland, CBS meetings started in the spring of 1984, and Poage started attending that fall. The meetings were held Monday nights at Midland's First Presbyterian Church. They started with one hundred and fifty or so men singing a few hymns, followed by a talk by an assigned Bible teacher (always a local man). After twenty minutes, the men would divide into smaller core groups for deeper discussion of the text. Poage became an enthusiastic participant in CBS, and by 1985 had become a "core leader"—someone trained as a facilitator of the discussions. The subject when George W. first started attending was the Gospel of Luke. CBS participants are expected to spend up to two hours each week preparing responses to questions on the Gospel text given to them the previous week.

George W. was not a CBS participant in its first year, but something so profound happened the following year that made him a faithful and eager member—his life-changing 1985 encounter with Billy Graham. Graham himself has not spoken or written about this, so the substance of what took place has been pieced together from George W.'s comments to his friends and from his accounts of the incident to various reporters and in *A Charge to Keep*. The encounter took place during a Graham visit to the Bush family summer vacation retreat at Kennebunkport, Maine.

According to Barbara Bush, Graham visited Kennebunkport during two or three summer vacations in the 1980s. He had been a close friend of the Bush family for several years and was to become even closer when

Bush Senior became president in 1988, spending many nights as presidential guest in the White House. But Graham's summer visits of a few days each time became something of an informal Bible camp for the Bush children and grandchildren. Barbara recalls,

> Billy Graham would sit down in our living room and answer questions. It was a very moving time. The kids would ask things like, what about prenatal deaths? How could a good person die? Billy just took time to answer these things. It made a huge experience. I think that was a great opportunity for our children.[12]

Graham's visits were happening at a time when George W. was beginning to look at life, at faith, and especially at his own behavior. According to the president, it was not so much Graham's teaching during the fireside sessions that struck him, but the sheer presence and character of the aging evangelist (who was sixty-six in the summer of 1985). "The Lord was so clearly reflected in his gentle and loving demeanor," George W. wrote.[13] Graham and George W. took a walk along the beach at Walker's Point. George W. said that he recognized that he was "in the presence of a great man. He was like a magnet; I felt drawn to seek something different. He didn't lecture or admonish; he shared warmth and concern. Billy Graham didn't make you feel guilty; he made you feel loved."[14]

Graham seemed to have an uncanny ability to put his finger on key—often vulnerable—areas of the lives of those with whom he discussed deep and personal spiritual issues. George W. has declined to describe his conversation with Graham in detail, but Rove says that what struck George W. most powerfully was how closely Graham seemed to read the thirty-nine-year-old's character that summer. "For the president," Rove recalls, "it was the wonderment of Graham's watching him. Billy Graham was watching the interplay of [George W.] and his family, and he asked, 'Do you have the right relationship with God?'"[15]

That question, the walk, the power of Graham's godliness all seemed to shift the spiritual center of gravity in George W.'s soul. As he wrote later:

Over the course of that weekend, Reverend Graham planted a mustard seed in my soul, a seed that grew over the next year. He led me to the path, and I began walking. And it was the beginning of a change in my life. I had always been a religious person, had regularly attended church, even taught Sunday school and served as an altar boy. But that weekend my faith took on new meaning. It was the beginning of a new walk where I would recommit my heart to Jesus Christ.[16]

Secretary of Commerce Don Evans, a close friend since the 1970s, recalls George W. telling him that he had asked Billy Graham during the Kennebunkport weekend if some sins were worse than others. Graham, according to Evans's recollection of George W's account of the conversation, replied, "Well, sin is sin. You can't place one sin as higher than another sin."[17]

All of the president's close friends agree that the Graham encounter was the absolutely decisive event in moving George W. from what might be called an "assenting believer"—someone who agrees with the Christian faith and at some level has expressed assent to it—to what longtime confidante Karen Hughes calls "a follower of Christ."

When, therefore, did George W. become "born again" or a "follower of Christ"? Or to rephrase the question, at what precise point did he "come to faith"? Was it while praying with Arthur Blessitt in April 1984, or was it after Billy Graham's words sank into his soul in the summer at Kennebunkport more than a year later? Surely no human being can know, perhaps not even the president himself. Though George W. for a while used the terminology "born again," and probably "saved" as well, this is not the language heard around the White House today. In a subtle move away from too-close identification with faith jargon often associated strongly with Christian conservatives—or to use the pejorative term, the Religious Right—hardly anyone close to the president uses these terms today. Hughes puts it this way: "I think you'll find many of us uncomfortable with jargon. I believe you are a disciple of Jesus Christ or you are not. What I've always heard [President Bush] say is that he renewed his faith. The Christian faith is the process of the Holy Spirit converting you, and you become more Christlike."[18]

---

IN THE CASE OF GEORGE W., the fruits of his meeting with Graham began to come into full flower in the fall of 1985. His good friend Don Evans gave him a copy of the *The One Year Bible*,[19] a version of the Bible that organizes the text into daily readings so that a person can go through the entire Old and New Testaments in a year. George W. read with zeal. Together with Evans, he also began attending the weekly CBS meetings. As it happened, Don Poage was the core leader for George W.'s group, and he vividly recalls the future president's enthusiastic participation. "We were studying the Gospel of Luke," Poage says. "George W. was either very new to the faith, or he'd been having those conversations with Billy Graham, and he wanted to be equipped. He did his lessons, he asked great questions, and he had great answers. He was also refreshingly cynical."[20]

Cynical? Poage says that George W. displayed his cynicism once when the discussion turned to a recent statement by the evangelist Oral Roberts that unless his ministry received the needed sum of four million dollars, the Lord would "take him home" (that is, he would die). Bush had fun with this concept. He'd ask with a chuckle questions like, "What does this week's Scripture lesson have to say about that sort of thing?"

Poage says that though George W. was refreshingly unassuming and unpretentious, the reality of his power and importance that derived from being son of the vice president of the United States occasionally surfaced. Once, as the other men listened in wonder, George W. described a disagreement he'd had with his mother over what being "born again" meant. The matter had come up while they were discussing the faith of former president Jimmy Carter—a Southern Baptist who had first drawn attention nationally to the term "born again" during his run for the presidency in 1976. Barbara Bush, a staunch Episcopalian, hadn't been very impressed by "born again."

"Mother, it's in the Word," George W. told his fellow core group members he had said to her.

He told them her response was, "Let's call Billy Graham."

"Yes, Barbara, it's true; it's in the Word," Poage recalls Graham saying. "George W. had this smirk on his face. A couple of the guys looked at me and rolled their eyes."[21]

Smirk or not, Bush was taking his Bible studies, both in the weekly CBS sessions and at home, very seriously. "We were always keeping each other honest," recalls Don Evans, who was also reading *The One Year Bible*. "We were making sure that we were not dragging our feet. I mean, if it's April the twenty-third, you're on April the twenty-third, aren't you? You're not back on March first; you haven't been slipping or sliding on me? And boy, he didn't slide a bit. I don't know how many times he's read the Bible. He always had it when I saw him, even along the campaign trail during that grueling two-year period we spent together [1998–2000]. He just disciplined himself into the Word every day."[22]

George W. and Laura continued to be very active in the First United Methodist Church of Midland, absorbing some of the important contemporary Christian teaching of that day on how to raise families. Some of the material he studied was written by Focus on the Family's James Dobson. "As I studied and learned," George W. wrote later, "Scripture took on greater meaning, and I gained confidence and understanding in my faith."[23]

---

GEORGE W. continued to run every day, and he played basketball several times a week. But though his body responded well to the intense physical discipline of arduous daily exercise, it wasn't responding well to his continued drinking. Several people over the years had spoken to him quietly about this problem, including Laura (though it is unclear whether she ever gave George W. an ultimatum to stop). A close Midland business friend of the 1980s, who requested anonymity, said he told George W. outright, "George, you're drinking too much."

George W. knew this was true, but it hadn't seemed to alarm him. After all, though he'd had one run-in with the law over drunk driving (a decade earlier in Maine), he had not yet concluded that his entire life in various ways was influenced by the continuing evening rounds of alcoholic conviviality.

That all changed one morning at the Broadmoor Hotel in Colorado Springs. George W. had turned forty on July 12, 1986, but his very close friend Don Evans was hitting the same mark at the end of the month. The two couples, Don and Susie Evans, and George W. and Laura Bush, along with the Bushes' other longtime favorites, Joe and Jan O'Neill, flew off for a three-couple celebration of the "big Four-O" in the Rocky Mountains. The main event was dinner on the evening of July 27, 1986, which was Don Evans's actual birth date. Brother Neil Bush and longtime family friend Penny Sawyer joined the three couples.

Evans remembers the evening this way: "We went up there and had a lot of bottles of wine, I remember that. And you know, kind of *too* many bottles of wine. It wasn't anything obnoxious, but it was kind of silly behavior. And he woke up the next day—he didn't tell me this at the time—and that was it. Quit. No more."[24]

In *A Charge to Keep*, George W. provides more detail:

People later asked whether something special happened, some argument or accident that turned the tide, but no, I just drank too much and woke up with a hangover. I got out of bed and went for my usual run. For the past fourteen years, I had run at least three miles almost every day. This run was different. I felt worse than usual, and about halfway through, I decided I would drink no more. I came back to the hotel room and told Laura I was through.[25]

There is a paradox in this almost confessional admission. The very fact that George W., who was well known around Midland for his jovial ways, had suddenly turned stone-cold sober provoked repeated efforts by suspicious journalists, then and later, to probe whether he had ever entered a chemically altered state using substances other than alcohol. What may have prompted the flurry of speculation about his possible bad habits before age forty was precisely the Bush family's reluctance in public to be confessional about anything. Some people wondered that, if George W. were suddenly owning up to too much drinking, perhaps there were other skeletons in the family closet too.

The decision to stop drinking, though perhaps not specifically a "spiritual" decision, had profound spiritual consequences. What it seemed to do was quiet down a part of George W.'s life that, though not in and of itself harmful, had constantly interfered with serious career building up to that point in his life. Describing what happened after the momentous decision, which he freely admitted might have been regarded at first with some skepticism by his wife, George W. made it clear that his entire life was affected by his Broadmoor Hotel turnaround. Though he says he didn't advertise it, his friends certainly noticed the change. He wrote this:

> I didn't change habits or do anything different to help me quit. But inwardly, I felt different. I had more time to read. I had more energy. I became a better listener, and not such an incessant talker. Quitting drinking made me more focused and more disciplined. I now say it is one of the best things I have ever done.[26]

Anyone who becomes sober after a lifetime of alcoholism will recognize the almost spiritual sense of change that sobriety brings. George W. was not an alcoholic in the clinical sense; so what he experienced was not a break with a lifestyle dominated by an unmistakable illness. Rather, it was, by a rather striking single act of self-discipline, a decision by George W. to reorient his life. This decision, in turn, began to bring real power to all the spiritual influences that had started changing his life since his encounters with Blessitt, Graham, and the CBS meetings.

Almost certainly, the most powerful expression of George W.'s act of will to quit drinking was deciding once for all that he would never, even with his closest friends, do what everyone simply accepted as part of his natural disposition—namely, to permit the charms of Bacchus to shape his personality night after night, month after month, year after year. George W. had, through the encounters described, arrived at a powerful understanding of what the Christian faith really means. Every day for several years, his mind and spirit had been absorbing Christian truths from the Bible. But now, unencumbered by old, strong, alcohol-induced habits, he was free to live out those truths far more powerfully than he must originally have imagined possible.

---

AS LAURA BUSH HAS SAID MANY TIMES, if there is one thing George W. seems to be good at, it is timing. The second half of 1986 was a year of testing for Bush Senior, who was assembling the team that would direct his 1988 presidential bid. The man who became the mastermind of the 1988 election of President George Herbert Walker Bush was Lee Atwater, a take-no-prisoners political operative who, in the course of the onset of an ultimately fatal cancer, went through deep contrition about some of his political dirty tricks of earlier years.

George W. was assigned the role of senior advisor to the Bush Senior campaign. In fact, by his own description, he was the campaign "loyalty enforcer." Conveniently enough, George W. was able to put his own business affairs into a holding pattern before moving the family to Washington. In 1984, Bush Exploration, foundering badly in the dismal downturn of the Texas petroleum industry, was taken under the wing of Spectrum 7, an oil-investing fund that itself began to run into trouble a few months later. George W. then worked hard to have Spectrum 7 bailed out by a bigger fish in the Texas pond, persuading Harken Energy, which specialized in taking over struggling energy companies, to bring Spectrum 7 into its fold. It was a win-win situation: Harken had the son of the vice president on its board, and George W. was given the financial means to move to Washington.

George W. and Atwater worked closely and well together. But the younger Bush also became close to another key figure in the 1988 Bush

Senior campaign, Doug Wead, writer of twenty-six books, motivational speaker and ordained minister of the Assemblies of God Church. Wead was brought on board the Bush Senior campaign because of his close association with the world of American evangelicals. This group had voted solidly for Ronald Reagan in 1980 and 1984 and had mixed feelings about Bush Senior. Wead was needed to secure the connection with the evangelical bloc.

According to Wead, George W. was instantly comfortable with all of the evangelical figures to whom Wead introduced him. He knew their language, and it was obvious to them all that his conversion experience had been genuine and profound. He certainly understood evangelical Christian theology better than his father. According to one tale, George W. was in a meeting with Bush Senior and other campaign advisors when the issue came up of how evangelicals believed a Christian would get into heaven. As it is told, Bush Senior hemmed and hawed about various virtues before George W. cut him off with words to the effect of, "You get into heaven because you are born again, Dad."

Wead prayed with George W. and read the Bible to him the night in February when his father placed third to Senator Bob Dole and Christian broadcaster Pat Robertson. They discussed an array of Christian and spiritual topics as they hopscotched around the country lining up evangelical support for Bush Senior, first trying to ensure that Pat Robertson, Bush Senior's religious conservative primary opponent, wouldn't snatch victory from him among evangelical Republicans, and second, that the nation's evangelicals would not sit on their hands when it came time to vote in the general election. In the process, George W. learned invaluable lessons about what would later become the most important political base of his own run for the presidency. Speaking on the PBS program *Frontline* during the 2000 election season, Wead described what he observed of George W. twelve years earlier:

When G. W. meets with evangelical Christians, they know within minutes that he's one of theirs. Now, most presidential candidates, they have to probe, and they have to look, try to find common denominators that they can say, "Well, he's kind of ours, he just doesn't know it;" or, "He's ours but he doesn't understand the culture." And with G.W., they knew it was real. I don't know how to explain that without defining the whole subculture itself, which you can't do in thirty-second answers. But they knew it.[27]

Wead also observed how George W.'s young but rapidly strengthening faith held up in the face of a perennial challenge of political campaigns—sexual temptation. An attractive female campaign staffer at one point had clearly set her sights on the handsome and politically powerful son of the candidate. But George W. rebuffed her so abruptly that she complained to another prominent Republican figure involved in the campaign that she had been hurt. George W., according to Wead, was unrepentant when that man, a prominent public figure, relayed the woman's grievance. "Good. I'm married. Not interested. Case closed," he reportedly said. "I hope she feels bad. Good. Glad she got the message."[28] George W., of course, had been harsh with the woman, but he was displaying some of the iron in his soul that would emerge much later in a different context.

But George W. was also ruffling other feathers, living up to his reputation as the feisty one of the Bush children. He often snapped at reporters, and he made himself something of a gatekeeper for access to his father. Years later, a reporter who had found himself in a testy exchange with George W. told the younger Bush, then preparing inwardly for a presidential run in 2000, "Your dad would never have been that feisty; he was too polite." It's revealing that George W. tells this story, in a sense against himself, in his 1999 autobiography, *A Charge to Keep*.[29]

Worried about what would happen to him once the campaign was over and his father, it was to be hoped, was occupying the Oval Office, George W. asked Wead to write a memo summarizing research on what had happened historically to the children of presidents. Wead's forty-four-page, eleven-chapter answer wasn't at all encouraging. Alcoholism, suicide, and emotional breakdown were among a slew of the problems that seemed to beset with alarming frequency the presidential offspring during America's two-century history. Wead's account was later turned into an informative and interesting book called *All the Presidents' Children*.[30]

Bush Senior, of course, won the 1988 election with a convincing 53 percent of the vote. The victory may have been due in part to an upbeat introduction of the vice president that Wead wrote for publication early in 1988 called *George Bush: Man of Integrity* to persuade evangelical voters that he really was one of them, even if he didn't look or talk like a Southern or Midwestern Christian conservative. When the election was over and preparations were being made for a church service following the inauguration, Bush Senior showed that he had every bit as much Christian conviction as his born-again son. In his "Open Letter to the Clergy" of Washington National Cathedral, an Episcopal church, Bush Senior expressed gratitude to the bishop of Washington for hosting the event in the gigantic cathedral in the nation's capital. Then he added,

> We will be united in praise to God for the blessings which have endowed [sic] our Nation, and in asking for leadership as we face the challenges of the future.
>
> Worship is basic to my own life. Our family has endeavored to uphold our faith by participation in the life of our Church. I am particularly pleased that the American Bicentennial Inaugural will end on a note of asking God's guidance on the new beginning which opens before us.
>
> As the bells ring across our Land on January 22, may their joyous sound express our gladness for the blessings the Lord has given and equally express our renewed commitment to seeking goodwill and peace among all peoples. Sincerely, George Bush.[31]

This was a sincere, spontaneous expression of Christian faith by a man who had hitherto often seemed uncomfortable if asked to speak on any personal matters, especially on matters of personal faith. In these comments, he was not a political conqueror speaking for the benefit of attending scribes writing for posterity; he was the patriarch of the Bush family reasserting a conviction of faith handed down over generations. He was, in effect, part of a legacy that already included his son.

In the hectic months before the election, George W. had demonstrated his political usefulness by lining up massive electoral support of evangelical Christians for his father, and he did so not just through the connections provided him by Wead, but because his own Christian conversion experience clearly resonated with America's conservative evangelicals. George W. had demonstrated, in ways that were to impress Wead for nearly two decades, remarkable political instincts, prowess, and decisiveness.

When the election was over, though, George W. was faced with a perhaps greater challenge: to demonstrate that he could do other things than give good political advice or win over political allies for his dad. He was forty-two and newly recommitted to a faith he had ignored for a few years but had always respected. But he was singularly without academic, business, or electoral political achievements. It was time to see if George W. could impress Texans with the fact that there was more to him than just joking bluster or skillful implementation of successful political strategies. He had certainly grown up in several important ways, but if his faith counted for anything, he needed to live it out in the real, rough world of life in Texas once again.

# 5

## FROM A SHRUB TO A BUSH

*He had changed in significant ways . . . His whole personality*
*had been transformed . . . Christ had entered his life.*

—MERCER REYNOLDS

I	T'S NOT ALL THAT DIFFICULT, once a man has been elected president, to figure out how he got there. By then, it's clear that his springboard was a particular previous elected office, and that he couldn't have gotten elected to *that* position if he hadn't achieved a degree of prominence in such-and-such job before that. Some politicians in high offices, including the presidency, seem to have had the stamp of political ambition tattooed on their brow. But that was not true of George W. Bush in 1989.

As his father settled into his role as the nation's CEO, there was absolutely nothing in George W.'s career, or in his perceived skills, suggesting even the remotest possibility of his achieving a high office, much less the *highest* office in the land. To be sure, he was outgoing and good with people, he had an astonishing memory for names, and he had a famous last name. But *presidential?* Even his closest friends would have laughed at the suggestion that George W. would occupy the Oval Office just eleven years after his father began his own four-year term.

Of course, George W. was genuinely interested in politics. He had, after all, run for the U.S. Congress in 1978. It probably galled him that he had been beaten, but he certainly learned some important lessons from that campaign. (One lesson: When trying to win votes in rural America, never let your opponent portray you as a city slicker). He had become good friends with Lee Atwater, the political genius largely responsible for Bush Senior's successful campaign in 1988. He had campaigned vigorously for his father in that election year. He had come to know and take enormous pleasure in the company of another rising young political expert, Karl Rove, a man who was to play a vital—some would say the *decisive*—role in George W.'s political career from the 1990s on. George W., with his penchant for assigning nicknames, decided at some point that Rove would have the not-so-flattering sobriquet of "Turd Blossom."

On the other hand, unlike many who preceded him to the White House, George W. wasn't a lawyer, he wasn't a successful businessman, he wasn't a writer or academician, he wasn't a retired senior military officer, and he hadn't been elected to any office at any level of local, state, or federal government. In effect, he hadn't *done* anything significant. Even Ronald Reagan was a prominent actor and had been president of the Screen Actors' Guild before running for the governorship of California in 1964. He was quite well known on the corporate speaking circuit, and even Reagan's adversaries had to concede that he had some prominence in public life before entering the serious political arena at the state level.

George W. was certainly aware of his own lack of achievement. Some Texas friends suggested that he was in a good position to run for the governorship of Texas in 1990, but George W. wisely rejected that counsel. He didn't want to appear to be running on the name recognition of his father, a sitting president. And if he ran and lost, he didn't want to be an embarrassment to his father either. George W., soon after returning from Washington and moving into a comfortable house in north Dallas, realized that he needed to be about something serious quite soon if he were to have any kind of a political future.

An opportunity presented itself surprisingly quickly in the spring of 1989. He decided to put together a consortium to purchase the Texas

Rangers baseball team from Eddie Chiles, a friend of Bush Senior and a self-made millionaire who owned the controlling interest. Chiles reportedly had been approached by many potential buyers but wanted to see what George W. could put together, because of his great admiration for Bush Senior and because he thought George W. had the energy needed to organize a successful buyout.

Chiles's judgment was sound: George W. helped pull together a consortium of wealthy Texas men that eventually paid seventy-five million dollars for the team. George W.'s own contribution was $606,301, approximately one-third of his then net worth.[1] Once the deal was signed, George W. became the consortium's managing general partner, drawing a salary of two hundred thousand dollars. He became the public face of the Rangers, dealing with the media and resolving management issues. It turned out to be a highly profitable arrangement. When the Rangers franchise was sold several years later, George W.'s share had risen to around fifteen million dollars.

But he earned his keep for the Rangers. He helped arrange a bond issue to raise funds to build a new, state-of-the-art stadium, The Ballpark in Arlington, which opened in 1994. Mike Reilly, a Texas real estate broker and part owner of the Rangers, said, "The bond election, the ballpark, the financing technique—that was all George's deal. He quarterbacked the whole thing, but he never took the credit."[2]

The new business connection was both timely (now that he was back in Dallas he needed a new job) and providential. "It solved my biggest problem in Texas. There's no question about it, and I knew it all along," he told a reporter from the Long Island newspaper *Newsday.* "My problem was, 'What's the boy ever done?'"[3] By "problem," George W. was referring, of course, to the political liability of not being a recognized feature of public life in Texas, except as the eldest son of the current president of the United States. If he were ever to run for public office again, being known for his role in managing the Rangers would at least count for something.

A Man *of* Faith

IN FACT, IT COUNTED FOR A LOT. George W., a lifelong aficionado of America's favorite sport, loved nothing more than to attend the games, sitting behind the players' dugout, signing autographs, shooting the breeze with the players, and getting to know every single person who worked in the stadium, from hot-dog salesmen to groundskeepers.

Even George W.'s Christian faith came into play, to the annoyance of some. Molly Ivins, a strong critic of George W. from the years when he was in Texas, complained in her book *Shrub: The Short but Happy Political Life of George W. Bush,*

> In fact, the Rangers got rich. Not the old-fashioned way, with savvy scouts handicapping prospects at high school and college games across the nation; Bush pushed Ranger scouts to sign Christian athletes, rather than the coursing egos who gave sports a bad name. Johnny Oats, the Rangers' God-fearing manager, is one example of the Christian athletes sought out by Bush.[4]

But there were still carryovers from his earlier life. He was still smoking, and he had not abandoned his good-old-boy habit of chewing tobacco and spitting it into a Styrofoam cup. His language was still often rough-edged, and his outgoing, cocky-seeming public style might not have conveyed much spirituality. Inwardly, though, he was changing.

For one thing, George W. and Laura were going to church nearly every week of the year, except when they were out of town. Following their 1977 marriage, George W. had joined the United Methodist Church (UMC) with Laura, and they have been faithful members ever since. When George W. and Laura moved into their new Dallas home on Norwood Road in 1989, they attended Highland Park United Methodist Church. In 1995, Rev. Mark Craig became senior minister of the church and friends with George W., a friendship that continued even after Bush moved to the governor's house in Austin.

George W. and Laura's membership in the United Methodist Church cannot be overestimated as an important source of George W.'s spiritual interests and direction. In no way part of the Religious Right, the UMC in the United States is a mainstream Protestant denomination that has been in the country since before the Revolutionary War. For many decades, both in political and theological spheres, the leadership of the UMC has often been left of center. But the UMC, like the Episcopal Church, U.S.A.—the denomination in which Bush Senior was raised for part of his childhood— also is a very diverse entity. Some parts of it are liberal-leaning in theology, politics, and social policy, while other parts are theologically conservative, evangelical, and far more sympathetic to conservative Christian points of view.

The denomination's founder, John Wesley (1703–1791), was a contemporary of America's greatest theologian, Jonathan Edwards (1703–1758), and both men are credited with launching the great upsurge, on both sides of the Atlantic, of Protestant Christian evangelicalism in the first half of the eighteenth century. Edwards had spiritual roots deep within Puritan pietism and was solidly Calvinist (which stresses God's role in predetermining some souls to be saved and others not). Wesley and his followers, though, held that salvation is available to all and attainable by anyone through an act of will—that is, through a conscious choice to accept the Christian faith.

This viewpoint was dubbed Arminianism after "Jacobus Arminius who opposed the absolute predestination of strict Calvinism and maintained that salvation was possible for all."[5] In its more forceful form, Arminianism had obvious consequences for the development of Methodism both in England, where it began, and in the United States. The name "Methodist" was first attached to Wesley and a group of close friends at Oxford University who, in the 1730s, tried to establish principles—or methods— of holy living through a rigidly disciplined approach to prayer, Bible study, corporate fellowship, and lifestyle.

The decisive event in Wesley's life, which was to affect the entire development of Methodism thereafter, was his visit to a church of the Moravian Brethren. (This group of pietist Christians sprang from revival movements in Moravia—today part of the Czech Republic—and their missionary zeal established churches in England and other parts of Europe.) While attending the Moravian meeting in Aldersgate, London, on May 24, 1738, Wesley went through a profound conversion experience while listening to the reading of Martin Luther's preface to St. Paul's Letter to the Romans. Wesley later recalled it this way:

> About a quarter before nine, while he was describing the change which God works in the heart through faith in Christ, I felt my heart strangely warmed. I felt I did trust in Christ, Christ alone, for salvation; and an assurance was given me that he had taken away *my* sins, even *mine*, and saved *me* from the law of sin and death.[6]

To be strictly accurate, George W.'s Christ-Philosopher comment in the December 1999 debate in Iowa was completely in line with a British and American Protestant tradition harking back more than two and one-half centuries, long before American Christian conservatives even began playing a role in the political arena.

But Methodism, as it developed in both England and America, was far from purely pietistic. Early American Methodists played a major role in the struggle against slavery and in providing a church with which African American Christians could identify. Today's major African American denomination in America—the African Methodist Episcopal Church—grew directly out of early Methodist efforts to encourage Christian evangelism among slaves and ex-slaves. Methodist churches stressed the need to develop social welfare, medical, and educational resources for the poor. They also fought vigorously for improved working conditions during the harsh decades of rapid industrialization in the late nineteenth and early twentieth centuries. In 1757, Wesley himself said, "I love the poor; in many of them I find pure, genuine grace, unmixed with paint [i.e. makeup], folly and affectation." At the age of eighty-eight, in 1791, he was willing to walk the streets of London with a collection box for various projects among London's poor[7]—a rather early example, perhaps, of "faith-based initiatives."

Methodism grew rapidly in the United States, and from the mid-nineteenth century until the turn of the twentieth century, when it was bypassed by Catholicism, Methodism was the largest denomination in the country. It remained the largest Protestant church until the 1970s.[8] Methodists had supported the war effort during World War II, but the international peace idealism that developed strongly at the end of that war, combined with an emphasis on domestic social reform—sometimes called the "social gospel"—began to move Methodism in the United States in a more liberal direction socially and politically. The denomination approved the ordination of women in 1954, and the present-day organization, the United Methodist Church, resulted from the merger in 1968 of the two major branches of American Methodism—the Evangelical United Brethren Church and the Methodist Church.

Methodists are governed by bishops, a throwback to the day when the earliest Methodists, including John Wesley himself, ardently considered themselves part of the Anglican tradition. But individual Methodist churches have a much wider scope in deciding the nature of their theology, worship, and even social and political perspective than, for example, is generally possible within Anglicanism's American component, the Episcopal Church, U.S.A. Individual Methodist churches in the United States, therefore, may be resolutely evangelical in terms of emphasis on personal conversion and piety in Christian living but may also, with equal conviction, be strongly committed to social works programs.

This was true of Highland Park United Methodist Church when George W. and Laura attended in the period 1989 to 1995. George W. was, as usual, active in various church committees, in particular a program aimed at low-income, largely Hispanic families in Dallas called the Wesley-Rankin Community Center. Founded in 1902, Wesley-Rankin serves about fifteen hundred adults and children in everything from daycare to adult computer literacy to senior citizen activities. Highland Park Church has played a central role in operating Wesley-Rankin and supporting it financially.

George W.'s involvement in Wesley-Rankin was major. "He was huge, he and his wife, in the Wesley-Rankin center here," says Rev. Mark Craig, still the church's senior pastor today. "I think his heart went out to this community, and certainly his wife's as well." Laura Bush, according to Craig, was active in the church's United Methodist Women's Movement.

Yet for all of George W.'s growing visibility as co-owner of the Texas Rangers baseball team, Craig says the couple made no effort to be the center of attention at Highland Park. "He was just like other members of the church," Craig said. "He and Laura would show up, they worshiped, they were faithful, they helped their church, they helped other people, and that's what they did. I never saw in the history of our church or in my experience of [George W.] that he tried to get the spotlight on himself."[9] George W. contributed "generously" in financial terms, in Craig's words, to the Wesley-Rankin Center.

Sometime in the early 1990s, George W. gave up smoking, the last symbol of a lifestyle centered around rather heavy drinking that he had consciously abandoned in 1986. Mercer Reynolds, a business friend who knew George W. in the early 1980s, said he was struck by the changes in personal lifestyle. Reynolds recalled,

I could tell that he had changed in some significant ways. He was more caring; he appeared to have genuine interest in other people. He had given up drinking. He appeared more devoted to his family. He had started studying the Bible . . . His whole personality had been transformed. It was like Christ had entered his life. The Holy Spirit had taken over."[10]

---

A REGULAR GUY THOUGH HE MAY HAVE APPEARED to his pastor, George W. was also the son of the president, who in January 1991 had taken the nation into a war to liberate Kuwait from occupying Iraqis. As such, he was only a phone call or two away from the world's highest-level politics. In the late fall of 1991, he was called in to deal with an increasingly bothersome problem in the White House. White House Chief of Staff John Sununu had angered some cabinet members and several senior staffers with a management style they found abrasive. Sununu had also pushed out Doug Wead, a longtime George W. associate whose contacts in the American evangelical community had been so useful in the 1988 election. George W. was now called in, with his father's obvious approval, as the "enforcer" to ensure that Sununu exited promptly and without fuss. And so it was, Sununu resigned on December 3, 1991.

The following year, 1992, was an election year for Bush Senior, and George W. took time off from the Rangers to try to crank the campaign into gear. But not even his energy, drive, and toughness could make it happen. A fellow Texan, wiry billionaire Ross Perot, entered the political fray and ensured that, by getting 19 percent of the total national vote of 103 million that November, the election went to Democrat Bill Clinton. Though George W. campaigned hard for his father, Bush Senior to some observers seemed strangely disconnected from the race, as though he were tired of politics. In a scene replete with rich poignancy, as the Air Force One Boeing 707 headed back to Washington, D.C. on the last day of the 1992 campaign, the Oak Ridge Boys, a country group that had supported Bush Senior in his reelection bid and had performed at the White House, started to casually perform for the weary campaigners and quickly settled into gospel song. As they broke into "Amazing Grace," both Bush Senior and George W. had tears in their eyes.[11]

More tears fell in the Bush family when matriarch Dorothy Walker Bush died soon after, at the age of ninety-one, on November 19, 1992. She had been the rock of spiritual formation in the Bush family for three generations, and, at the end, her whimsical sense of humor triumphed also: mourners were asked to wear bright colors, not black—to reflect the Christian belief that death is the entrance to an eternity of joy and freedom from suffering.

George W. seemed to embrace this optimistic view, for he did not allow his grandmother's passing to dampen his *joie de vivre*. Just two months later, in January 1993, he realized an ambition that he had held for most of his adult years as a recreational runner: he ran the Houston marathon, finishing with a respectable time for a first-timer (now forty-six, after all) of three hours, forty-three minutes.

---

POLITICAL FRIEND KARL ROVE, a.k.a. Turd Blossom, had another kind of running in mind—for the governorship of Texas in 1994. George W. said that he first seriously thought of running for governor in May 1993 as he watched the overwhelming victory unfold of Republican candidate for the U.S. Senate Kay Bailey Hutchison. That had been a special election to replace the Senate seat vacated by Lloyd Bentsen when he was tapped by President Clinton to be secretary of the treasury. As George W. came on-stage at the Anatole Hotel in Dallas to introduce the victorious Hutchison, young Republican activists in the audience shouted, "Run for governor!"

But it was an uphill battle in many ways. The incumbent, Ann Richards, was a popular daughter of the soil, a quick-witted—and often acerbic—speaker whose most infamous quip during the July 1992 Democratic Party Convention in New York City, was at the expense of then President George H. W. Bush. "Poor George," she drawled slowly, so as to draw out the punch line, "he can't help it . . . he was born with a silver foot in his mouth."[12]

It was a meanspirited put-down that stung the Bush family. Some Texans speculated later that it had been a deciding factor in motivating George W. to run against her. What political analyst Karl Rove saw, though, was not the settling of family accounts but the emergence of a tide of Republicanism in a state that throughout most of its history had been solidly and overwhelmingly Democratic in its choice of representatives, senators, and governors. He had seen George W.'s convictions grow and deepen in ways Rove almost certainly hadn't anticipated.

Rove remembers conversations in 1993, early in the planning for George W.'s campaign:

If you listened as I did in 1993 and heard him talk about juvenile justice and educational reform and welfare reform, you heard an entirely different voice from the normal, customary political candidate. If [they] talked about things like juvenile justice reform, it was, "You find the bad apples and you lock 'em up." Instead [George W.] talked about how we need to save a generation of young people by letting them know that love and discipline walk hand in hand. When he talked about welfare reform, it was about how basically we were consigning people to a life of hopelessness and despair rather than helping them become all they were intended to be in this world. When he talked about education reform, it was in terms of leaving no child behind, about how we had a disparity between the haves and the have-nots, and how every child was worthy of dignity and respect, and how every child could achieve great things, and how we had a society, though, in which we were making decisions to shuffle them off. And I heard it, because it was clearly not just informed by political thought; there had to be deeper values that informed it, so that all of that came from the same perspective and came so unconsciously and with clarity and without any reticence. I mean, to stand up and run for office and say we need to save a generation of young kids by teaching them (that) love and discipline go hand in hand. . . . It's a little bit odd to have a political candidate up there using the word love.[13]

In effect, according to Rove, by the time George W. was serious about running for a nationally significant political office, Bush's faith convictions were leading him to look at politics through a lens that, while keeping conservative political convictions in focus, softened their edges with an expression of social conscience. This viewpoint, which George W. from then on held almost exclusive rights to, became known as "compassionate conservatism." For George W., it was less a theoretical reconfiguring of philosophical and political principles than an effort to instinctively articulate personal faith convictions—convictions holding that Christians should always try to help the disadvantaged—in the language of accepted political philosophy.

Rove sat George W. down in 1993 and asked him, very simply, to write down his reasons for running for governor of Texas. Rove said he wishes he'd kept that piece of yellow legal pad paper. He recalled that George W. scrawled, "The principal reason I want to seek office is to bring about a cultural change from a culture of the 1960s, which said, if it feels good do it, to a culture of personal responsibility."[14] In this, George W. was unmistakably articulating his two-decades-old disgust with what he viewed as East Coast liberal guilt over the fact that some people's lives were difficult. It also involved his sense that, through faith, individuals can change their own lives, as he had done, or be helped by people of strong faith to change. In his autobiography, George W. wrote this of the campaign: "Most of all, I worried about changing the culture, a culture I described as saying, 'If it feels good, do it, and if you've got a problem, blame somebody else.'"[15]

But though he was strongly motivated by these convictions to run, even his own family doubted that he would be able to oust Ann Richards, whose approval rating was running at 58 percent when George W. threw his hat into the ring. Barbara Bush bluntly told her son that he couldn't beat Richards. Even Don Evans, longtime pal and Christian buddy from Midland, had doubts, but he kept them to himself and soldiered on in support of the election bid.

One family member, George W.'s sister Doro, wondered if her irrepressible and sometimes notoriously feisty brother could keep from losing his temper in public. The Democrats, of course, also wondered, and they tried in many ways to push him off-balance. The Richards campaign unveiled the epithet "shrub," meaning "a little bush," to irritate him, and Richards herself needled him with some of her own caustic rhetoric, at one point referring to him as "some jerk." But amazingly, George W. didn't rise to the bait or lose his cool during the 1994 campaign. He campaigned with a disciplined and simple platform: tort reform, education reform, juvenile justice system reform, and welfare reform. Nine years after the walk on the beach with Billy Graham and eight years after the Broadmoor Hotel decision to refrain from alcohol for the rest of his life, George W. had learned how to master his temper, most of the time, particularly in public. No doubt this feat was the fruit of a discipleship walk of daily prayer and Bible reading that was already an ingrained habit for him.

―――――――――――――

GEORGE W. DEFEATED ANN RICHARDS in November 1994 with an impressive 54 percent of the vote. It was the largest gubernatorial victory margin in Texas in twenty years and only the second GOP win since Reconstruction after the Civil War.

On inauguration day in 1995, the day began with a church service in Austin at which one of George W.'s favorite hymns, "A Charge to Keep," by Charles Wesley, was sung. George W. knew the words by heart, for he had sung the song many times in the Methodist churches over many years:

> A charge to keep I have,
> A God to glorify,
> A never dying soul to save,
> And fit it for the sky.
> To serve the present age,
> My calling to fulfill;
> O may it all my powers engage
> To do my Master's will![16]

Many times since his first Texas gubernatorial inauguration, George W. has referred to the song and its moving words, along with a painting, which now hangs in the Oval Office, of the same name and inspired by the song. On the back cover of *A Charge to Keep*, there is a reproduction of the painting showing a determined rider—ahead of two other riders— urging his horse up a steep, narrow path. The rider even bears a superficial facial resemblance to George W. himself. In April 1995, the new governor sent this memo about the painting to his staff:

When you come into my office, please take a look at the beautiful painting of a horseman determinedly charging up what appears to be a steep and rough trail. This is us. What adds complete life to the painting for me is the message of Charles Wesley that we serve One greater than ourselves.

Then follow words from the book itself: "A *Charge to Keep* calls us to our highest and best. It speaks of purpose and direction. Many hymnals associate it with a verse from the Bible, 1 Corinthians 4:2: 'Now it is required that those who have been given a trust must prove faithful.'"[17] The newly elected governor was not requiring that members of his administration give public assent to any part of his own Christian faith. But George W. was demonstrating that he was not embarrassed to put down in writing the faith that was the source of some of his political convictions.

Just before the inaugural ceremony, Barbara Bush handed her son an envelope containing a letter from his father and cuff links that Prescott Bush had presented Bush Senior when the latter was awarded his navy flying wings in June 1943. In the letter, Bush Senior said he was now handing down his "most treasured possession" to his eldest son. "You have given us more than we ever could have deserved," he wrote in conclusion. "You have sacrificed for us. You have given us your unwavering loyalty and devotion. Now it is our turn. We love you. Devotedly, Dad."[18]

Billy Graham gave the invocation at the swearing-in ceremony and referred to the "moral and spiritual example [George W.'s] mother and father set for us all." George W. placed his hand on a Bible that had belonged to legendary Texas hero Sam Houston when taking the oath. Then, in keeping with what he had written for Karl Rove, he used his ten-minute inaugural address to introduce to his Texas audience his goal of cultural change. "For the past thirty years," he said, "our culture has steadily replaced personal responsibility with collective guilt. This must end. The new freedom Texas seeks must be matched with renewed personal responsibility."[19]

The speech was interpreted by some as a subtle attack on Bill Clinton's reputation for lack of self-control in some areas of his life even before he became president (the Monica Lewinsky scandal was not to break for more than two years yet). It may well have been. But more importantly, it was a call to arms, at least within the state of Texas, to begin moving American culture as a whole in a different direction, away from what George W. and many conservatives believed was the mistaken path it had set upon three decades earlier. It was no surprise that not everyone climbed aboard this particular bandwagon.

————————

THE PHRASE "COMPASSIONATE CONSERVATISM," which George W. appropriated to describe his approach to solving social problems by mobilizing faith-based institutions to do much of the dirty work, has been claimed by several different people as their coinage.[20] Originally a campaign slogan used by Bush Senior's aides during his 1988 campaign to characterize their candidate's approach to social policy, George W. latched on to it during his first term as governor (1995–1999). It described his efforts to mesh a compassionate social philosophy that was obviously influenced by his understanding of Christian charitable work with a conservative view of the need for discipline in the lives of individuals and societies. George W. writes in *A Charge to Keep*:

> The philosophy is engrained in my heart. The words came from a discussion I had with a reporter several years ago. The reporter was trying to label me. "I am a conservative," I told him. "But you have done things differently," he argued. "Insisting on educating every child and leaving no child behind is not a concept usually associated with conservatives," he said. "Well, then, call me a conservative with a heart," I replied. None of us can remember the exact date when that conversation took place, but from it grew the brand name my philosophy now wears. I didn't invent the phrase, but I adopted it, and I have made it my own.[21]

George W. had surely absorbed the principles of compassionate conservatism from his observation of, and participation in, programs administered by churches to assist the disadvantaged. But early in his governorship, he came to have several meetings with a man, surprisingly enough from the academic world, who seemed to intuit what George W. believed and who was able to express it with great forcefulness. The man was Marvin Olasky, a professor of journalism at the University of Texas at Austin with an intriguing spiritual and ideological odyssey of his own.

Born into a Jewish family and educated at Yale, Olasky's early allegiances were to Marxism ("Bar mitzvahed at thirteen, atheist at fourteen," he has often quipped). In fact, he was at one time a card-carrying member of the Communist Party of the United States. But after trying to brush up on his Russian by reading a Russian New Testament, he began to question whether Lenin's screechy diatribes against religion were actually valid and found himself strongly drawn to the Christian faith. For many years since that change of heart in the 1970s, Olasky has been an active churchman, most recently in the conservative Redeemer Presbyterian Church in Austin.

Olasky came upon his insights into American "compassion" while investigating ways in which earlier generations of Americans had dealt with difficult social issues like poverty. His research convinced him that if social welfare endeavors and expenditures are separated from efforts to be engaged in the lives of recipients, even the most high-minded programs are doomed to failure. In a manner that exactly articulated George W.'s intuitive views, Olasky thought that the concept of personal responsibility was far more valid than the concept of entitlement. Olasky once told the news service United Press International, "We must challenge people to get out of poverty, and we should do so by mentoring and tutoring."[22]

George W. first met Olasky in 1993, and Olasky's views reinforced in the governor's mind those of leftist-turned-conservative writer and commentator David Horowitz, who views the 1960s as the source of social policy based on guilt and on calls for massive government welfare spending. This approach, according to Olasky, ensured the continuing existence of a permanently dependent underclass. Rove had discovered

Horowitz and another influential debunker of the 1960s, Myron Magnet, and urged George W. to read their works. Rove was very taken with Magnet, whose book *The Dream and the Nightmare* reinforced Rove's notion, shared by George W., that one of the disastrous cultural errors in the United States during the 1960s was the view of society as one great morass of "victims." Rove arranged for Magnet to fly to Texas and meet with George W. and the governor's staff. Their welcome of him was enthusiastic.[23]

Olasky met frequently with the newly elected governor in the first two years of his tenure. When *The Tragedy of American Compassion*—Olasky's major statement on the failure of contemporary welfare and the importance of a faith component in social work—came out, it was warmly endorsed by Republican House Speaker Newt Gingrich as a must-read for his party's newly elected House Representatives.[24] Olasky not only helped George W. articulate the philosophy of compassionate conservatism with which he chose to become associated, he also identified what became known in Texas, and later nationwide in the Bush administration, as "faith-based initiatives."

---

IT WAS NOT, HOWEVER, A MATRIX OF SOCIAL THEORY that stirred George W. to action on his faith-based initiatives. It was, rather, a very practical problem that an organization called Teen Challenge was facing: renewing its state license for running a worldwide drug and alcohol rehabilitation program in Texas. Despite its name, the organization's work was with adults as well as teenagers. Its founder was Dave Wilkerson, a pastor from rural Pennsylvania who had begun pioneering Christian pastoral ministry to the gangs of New York in the late 1950s. Wilkerson, a Pentecostal minister whose Times Square Church today stresses both overseas missions and outreach to New York's poor, pioneered bringing heroin addicts off their habit through intensive prayer, close monitoring, and counseling sessions.

What irritated George W. was a forty-nine-page report by the State Drug and Alcohol Agency that listed a series of technical violations by the Teen Challenge center in Texas. Some alleged violations were potentially serious (inadequate staff training for medical emergencies), but others were quite trivial, which George W. ridiculed as "ranging from frayed carpets to torn shower curtains."[25] George W. was particularly annoyed by the bureaucratic nitpicking that paid no attention to the actual results of the Teen Challenge program that had been highly successful in Texas, as in other parts of the United States and the world, in inducing men and women to leave alcohol and chemical dependency and in preparing them for a productive life afterward. (The Teen Challenge website, www.teenchallenge.com, displays independent, academic studies showing a success rate of drug and alcohol rehabilitation as high as 86 percent.)

In response, the governor recommended several changes to state laws governing rehabilitation programs. The most significant change was to protect from state interference any institution that made faith the primary instrument for changing behavior and lifestyle of addicts and youth offenders or to remove such institutions from state oversight.

George W. also made a striking initiative in prison reform by introducing a faith-based prisoner rehabilitation program pioneered by the Christian organization Prison Fellowship, founded by former Watergate-era felon Charles ("Chuck") Colson, once popularly described as "Nixon's hatchet man." The former Nixon aide, whom Bush Senior mentioned with special dislike in a 1974 letter to his sons, had developed a worldwide ministry to prisoners after his own dramatic Christian conversion in the mid-1970s.

One of Prison Fellowship's reform programs in Brazil had turned around the notoriously dangerous Humaita Prison in Sao Paulo by introducing an intensive, though voluntary, program of Christian teaching and fellowship. From this, Prison Fellowship developed its own version for American prisons—InnerChange Freedom Initiative. The program is now operational in prisons in four states—Texas, Kansas, Minnesota, and Iowa. George W.

took a risky step as governor by permitting a pilot program at the Carol Vance Unit near Houston. George W. was so interested in InnerChange that he visited the prison in the program's first year and was photographed joking and singing "Amazing Grace" with some participants. "We're all human; we all make mistakes," he told watching reporters.[26]

The voluntary program requires inmates to commit to 24/7 participation in a daily routine of work, study, Christian fellowship, teaching, and private devotions for the entire waking day and for periods of up to eighteen months. Prison Fellowship cooperated with the University of Pennsylvania to conduct a study of the program, released in June 2003, which reported that inmates who completed the program had a 50 percent lower recidivism rate than the general prison population. The apparent success of the program heartened supporters of President Bush's faith-based initiatives. It appeared to show that, if practiced diligently, the principles of a disciplined, faith-centered approach to the major social issue of crime could have results far superior to any existing state and federal prison programs. Some critics, however, argued that the report also showed that those who had dropped out of the program were actually re-incarcerated at a higher rate than the general prison population. In effect, if you completed the course and it "took" with you, you were in better shape; but if you tried it and dropped out, you might be worse off.[27]

George W.'s overall social program in Texas was his first experiment in trying to induce government to work cooperatively with faith-based institutions when those institutions seemed to be effective in helping solve social problems. Though George W. was obviously conservative in most of the new developments he sought to encourage the Texas legislature to adopt, he was not so easy to categorize, as some mainstream reporters noted as the governor approached the end of his second term.

An in-depth report by the *Chicago Tribune*, for instance, that was reprinted in several American papers early in 2000, when George W. was already running hard for the presidency, summed up his governorship this way: "Bush is not easy to pigeonhole on many major issues, and at times his efforts to straddle issues can appear tortuous." The newspaper, in a lengthy report that included substantial new reporting on many aspects of George W.'s life, noted that the governor had signed a bill allowing Texans to carry concealed weapons, yet he had also raised the age permissible for the carrying of handguns to twenty-one. George W., the article went on, had not supported California's Proposition 187, which denied education to the children of illegal immigrants, and he had signed a bill guaranteeing access to Texas state universities to any high-school graduate in the top 10 percent of his class.[28] He did impose tighter restrictions on access to abortion, especially for minors, but he did not at the time come out in favor of a constitutional amendment to ban abortions altogether. Perhaps that's because Laura Bush has been reported by some close to the family as being pro-choice, althouth she hasn't said so publicly, as indeed Barbara Bush, has been reported to be.

---

WHERE GEORGE W.'S FAITH EXPERIENCED its severest test in the public policy arena in the case of Karla Faye Tucker, a convicted murderess who underwent what seemed to most observers to be a genuine and deep-rooted conversion to the Christian faith while on death row and who had expressed deep remorse for her crime. Tucker had been interviewed extensively by both American TV and print reporters and by many foreign journalists. Her case seemed particularly poignant because she had an appealing personality and was attractive. While on death row, she had married the prison chaplain. Christian news organizations like CBN's *The 700 Club* presented her as a classic example of the redeeming power of God's grace in a person's life after confession, repentance, and faith in Christ.

In fact, Pat Robertson, founder of CBN and one of the most outspoken figures among America's conservative Christians, put his prestige on the line by appealing to Governor Bush to stay Tucker's execution. Other appeals from overseas poured in, including one from Pope John Paul II. After all, Tucker's supporters argued, George W. ought to be more appreciative than most people of the power of a Christian testimony to transform a person's life; he had often spoken—and would much later speak famously—of how Christ had changed his own life.

Even Doug Wead chimed in, contacting George W. and arguing that the execution of Tucker, should it happen, could backfire among evangelical Christian voters who, though usually pro-death penalty, would probably interpret the Karla Faye Tucker case as just the situation when the authorities should show mercy.[29]

But George W. resisted the appeals to clemency, and the execution went ahead in early February 1998. In his autobiography, the fifteen pages he devotes to explaining why he didn't order a stay of execution reveal how affected he was by the storm of disapproval that his decision evoked among many of his fellow Christians. While reaffirming that he supported the death penalty and admitting that one of his daughters, on learning of the case, had expressed to him her opposition to his position, George W. acknowledged that he appreciated the moral validity of those arguing for a reprieve from execution for Tucker. He wrote, "A lot of my friends in the evangelical community were deeply concerned. They felt Karla Faye Tucker was a living witness to the redeeming power of faith, and they were praying for her. I could feel their anguish."[30] George W. added, "The environment became more and more charged."[31]

Many people, who otherwise admired him, became deeply concerned later. In a conversation with the conservative reporter Tucker Carlson in *TALK* magazine (now no longer published), George W., according to Carlson, mimicked Karla Faye Tucker as though she had been pleading for clemency during an interview on CNN by Larry King.[32] (In fact, on the CNN program, Tucker did not make any direct appeals for clemency.) Tucker Carlson, the reporter, insists that his conversation with George W. did take place as originally described.[33]

If George W. did mock Karla Faye Tucker, it is not clear what provoked him to do so. Nonetheless, George W.'s more reasoned explanation of why he could not grant clemency to Tucker on grounds of Christian compassion is an interesting one. In his lengthy autobiographical account of the controversy, George W. gives considerable space to

Tucker's own eloquent words in arguing for her life. "I can't bring back the lives I took," George W. quotes her as saying. "But I can, if I am allowed, help save lives. That is the only real restitution." George W. admitted that this argument was "compelling." But in his autobiography, he provides reason for *not* being persuaded by this argument, and his reasoning ought to be a source of comfort to followers of other faiths worried that Christianity might enjoy an unfair advantage under the law if the governor of a state were a person of strong Christian convictions. He wrote, "If I accepted that Karla Faye Tucker was a changed person because of her faith, how should Texas respond when a Muslim or a Jew—or a Christian man—made the same argument?"[34] It is a valid point. On the principle of maintaining a level playing field in the public arena for all faiths, neither Christianity nor Judaism nor Islam, nor any variety of either religion or unbelief, should have any advantage under the law.

The Karla Faye Tucker affair, curiously, became a handle for some opponents, especially after George W. became president, to criticize his Christianity. Some critics claimed that the New Testament teachings of Jesus Christ, along with the fact that Jesus himself was executed unjustly, indicated that all Christians should oppose the death penalty. Many used as evidence the fact that Texas, during the years of George W.'s governorship, had executed more prisoners than any other state in the nation to assert that George W.'s Christian profession of faith was not genuine.[35] Ironically, those same critics at the same time appeared to refuse to accept the authority of the New Testament as a valid criterion of judgment in any other political domain, domestic, or foreign. The sincerity of someone who applies Christian texts in such an inconsistent way is surely questionable.

---

IN HIS PRIVATE FAITH LIFE while governor, George W. continued to attend a United Methodist church with Laura and his daughters. This time, it was at the Tarrytown United Methodist Church in the western part of Austin. The senior pastor was Dr. Jim Mayfield, an accomplished poet in his spare time, who had moved to Tarrytown in 1988.

Mayfield says that George W. and his family attended Tarrytown regularly: "He was *very* regular," although sometimes the girls didn't come. At first not quite certain how he, as pastor, should relate to the governor, Mayfield said to George W., "When you come in the door of the church, my perception is that you come in as George Bush, child of God, and the 'governor' label isn't what comes in the sanctuary." The governor readily agreed. "He said, 'That's exactly right,' and we saw eye to eye on that one right away," Mayfield said. "And it became apparent right away that that's who he was. He was a real person." George W. also expressed appreciation to Mayfield that the pastor would do everything he could to avoid ever embarrassing the governor.[36]

Mayfield said he was especially touched that on Christmas Eve 2000, when the governor had already become the president-elect, George W. attended one final service and was one of the lay congregants serving communion. A four-year-old girl in the congregation was seated in the crowded church next to the pastor, who began to talk to her. The little girl knew who George W. was and was aware that he was leaving Austin. "I think we ought to tell him not to leave," the little girl, Elena, said.

"I said, 'Really?'" Mayfield remembers responding.

"Yes, I like him," Elena replied. "He talks to me."[37]

George W. also talked to Mayfield during some visits the pastor made to the governor's office. Mayfield—politically independent but more inclined to the Democratic than the Republican Party—was not bashful about expressing his own political views at times on a variety of subjects, though he says their conversations were never confrontational. Mayfield expressed concern to Governor Bush about what he felt was the excessive use in Texas of the death penalty, though he was not totally opposed to capital punishment as such. Mayfield says that the conversation was "not an emotionally confrontive" one.

During one of Mayfield's visits, George W. pointed to the *A Charge to Keep* painting in his office and explained that by "charge" he didn't mean trying to do many things in a short time but being conscious of having a responsibility placed upon him from above. George W. then quoted in full the words of the hymn that was so special to him. Then he pointed to another painting in the office, of Texas hero Sam Houston dressed in a Roman toga amid the ruins of Pompeii. George W. commented, "Oh, I keep that one up there to remind me: I'm only one bottle away." He explained to Mayfield that Houston had been known by the Cherokee Indians as a big drunk.

Summing up his thoughts about George W. as both a Christian and a political leader, Mayfield said,

> It became very clear to me that he had an intuitive understanding of himself as a man of faith and a governor, and that he was almost a classic embodiment of what Martin Luther talked about [on the integration] between office and person in discussing the role of a prince. When I mentioned Luther's idea to him, he was interested, and I arranged to have some excerpts from Luther's writing on the subject sent to him.[38]

---

BY THE END OF GEORGE W.'S FIRST TERM as Texas governor, he had successfully wooed many in ethnic communities that generally voted Democratic *en bloc*. Among the most impressive of his political converts was the Hispanic community, which voted for him by 49 percent when he ran for a second term, one of the largest Hispanic votes for any GOP candidate ever. But his crushing defeat of his Democratic opponent, Gary Mauro, of 69–31 percent in 1998 was a decisive victory and served notice that, underestimated though he had often been, George W. was an astonishingly successful Republican vote getter.

The victory, along with the success in the second attempt of his brother Jeb to win the governorship of Florida, suggested that the Bush family, whose patriarch Bush Senior had been defeated in the 1992 presidential race, was braced for a convincing comeback on the American political scene. There had been talk throughout 1998 of a possible presidential bid by George W. in the 2000 elections, and many Republican backers came forward generously in the last few months of 1998.

But something profound happened to George W. during his second gubernatorial inauguration in 1999. George W. himself describes the church service in downtown Austin's First United Methodist Church as a "defining moment," in spiritual terms, for his life to that point. The preacher was Rev. Mark Craig, who had come in from Dallas and was conscious of preaching not just to the newly reelected governor but to an entire family dynasty of Bushes (absent Jeb, newly elected and inaugurated in Florida, who was putting together his own administration). Before him, filling the first three rows of the church, were the former president of the United States and his wife, Barbara, as well as the governor's twin daughters, Barbara and Jenna, two of his three brothers, their spouses and children, and a galaxy of aunts, uncles and cousins.

"I've heard powerful sermons, inspiring sermons, and a few too many boring sermons," George W. wrote later, "but this sermon reached out and grabbed me, and changed my life." Craig spoke about the need to regard every moment of one's life as a challenge and to use every moment with profound responsibility. There were, he said, eighty-six thousand four hundred nonrefundable seconds every day: "Use them or lose them."[39] Then he seemed to address George W. directly, describing the governor's reelection as "a beginning, not an end." People everywhere, Craig went on, were "starved for leadership, starved for leaders who have ethical and moral courage. . . . America needs leaders who have the moral courage to do what is right for the right reason."[40]

Barbara Bush approached George W. after the service and said that Craig was speaking directly to him. George W. commented, "The sermon spoke directly to my heart and my life." Craig had spoken of the need to "do the right thing for the right reason." Now, George W. added, "It seemed the pastor was challenging me to do more."

What George W. believes happened during Rev. Mark Craig's sermon was that the Almighty was speaking through the pastor to encourage him to run for the presidency of the United States. He had been wrestling with the decision for several months, debating not just the political challenges involved but the lifetime changes it would mean for his entire family. Craig, ruminating on the sermon in January 1999, says he believes it was the "greatest sermon" he had ever preached.

> I guess deep down I wanted something to happen. I think he was at a pivotal time in his life, where he was looking for direction. I would call it a magical moment, because you could see it in the former First Lady's eyes. You could see her whispering to her son, and you could see a glimmer in his eye, and some tears. After the sermon, people came up and said, "You know, he's gonna run now." I mean, there was a sense among everyone there that something had happened."[41]

It had. But was George W. prepared for what was in store?

# 6

## Preacher, Politician, and President

*When you walk the walk,*
*people of faith will walk right with you.*

—George W. Bush

Rev. mark craig's sermon on the morning of George W.'s second gubernatorial inauguration was pivotal in helping him decide to run for president. And yet, the road leading up to this milestone was marked by important friendships with several other clergy who also encouraged him in this direction. These men of the cloth hailed from widely divergent political and denominational backgrounds, but they all had essentially the same message for George W., whether implicit or explicit: there was a calling on his life, and it was to the highest office in the land. Without their guidance, counsel, and prayer, the forty-third president of the United States might not have been George W. Bush. And their role as trusted friends and personal advisors went beyond just persuading him to make a bid for the White House. Indeed, they have become even more important to George W. as his administration has faced historic and unprecedented trials.

No other recent American president seems to have sought out the counsel of clergy and nurtured those friendships, even after he was firmly in the White House, in quite the way that George W. has. Other presidents, to be sure, called on prominent clergymen in earlier administrations. Rev. Billy Graham has been close friends with at least eight presidents, and he has been invited to stay as an overnight guest at the White House by most of them. He was, perhaps, closest to Lyndon Johnson, praying with and counseling him in the White House and at Johnson's farm in the Texas Pedernales. George W., too, when he was Texas governor, remained close to Graham, but the advancing age of the famous evangelist made it difficult to have the kind of frequent, intimate fellowship that Graham shared with earlier occupants of the White House. According to Bush's close aide Karl Rove, although George W. did have several conversations with Graham during his governorship, only some were in person; most were by telephone.

George W. has also differed from his White House predecessors, and from most other major American political figures, in his choice of friends among Christian clergy. He was—and remains—almost startlingly ecumenical. Of course, as he notes in *A Charge to Keep*, he grew up in an Episcopalian home with parents who, for many years, also attended a Presbyterian church. He was an Episcopalian altar boy (in Houston), but after his marriage in 1977, he switched his affiliation to the Methodist church. Even before becoming governor of Texas, his family's prominence enabled him to meet a broad range of Christian pastors from many backgrounds. Some of his Christian friends today, in fact, are inherited from Bush Senior.

The friendship with Rev. Craig, though, was very much his own and had its beginnings when George W. and Laura attended Craig's Highland Park Methodist Church in Dallas in their pre-Austin days. It was a friendship that went beyond the normal range of pastoral care and continued through George W.'s two terms as governor and into his presidency. Craig, who says he seldom accepts outside speaking engagements, made an exception when Bush asked him to speak at the morning chapel service before George W. was sworn in for the second time as Texas governor. He made another exception two years later when he was invited to preach again just before George W. was inaugurated as president of the United States, in January 2001. Craig was asked to give the "homily," a low-key encouraging sermon, at St. John's Episcopal church—also known as "the church of the presidents"—just across from the White House in Lafayette Square.

Craig and his family, like many other Christian friends from Texas, were invited to attend the inauguration and the day's receptions as special friends and family members of the president. Later, he kept in touch with President Bush at the White House through infrequent phone conversations. Craig, in many ways, had touched something in George W. while in Texas, and it endured through a tough campaign and the emotional see-saw during the weeks-long wait for the results of the disputed Florida votes after the November 2000 general election. But Craig was certainly not unique in the Christian friendship he developed with the future president while George W. was still Texas governor.

─────────────────────

ONE CLERGYMAN WHO PLAYED A SIGNIFICANT ROLE in praying with George W. as he sought divine guidance about whether he should run for the presidency was Rev. James Robison, a Texas evangelist. The child of a woman who had been raped, he was raised for the first five years of his life as a foster child by a Baptist pastor. Robison, formerly a Southern Baptist, was a dynamic evangelist in the 1970s but said later that the hard work, fame, and temptations caused him to "burn out." His ministry then seemed to change direction somewhat, expanding and crossing denominational lines. Robison believes that Christians can hear God speak to their hearts, although what is heard should clearly be in harmony with the Bible.

Based on his relationship with Ronald Reagan and his assessment of Reagan's political needs in the 1980 election, Robison concluded that Reagan would choose Bush Senior as his running mate. His prediction was a surprise to Bush Senior. Robison met George W. for the first time in 1992, but says at that time he did not discern any great spiritual dynamic. After George W. became governor, the two reconnected and Robison says he was struck this time by the sincerity and power of George W.'s testimony about his own changed life.

According to Karl Rove, Robison helped arrange a series of prayer meetings for George W. in 1998 and 1999 in churches where the governor had an opportunity to meet leaders of both large suburban megachurches and some of the most powerful inner city African-American congregations. Robison recalled, "Then I arranged one in the governor's mansion. That evening after the meeting, I saw Karl Rove and he commented, 'The governor seemed to walk in an aura of peace [after your prayer meetings ].' Karl said, 'Please keep doing them.'"

Late in 1998, Robison says that George W. told him he was praying about running for president. During 1999, George W. appeared twice on Robison's daily TV program, *Life Today with James and Betty Robison*, and the evangelist prayed on the air for George W. According to Robison, Governor Bush expressed appreciation for the gesture, and they stayed in close contact with frequent phone calls during the presidential campaign of 1999–2000. "One thing that meant a lot to me," said Robison, "is that we prayed before every debate together, over the phone."

---

ONE OF THE PRAYER MEETINGS ROBISON ARRANGED in early 1999, just before George W. announced his presidential bid, was in the church of Dr. Tony Evans, senior pastor of the six-thousand-member Oak Cliff Bible Fellowship Church in Dallas. Evans, an African American who has been a frequent speaker at nationwide gatherings of the Christian men's movement Promise Keepers, is also founder and president of the Urban Alternative, a national organization that seeks to bring about spiritual renewal in urban America through the church.

Evans first met George W. in 1996 in Greenville, Texas, one of the small towns in several parts of the South where predominantly African American churches were burned in an apparent wave of arson. Evans, well known all over Texas as a dynamic speaker, and George W., then governor, had both been invited to address a church meeting to show support for congregations of the damaged or destroyed church buildings. Evans struck a deep chord in Bush when he talked about churches as the best social sources available for delivering aid in any community. Evans recalled, "He shared with me afterwards that the talk that I gave was the inspiration for his faith-based initiatives program as governor in Texas."

Rove confirmed Evans's comments, noting that President Bush has several times referred to the profound impression that Evans's remarks that day made on him. Rove recalls Bush as quoting from Evans's speech in Greenville on several occasions: "On every street corner there are places that know how to deliver help to people in the neighborhood, where you can turn for help. They're called churches."[1] Evans invited George W. to speak in his Dallas church, and Evans talked and prayed with him when George W. first told him that he was considering running for the White House. "First, he wanted to know if God was confirming that this was the thing that he should do. Second, he wanted to get a clergy perspective of what the issues were that should be addressed,'" Evans recalled.

"Most African Americans will not vote Republican," Evans candidly acknowledged. "But once they see him and hear him [George W.], they are very impressed." Evans is understandably supportive of the faith-based initiatives program launched by the Bush administration and says the president "is doing a tremendous job." He added, "He has grown spiritually in office." Despite his move to Washington, George W. has maintained his friendship with Evans, inviting him several times to the White House and praying together. The president has also traveled back to Texas to speak at keynote events in Evans's church.[2]

---

EVANS IS NOT THE ONLY AFRICAN AMERICAN PASTOR with whom George W. established a warm, close relationship while governor and who has been invited several times to the Bush White House. Another is Rev.

Kirbyjon Caldwell, a brilliant, charming, and very funny pastor who
heads the largest Methodist church in the United States—Windsor
Village United Methodist Church in Houston. Caldwell, an M.B.A.
graduate of the Wharton School, the University of Pennsylvania's prestigious business school, was on the fast track to megabucks on Wall Street
in the late 1970s when he sensed a nudging to give up his business career
and become a full-time pastor. After completing a four-year theology
program at Southern Methodist University in three years, Caldwell
served as assistant pastor at churches near Dallas and Houston before
accepting the pastorate of Windsor Village.

Caldwell's preaching and personal style is a blend of Scripture, positive affirmation, and inspirational stories of people who have transformed
their lives through faith and perseverance. He calls on listeners and
readers to learn what faith is by practicing it in their own lives. In his
bestselling book, *The Gospel of Good Success*, he writes,

You, too, have invisible bridges waiting to support you in crossing the
seemingly bottomless chasm between your present and God's vision for
your optimal future. But you'll never see bridges, much less walk across
them, until you have the Faith and courage to embark upon the Faith
Walk. Those who desire Holistic Salvation walk by Faith, not merely by
sight. Like Indiana Jones and Sir Lancelot, you can attain the impossible,
cross the uncrossable, defeat the invincible. But the first step is Faith.

Faith combines with action in an incredible explosion of power. Every
great achievement is the result of a Faith Walk—a one-step-at-a-time
trudge toward the God-given Vision for your preferred future. Whether it's
the Vision of the great explorers who crossed mountains, continents,
oceans, and eventually moons, or the inventors and entrepreneurs who
revolutionized twentieth-century business and industry, Faith in the power
of God is a prerequisite for achieving the vision.

A Faith Walk is a journey that has the ability to rocket every aspect of
your existence into brave new realms. By aligning your desire with God's
preferred state for your future and by walking confidently and obediently

toward that Vision, you will find the impossible becomes possible in startling ways.[3]

George W. so admired what Caldwell had done in his Methodist church and in a social services center called the Power Center on the outskirts of Houston, that in September 2003 he traveled there to speak at the tenth anniversary of its opening inside a former K-Mart store. The department store building in a run-down area had been transformed into a facility housing a private Christian school, a branch of the Houston Community College, office space for small businesses, a pharmacy, a hair salon, a federal public-assistance office for women and children, and the area's only bank.

When Caldwell introduced George W. to the audience—an unusual mixture of prominent Houston African Americans and wealthy Texans who had contributed significantly to this and other causes—it was clear that the two enjoyed a close, even bantering relationship. Referring to George W.'s few months in 1973 helping young African Americans in Houston's low-income Fifth Ward, Caldwell said, "This man literally pastored the people." The audience applauded warmly.

When the president spoke, he described Caldwell as a friend so close that he was able to call on him by phone to pray before presidential election debates in 2000. George W. made special mention of Caldwell's church, saying that he was particularly grateful for the prayers of the congregation. "I feel them and it means a lot," he said. "The most powerful resource of all is the ability to transform lives through faith." Then George W. added what has become almost a mantra: his view of how faith can change people's hearts, and, by changing hearts, change society. He said, "I've been searching for that bill, by the way, ever since I've been in government—the bill that says you'll love somebody."

The president's presence at the celebration of the church's social services center might have been, in part, George W.'s way of returning a favor. At the Republican Party National Convention in August 2000, it was Caldwell who—though not a Republican—introduced a biographical video of George W. just before Bush's speech accepting his party's nomination to be the Republican presidential candidate. At the time, Caldwell was well aware that the Republican Party, in his words, had a "terrible reputation" in the African American community. He explained his participation in the Philadelphia convention this way:

> When I was originally asked by President Bush to introduce him at the convention, I was surprised, if not shocked, because I am not a Republican. But if I had told him, 'No, I don't want to introduce you,' the primary reason I'd have had was because he was a Republican. Since I'm not a label guy—I'm a content guy—the Republican label alone was not enough reason for me to tell him no.[4]

In fact, Caldwell disagreed with George W. during his governorship of Texas on the key issues of abortion, affirmative action, and gun control.

But those policy differences have not stood in the way of a deep personal friendship between the two men. Caldwell has stayed overnight in the White House several times since January 2001, and his relationship with George W. appears to many White House insiders to be perhaps the closest spiritual friendship the president has maintained since taking office. Interestingly, Caldwell was the only close spiritual friend who would not speak to me privately about George W.'s faith while I was writing this book and the only prominent figure whom the president specifically omitted from a list of close friends or relatives who were encouraged to agree to be interviewed for this book. When I speculated to one senior White House official that it was because Caldwell was George W.'s closest prayer friend since he became president, he nodded agreement.

President Bush clearly wants to protect the pastor from criticism by members of his church and the African American community in Houston that Caldwell, a professed Democrat, is hobnobbing with a Republican. Rove recalled that when George W. prayed with prominent Texan African American and white megachurch pastors in Houston in the late 1990s, one of the white pastors present wanted to publicize the event, arguing that it would bring George W. political brownie points if

George W. Bush speaks to reporters on April 18, 1989, when the sale of the Texas Rangers is approved.[1]

Young George W. Bush with his parents, George H. W. Bush Sr. and Barbara Bush[2]

George W. and Laura Bush with daughters Barbara and Jenna at Kennebunkport.[3]

President Bush offers a tribute to Martin Luther King Jr. at the First Baptist Church of Glenarden in Landover, MD, on January 20, 2003. Pastor John K. Jenkins Jr. stands by.[4]

Texas Governor George W. Bush and wife Laura in the inaugural parade for his second term in Austin, Texas, on January 19, 1999. The Texas capital is in the background. [5]

Republican presidential hopefuls line up prior to the GOP debate, December 13, 1999, in Des Moines, IA. From left, Steve Forbes, Alan Keyes, George W. Bush, Orrin Hatch, John McCain, and Gary Bauer. [6]

President Bush and the first lady steal a moment alone while touring the Hermitage in St. Petersburg, Russia, with Russian President Vladimir Putin.[7]

Bush and Chaney families pray during a church service at the National Cathedral in Washington on January 21, 2001.[8]

President George W. Bush, right, and Israeli Prime Minister Ariel Sharon laugh together during a news conference in the Rose Garden, July 29, 2003. [9]

President Bush, right, and British Prime Minister Tony Blair at Hillsborough Castle on April 7, 2003. [10]

President Bush surprises United States troops for Thanksgiving in Baghdad, Iraq, on November 27, 2003. He serves a platter of turkey and fixings to the soldiers. [11]

President Bush asks for a moment of silence for victims of the World Trade Center attack on September 11, 2001.[12]

he were shown praying with African American pastors. "No, no," Rove reports George W. responding. "You take care of the spiritual things. I'll take care of the politics."[5]

Almost certainly one of the reasons men like Caldwell and Evans are willing to take the heat for befriending a Republican president is that they know Bush bends over backward not to appear to be trying to make political hay from the relationships. In particular, he wants to avoid criticisms based on suspicions that his friendship with Caldwell is a ploy to curry favor with African Americans. While acknowledging that George W., even today, keeps many of his own spiritual friendships and contacts very private, this White House official agreed that Kirbyjon Caldwell may well be the closest clergyman friend that President Bush has.

Despite George W.'s precautions, Caldwell has had to weather criticism of another nature but stemming, nonetheless, from his close relationship with the president. Caldwell came under fire when he gave the invocation at President Bush's inauguration in Washington, D.C., in January 2001. Eschewing politically correct generic prayer, Caldwell called down, Pentecostal-style, protection for President George W. and First Lady Laura Bush: "We decree and declare that no weapon formed against them shall prosper." The prayer might have been acceptable to almost everyone, except that Caldwell ended his benediction with the words, "In the name that's above all other names, Jesus the Christ, let all who agree say amen." He later told a Religion News Service reporter, "There does come a time when you need to stake your claim. I always prayed in Jesus's name. No need to change it now."

---

GEORGE W.'S CIRCLE OF CLERGYMEN FRIENDS when he was Texas governor went well beyond Craig, Caldwell, and Evans. In fact, he established such good relations with pastors of both large, white and African American churches in Houston, Dallas, and Austin that they sometimes invited him to preach from their pulpits. One of his most remarkable sermons was delivered in the gigantic sanctuary of Houston's Second Baptist Church on Woodway Drive on March 9, 1999. The previous Tuesday, he had indicated that he would announce on Sunday an exploratory committee on whether he should run for president. The church's senior pastor—popular, convivial, and otherwise healthy-looking Rev. Ed Young—nearly had a heart attack when he learned of the plans for the Sunday announcement. The savvy Young then invited George W. to his expansive personal office and library on the top floor of the church building, and Bush opened up to him immediately. "I believe I am called to run for the presidency," he confided to the startled minister as soon as he sat down in a comfortable arm chair. Young says alarm bells immediately went off in his head, and he made it very clear that the invitation to preach would be withdrawn if George W. were planning to use the pulpit to announce political plans. George W. reassured him that he had no such plans.

The sermon George W. preached, included in whole in the back of this book, was a well-crafted, almost classic expression of the key points of his faith and how he thought faith should be related to political life. After telling a joke about the difference between Methodist baptism (by sprinkling) and Baptist baptism (by total immersion), he opened up broadly to his audience. He said,

> You and I are here because we believe that faith can change lives. We know faith can change Texas, and we know faith can help change our culture. Faith is the framework for living. It gives us a spirit and heart that affect everything we do. It gives us hope each day. Faith gives us purpose to right wrongs, to preserve our families, and to teach our children values. Faith gives us conscience to keep us honest, even when nobody else is looking. And faith can change lives. I know firsthand, because faith changed mine.[6]

George W. referred briefly to his well-known meeting with Billy Graham at Kennebunkport in 1985. He spoke of various faith-based initiatives in Texas, including the InnerChange prison ministry of Prison

Fellowship. He also repeated his strongly held conviction that the greatest weakness of government programs to improve social conditions was that they failed to transform people's attitudes toward other people. He said,

> Here's what government cannot do—what seems to be the false hope of the last thirty years; government can't make people love one another. I wish we could; I'd sign that law. Or if someone could tell me how much money it took to cause people to love one another, we'd pass it, we'd pass that budget, the "love budget." But the truth of the matter is, love comes not from government. It comes from the hearts and souls of decent Texans. Cultures change one act of compassion at a time. That's how cultures change and each of us must participate.[7]

This, of course, was a restatement of George W.'s thoughts on faith, faith-based social change, and cultural change that had emerged from his meetings with Olasky, with Magnet, and with his Texas clergy friends.

Then, in an unusual digression, George W. turned his focus to a trip to Israel he had made a few months earlier. Though not the focal point of his March 1999 sermon, his remarks were an early indication of what would underpin his administration's policy toward Israel. "We're all God's children. We're all bound by the power of faith," he said.[8]

At the time of George W.'s December 1998 trip to Israel, few political observers in the United States doubted that he would formally declare his bid for the White House, but he was in an unusual in-between period: he had already been reelected governor by a massive majority of Texans, but the inauguration—and Rev. Mark Craig's pivotal sermon—would not take place until two months after the election. Though as governor, George W. had visited Mexico, and in 1975 he had visited China, he was a neophyte in foreign affairs, especially compared, for example, with another prominent Republican presidential contender, Senator John McCain. If he were going to be president of the United States, George W. needed to boost his knowledge, preferably through firsthand experiences, and the perennial trouble spot of the Middle East was an obvious choice.

George W. and Laura flew to Rome during the 1998 Thanksgiving holiday, meeting up with one of their daughters, who was visiting the city with a school group. There they were joined by three other Republican governors—Massachusetts' Paul Cellucci, Montana's Marc Racicot, and Utah's Mike Leavitt—a few staffers, and some of Bush's American Jewish friends, and the group headed to Israel. The trip was sponsored by the National Jewish Coalition, a Republican-oriented American lobby group that strongly supported the policies of Israel's conservative then prime minister, Binyamin (Benjamin) Netanyahu. One of the first social events was a dinner in Jerusalem with Netanyahu on November 30. The delegation also met with President Ezer Weizman, Defense Minister Yitzhak Mordechai, and leaders of Israel's Labor Party opposition.

A highlight of the trip was a helicopter tour of the West Bank—or Judea and Samaria, as many Israelis call it—conducted by then foreign minister Ariel Sharon. As the helicopter flew low over the Judean hills, "Arik," who rose to the rank of major general in a twenty-five-year career in the Israeli Defense Forces, pointed out with great glee the locations of combat operations in which he had fought as a soldier in his early teens, before the 1948 establishment of the state of Israel.

George W. later said that he had been surprised, as many Americans are, by how small Israel is. More important, however, than broadening his understanding of this small but politically significant land was that, over dinner and in conversations aboard the helicopter, he seemed to bond strongly with Sharon. When Sharon parted company with the Americans for the last time before their return to Tel Aviv, an Israeli familiar with the visit said that George W. shook Sharon's hand warmly and said, prophetically, "You know, Arik, it's possible that I might be president of the United States, and you might be prime minister of Israel." Sharon, according to this observer, laughed and said it was very unlikely that he, a controversial figure in Israeli politics, would become the country's prime minister. (Sharon had been forced to resign as minister of defense in the early 1980s due to the political fall out from an incident during which Lebanese Christian militia forces had massacred Palestinian civilians in the Sabra and Shatila refugee camps of Beirut while Israeli forces, controlling greater Beirut at the time, stood by and did nothing to prevent the killings.) But Sharon did, in fact, become Israel's prime minister, in a special election in February 2001.

Prominent Israeli journalist Uri Dan, who has been a close friend of and sometimes spokesman for Sharon for many years, recalls receiving a phone call from the foreign minister on the evening of December 1, 1998, after he had finished showing his American guests the West Bank by helicopter. How had the tour gone? Dan asked.

"Exceptional," Sharon replied. "I had the opportunity to explain to an important American personality who wants to know our security problems and our attachment to the land. I don't know any other personality in the leadership of Israel for the last quarter of a century who is ready to preach for the right of the country." Sharon was making two important points in his comments. The first was that he had identified one of the three governors as an "important American personality," namely, George W. The second was that Sharon, a senior Israeli official, was making an effective, conservative, Israeli nationalist case for Israel's need to protect its biblical heartland of Judea and Samaria. And he saw no one else but himself ready to defend that cause.

According to Dan, George W. showed great interest in what Sharon was showing them, was a good listener, and asked "thorough questions." The reporter said Bush expressed obvious admiration for what Israel had accomplished as a nation in a very short time, at one point saying to Sharon, "If you believe the Bible, as I believe the Bible, you know that extraordinary things happen."

It is apparent that a very significant personal friendship grew during those three days in the final weeks of 1998 between a future American president and a future Israeli prime minister. In February 2001, just weeks after his presidential inauguration, George W. was one of the first foreign leaders to phone Sharon after the Israeli's crushing election victory over the Labor Party and its political allies. "When we met the last time," Bush told Sharon, "I was not the president and you were not the prime minister."

The following month, after Sharon had completed the complex process of putting together his cabinet, he embarked on his first official visit to Washington. Uri Dan was there, and Sharon introduced him to the president. Dan recalled, "I cover all the visits to America. Never before between any American president and any Israeli prime minister was there such credibility and veracity. I saw the friendship between them then. That's the basis of their understanding each other and respecting each other."[9]

Their friendship also helps explain why President Bush has been strikingly supportive of the Israeli government in its various dealings with the Palestinian Authority (PA). Though George W. was the first American president to publicly support the concept of a Palestinian state (in a June 2002 speech), he has been adamant in his refusal to invite Palestinian president Yassir Arafat to the White House. Sharon in the past has refused to shake Arafat's hand, insisting that to do so would be to shake hands with a terrorist murderer. Senior White House officials say that one reason for the disdain for Arafat is the intense hostility toward him on the part of younger PA officials, who are disillusioned with his obvious ambivalence about the use of terrorist violence as an instrument of Palestinian policy toward Israel.

---

BEFORE BECOMING PRESIDENT, George W. made no public statement of his views on Israel, and as president he has carefully avoided any suggestion that he might be more sympathetic to Israel in the Israeli-Arab conflict because of his personal Christian beliefs. Other American presidents, from Harry Truman forward, have also sometimes expressed deep emotional responses to the very existence of the state of Israel.

Truman, for example, though probably not an evangelical Christian, referred at different times to what he had learned about the biblical nation of Israel in Sunday school classes. He sometimes thought of himself as Cyrus, the Persian king whose actions enabled Jewish exiles to return to Jerusalem and rebuild their temple there. In fact, Truman's decision to recognize the infant state of Israel in May 1948, in the face of strong opposition from the State Department, reflected an intuitive belief that Israel *ought* to be there.

Richard Nixon, brought up in a Quaker household, also had a sense of moral obligation to Israel that surfaced during the 1973 Yom Kippur War. Although Secretary of State Henry Kissinger wanted to modulate the United States military resupply of stretched Israeli forces on two fronts, Nixon preferred an all-out American program to transport by air as much military equipment as quickly as possible to Israel. Moreover, when Soviet leader Leonid Brezhnev threatened to mobilize Soviet airborne divisions in November 1973 to rescue the Egyptian Third Army surrounded by Israeli forces inserted by General Sharon across the Suez Canal, Nixon ordered worldwide alert status for all United States forces. This implicit threat that Moscow would find itself at war with the United States if it attempted any military intervention in the Middle East that endangered Israel's security, effectively forced the Soviets to back down.

Democratic president Jimmy Carter, a self-proclaimed born-again Christian, had a strong interest in biblical Israel, but he believed his role should be to broker, if possible, a peace agreement between the sometimes deadly enemies, Israel and Egypt. Carter's greatest achievement as president was, indeed, doing just that, playing midwife to the Egypt-Israeli Camp David peace agreement of 1979.

Ronald Reagan had a strong interest in Christian interpretations of "end-times" events that predicted a final battle of Armageddon, in which Israel would be in a battle for its survival against forces aligned with a worldwide dictator. When Israel invaded Lebanon in 1982, in an effort to eliminate terrorist rocket attacks on northern Israel by defeating the Palestine Liberation Organization (PLO), the United States was under pressure to restrain Israel. Reagan's administration found itself negotiating a deal under which the PLO was permitted to retreat unscathed from Beirut to Tunis while Israel was required to withdraw its forces in stages to the far south of Lebanon.

During the presidency of George Bush Senior though United States-Israeli relations chilled considerably when Secretary of State James Baker strongly criticized Israel's government for continuing to expand the presence of Israeli settlements—a term resented by many Israelis—throughout the West Bank.

Bill Clinton thawed relations with his warm affability to Israel's leaders and by convincing most American Jewish voters that, staunch Democrat though he was, he would always favor measures to keep Israel strong in the face of Arab enmity and terrorist attacks. Clinton, according to evangelical Christians who met with him, had a sophisticated knowledge of biblical teachings on a variety of issues, from war and peace to the death penalty to gay marriage. What he didn't seem to possess was a strong enough conviction about biblically based morality to influence him to behave differently on a personal level.

George W. Bush, by contrast, has for years aligned himself with what the Bible teaches on a variety of topics, including Israel. Though some Christians, including evangelicals, believe that the Bible is silent on today's reestablished state of Israel, others believe that Gentiles, especially Americans, have a moral obligation to support and defend modern Israel. For sound diplomatic reasons, President Bush cannot state publicly a view of Israel that might be considered theological. But a personal friend, who is a strong Christian and who knows George W.'s Christian views on many issues well, insists that, privately, the president does hold a biblically favorable view of Israel's existence.

This is a view that is endorsed by a significant community—probably the majority—of American evangelical Christians: they believe the United States has a moral duty to God to ensure that Israel is defended and that to turn away from this obligation is to court divine displeasure. This view is not at all the same thing as having a dogmatic "end-times" view of Israel as playing an apocalyptic historical role prior to the return of Jesus Christ. It says nothing about Armageddon or any of the other dramatic speculation about how events might unfurl prior to the Second Coming of Jesus Christ. Rather, Bush's sense of affinity with Israel is connected to his belief that God works though history and that God has never abandoned his love for the Jewish people. It is not rooted in any predictive scenario about how the end-time events will unfold.

This understanding of George W.'s spiritual viewpoint is important, because his strong Christian convictions got him into trouble with Jewish-Americans in a way that overshadowed the reporting of his 1998 Israel trip. In 1993, prior to his first run for governor, he told a reporter the story of his argument with his mother about who gets into heaven. This was a replay of a story that had already made the rounds—the one about Barbara Bush's telephone call to Rev. Billy Graham to settle a theological argument with George W. In the 1993 retelling, however, instead of saying "born-again," George W. said "Christian"—in effect, that only Christians could get into heaven. The implication was clear and unwelcome: God might well keep out of heaven anybody who isn't a Christian.

In the original version of the story, where "born-again" was the issue and not "Christian" versus Hindu, Jew, Muslim, or Buddhist, for example, the debate between Barbara and her son focused on what constituted authentic Christian faith. In the 1970s and 1980s, "born-again" was the preferred description of a person who had made a personal commitment to Jesus Christ, and the more public the better.

In all versions of the story, Billy Graham is consulted by phone, confirms George W.'s closely Scripture-based understanding of conditions for entering heaven, but he wisely cautions against using that as a basis for judging anyone else. The controversy over George W.'s position in late 1998 derived from an eight-thousand-word profile in the *New York Times* by Sam Howe Verhovek: "From a personal perspective," said Billy Graham, as recalled by George W., "I agree with what George is saying; the New Testament has been my guide. But I want to caution you both. Don't play God. Who are you two to be God?"[10]

On his return from Israel in early December 1998, George W. found that reporters were far more interested in pursuing this story than in his overall impressions of Israel. At a press conference December 4, 1998, in Austin, George W. sought to put the issue behind him. He explained, "My faith tells me that acceptance of Jesus Christ as my *Savior* is my salvation, and I believe that. It is not the governor's role to decide who goes to heaven. I believe that God decides who goes to heaven, not George W. Bush."[11]

But he was still not quite off the hook. Director of the Anti-Defamation League Abraham Foxman demanded—and got—a written apology clarifying George W.'s position. George W. wrote in his December 8 letter of apology:

> I never intended to make judgments about the faith of others. Judgments about heaven do not belong in the realm of politics or this world; they belong to a Higher Authority. In discussing my own personal faith as a Christian, I in no way meant to imply any disrespect or to denigrate any other religion. During my four years as governor, I have set a positive tone that indicates my respect for individuals from all faiths, all backgrounds and all walks of life.

Foxman said later that he accepted the apology and regarded the issue as now "behind us."[12]

George W. was almost certainly not dissembling in saying this. As is true of many devout followers of Christ, he does not seem to regard his own belief in the need for a personal commitment to Jesus Christ as an impediment to good relations with followers of other faiths. Before he became president, George W. seems to have felt no inhibition in expressing a strong affection for the Jewish people.

In a story George W. told both in his March 1999 sermon at Second Baptist in Houston, as well as in *A Charge to Keep*, Bush says he was deeply touched by a display of Jewish Christian affection on the Israel trip. The delegation visited the Sea of Galilee and the Mount of Beatitudes, by tradition the location of Jesus's Sermon on the Mount. In George W.'s recollection of that excursion—the last social event of the Israel trip—one of the Gentiles in the group told the story of kneeling at the Sea of Galilee, holding hands with a Jewish member of the group, putting their hands in the sea, and praying together. George W. described how the Gentile, after narrating this story, then spontaneously sang an old hymn. The words, quoted in full in *A Charge to Keep*, and apparently closely echoing George W.'s strong sympathies for the Jews, are revealing:

> Now is the time approaching,
> By prophets long foretold,
> When all shall dwell together—
> One Shepherd and one fold.
> Now Jew and Gentile, meeting
> From many a distant shore,
> Around an altar kneeling—
> One common Lord adore.[13]

In effect, George W. appeared to see great commonality of faith and a similarity in outlook between Jew and Gentile, or more specifically, Jew and Christian. He seemed to share the intuitive empathy that most American evangelical Christians feel for the Jewish people because of the common roots and shared Scriptures of their faiths. Many Jews have not been able to accept this feeling of affinity on the part of American Christians, remembering, understandably, not-so-distant times in Europe when some of their worst persecutors proudly proclaimed themselves to be Christians. But if there is one thing dramatically different about Christian evangelicalism, at least in the United States, in recent decades from earlier epochs, it is the strong component of sympathy for Jews and support for Israel. It appears that George W. feels the same way.

---

GEORGE W.'S IDENTIFICATION WITH THE JEWISH PEOPLE was but one more element in a decade-long transformation that started in the late 1980s when he began to behave more in the manner that Christians and non-Christians expect of someone who calls himself a follower of Christ. He stopped drinking, abruptly, in 1986. A few years later, he gave up smoking, as well as tobacco chewing. His language could still be what is charitably called "colorful," and even on the presidential campaign trail, he sometimes let out expletives when someone displeased him. In other areas, though, he was displaying both a generosity of spirit and personal acts that deeply touched close observers.

Adair Margo, an El Paso art gallery owner whose family has lived there for four generations, came to know George W. and Laura well during George W.'s governorship through Laura's interest in art programs in El Paso (her mother's hometown), as well as in other parts of Texas. The friendship between the Margos, devout Southern Baptists, and the Bushes was so close that they were invited to stay in the governor's residence in Austin and later in the White House. What they saw in the Bushes' home impressed them. For instance, the Bushes were unusually involved in the lives and welfare of their housekeeper, a single mother named Maria, and her daughter. At the official residence, Margo said, "The girls would be playing with her. Maria told me that they paid for [her daughter] Alex to go to a private Episcopal school in Austin. [The Bushes] would never say it. They say very little."

The Margos' own housekeeper has herself spent several nights in the White House, sitting at dinner with the president's family in the evening. "They would pray at meals. I was always impressed by how unashamed he was at prayer," Margo said. "He [the president] has this self-deprecating humor. He doesn't take himself so seriously. It is in their walk. Their walk is everything." ("Walk," as used here, is an evangelical Christian term for a lifestyle that is Christlike. George W. himself spoke of the "walk" in an interview with Beliefnet.com during the 2000 presidential campaign. "I'm mindful of telling people that when asked about religion I'm mindful of walking that walk," he said. "That's the best thing I can do as president. And when you walk the walk, people of faith will walk right with you."[14]

The Bushes' other close friends had similar comments. Though not a trait necessarily related to his faith, George W., in particular, has always been very loyal to longtime friends. Adair Margo was struck by this when, after becoming president, George W. continued to associate with people he had known when he was governor, when he was co-owner of the Texas

Rangers, and even earlier. "They don't forget their friends," Margo said. "It's not like they've moved up the ladder to more important friends. Where I live we don't vote, and when we do, we vote Democratic. But he made it clear that he was the governor of the entire state and would invest the time with people who didn't know him. He spent time in very modest neighborhoods."[15]

Some Texas friends who are strong Christians observed that as the 2000 presidential campaign got under way, George W.'s faith seemed to be more evident than ever before. One Texas lady (who prefers to go unnamed) whose connection with George W. goes back to her college days when she first became friends with Laura, recalled, "What has brought us closer is that during the presidential campaign his faith really most manifested itself. I began to observe things that had probably been there all along. I just recognized it: his faith was seemingly becoming even deeper, and it was certainly very real. He loved God's Word, and he had an active prayer life."

Laura's friend started to send encouraging notes with Bible verses on them as she felt it appropriate. She never received any acknowledgment during the campaign itself, but when she and her husband were invited to the White House for the inauguration festivities, the newly installed president came up to her and gave her a big hug. "You were very encouraging to me during the campaign," he said, "and you have to keep it up now that I am in the White House."

---

PERHAPS PART OF THE REASON for the growing evidence of George W.'s faith was that it was being severely tested on the road to the White House. The campaign itself was grueling, as all presidential campaigns are, and George W. found himself constantly stretched and challenged. During the primaries with the other Republican candidates, the cross talk had sometimes been sharp but never really brutal. But with the approach of the 2000 general election, George W. was facing Al Gore on the stump, and the pressures grew intense. During these times, he frequently phoned his Texas pastor friends, especially James Robison and Kirbyjon Caldwell. Caldwell said that almost every conversation with George W. included a time of prayer.

According to Don Evans, who periodically joined him on the campaign trail, George W. almost always had his Bible beside his bed—that early practice first observed by his mother when he was in his twenties. "The nights I was with him [in the same hotel], when I looked by the bedside, it was there. And he just disciplined himself into the Word every day," Evans said.[16]

The same observation was made by his campaign press spokesperson Karen Hughes, who later served as White House communications director and who, along with campaign aide Israel Hernandez, was with the candidate almost every day of the campaign. She remembers, "I knew early on that he read the Bible every day. During the campaign he'd sometimes talk about what he'd read that morning. He alternated between *The One Year Bible* and *My Utmost for His Highest* by Oswald Chambers. Sometimes he sent me a page copied from his [Chambers'] devotional. It was during the campaign that I became aware of how important his faith was to him."[17]

This comment may have been more revealing than Hughes realized. As his gubernatorial press secretary, Hughes was well aware of the strong friendships that George W. had formed with key Texas pastors and of the close personal friendship with longtime Bible study friends like Don Evans. She was also aware of the brown-bag, Bible study lunches in the governor's mansion and of the devout Christian staffers who, from time to time, offered George W. some Bible verses of encouragement. What she apparently had not seen was the faith under fire that George W. would first display during the campaign and then, far more vividly, when the United States was under attack.

But first, George W. faced the trying days following the November 7 election that failed to provide a decisive resolution of the political contest that had been in process since the spring of 2000. It was to be another thirty-four days before the Supreme Court finally ruled 5 to 4 against another hand recount of the disputed Florida votes, thus confirming that, though not the winner of the largest number of votes cast, George W. Bush had, through the Florida result, secured a sufficient number of the electoral college votes to be named the next president.

During this long and uncertain period—as agonizing for Democratic candidate Al Gore as it was for George W.—the Texas governor was caught between the need to appear "presidential," in anticipation of being declared the winner, and the need to appear humble and modest, awaiting the verdict of the people, so to speak. Laura's college friend remembers encountering George W. in this uncertain period between November 7 and the Supreme Court's December 12 decision and "marveling at his self-assurance and his calm." She observed that Laura also showed remarkable composure, refusing even to discuss issues such as inaugural ball gowns until it was confirmed that her husband had won the election.[18]

Several friends noted how philosophical the Bushes seemed to be about the possibility of returning to Texas to resume a "normal" life rather than a presidential one. On learning of George W.'s probable entry to the White House, his Texas friend and scriptural encourager passed on to him an appropriate word from Scripture: "In order that I may boast on the day of Christ that I did not run or labor for nothing," from Philippians 2:16. "It looks like you'll soon be awarded an earthly crown," she added. George W. smiled broadly. A few days later, as a CBS TV news crew was taking down its equipment after an interview with the now-confirmed winner of the 2000 election, she walked into the governor's mansion and greeted him with, "Merry Christmas, Mr. President."[19]

# 7

## A New Conscience and Civility

*America, at its best, is a place where personal responsibility is valued and expected. Encouraging responsibility . . . is a call to conscience.*

—George W. Bush

THE ORDEAL OF THOSE THIRTY-FOUR DAYS of electoral uncertainty during November to December 2000 must have reminded George W. Bush of the fragility of all political power. No doubt, it forced him to his knees, as it did millions of Americans who were deeply worried about the direction the nation might take if his opponent were elected president. George W. has always said that he has never prayed to "win" elections or to triumph in particular political conflicts. He told Barbara Walters in a *20/20* interview before the election of 2000, "I don't pray for votes (and) I don't pray for the stock market to go up. I pray for strength and patience and love and understanding."[1] But he must have prayed that, whatever else happened, he would somehow be up to the task if elected.

In *A Charge to Keep*, George W. made it plain that he regards political life as a whole to be a walk of faith. "I could not be governor if I did not believe in a divine plan that supersedes all human plans," he wrote, adding, "I've certainly never plotted the various steps of my life, certainly never campaigned for one office to try to position myself for the next."[2] Bush's critics and opponents would probably not argue with that, regarding his entire career as a succession of fortunate events made possible by the accident of his birth into a prominent and successful American political family. George W. has wisely never attempted, since assuming office, to speculate on divine purposes for the particular "call" upon his presidency. But it is likely that he looked at his presidency from its inception as a vehicle for carrying out God's purposes, even if he didn't have a clue what those purposes might be. In this belief, he is no different from millions of Christians in the United States and around the world who want their lives to be consecrated to God's purposes, even if few of them have a clear idea of what those specific purposes are.

George W. made sure that every possible pastoral blessing of clergy and liturgy might be on hand from inauguration day onward. At the church service in St. John's Episcopal Church in Lafayette Square before any of the public ceremonies on inauguration day, he had asked Rev. Mark Craig to offer the homily. According to one source, the president-elect spent a half-hour in the church in personal prayer, preparing himself to take the oath of office.[3]

Then, at the inaugural ceremony itself on Capitol Hill, in addition to Rev. Kirbyjon Caldwell's closing benediction, prayers were offered by Rev. Franklin Graham, standing in for his ill and infirm father, Dr. Billy Graham, who had been a feature of presidential inaugurations for decades.

George W.'s inaugural speech was both eloquent and pithy, lasting just fifteen minutes—one of the shortest inaugural addresses in decades. He called for a new era of civility in national politics and for the United States to lead the cause of freedom globally. As thousands in the attending crowds shivered in the damp cold of that January day, he called upon Americans to work for "a single nation of justice and opportunity." This, he said, was within their reach "because we are guided by a power larger than ourselves, who creates us equal in His image, and we are confident in principles that unite and lead us onward."[4] He alluded to faith-based social initiatives, which had been announced during his campaign and which he had already experimented with in Texas. Government had an important role to play, he said, then added, "Some needs and hurts are so deep they will only respond to a mentor's touch or a pastor's prayer. Church and charity, synagogue and mosque lend our communities their humanity, and they will have an honored place in our plans and in our laws."

During his speech, George W. also introduced his theme of the need to call people to personal responsibility—a key ingredient of his aspiration to turn America's culture around. "America," he said, "at its best, is a place where personal responsibility is valued and expected. Encouraging responsibility is not a search for scapegoats, it is a call to conscience." Summing up this short address, he cited a conversation between America's third president, Thomas Jefferson, and Virginia statesman John Page. "We know the race is not to the swift nor the battle to the strong. Do you not think an angel rides in the whirlwind and directs this storm?" Jefferson had asked. George W. had his own concluding response to that question: "We are not this story's author, who fills time and eternity with His purpose. Yet His purpose is achieved in our duty, and our duty is fulfilled in service to one another."[5]

On his return to the White House, even before the festivities that took up afternoon and evening, President Bush issued a proclamation calling the nation to a day of prayer and thanksgiving the next day, a Sunday. Then there was another church service, this time in the Washington National Cathedral and a sermon by Rev. Franklin Graham. In keeping with George W.'s own ecumenical Christian background—Episcopal, Presbyterian, and Methodist—the senior Methodist bishop of the Washington area, Rev. Felton E. May, was on hand, along with clerics from the Eastern Orthodox and Roman Catholic traditions. Jewish rabbis had also been invited. No observer of these events could have been left in any doubt that George W. Bush, forty-third president of the United States, took his Christian faith seriously and welcomed varieties of America's Judeo-Christian tradition to celebrate that seriousness with him.

---

THE CLINTON WHITE HOUSE in its early days was infamous for pizza deliveries and late-night policy seminars as young staffers, new to

Washington and new even to the political system in general, wrestled with policy priorities after twelve years of Republican rule in the nation's capital. President Bush did away with that casualness as brusquely as he might have chain-sawed through the underbrush at his ranch in Crawford, Texas. It was coats and ties only throughout the White House at all times for the men, and office suits or dresses for women staffers. He would not even allow himself to enter the Oval Office without a suit—a self-imposed discipline despite the hassles it caused when he needed to personally retrieve a document from the office after he had formally ended the workday and returned to the private quarters of the White House. He would change out of his after-work clothes back into a suit for the short walk to the West Wing and the Oval Office, then return to the private quarters and change back into casual clothes.

Punctuality became an obsession with President Bush—another striking contrast to his predecessor, who had kept Bush Senior waiting at the changeover of power in 1993 and also was late for the formal civilities of administration change on January 20, 2001, when George W. entered the White House. "Late is rude," George W. once tersely observed.

Other forms of civility were also strongly encouraged. It became quickly apparent that George W. was greatly irritated when cell phones went off among journalists or other staffers while he was having a meeting. A receptionist in the West Wing late in 2003 responded to a comment on the almost Victorian level of formal politeness throughout the White House with the words, "It starts at the top." In effect, though manners are not specifically connected to George W.'s personal religious faith, it was as though the discipline he brought to his own life of prayer and Bible study filtered down into the work habits of everyone who worked with him at the White House.

Cabinet meetings often began with prayer, usually by a cabinet secretary called upon by the president to perform that function. Of course, several members of George W.'s first cabinet were devout, even outspoken evangelical Christians, from Attorney General John Ashcroft to Secretary of Commerce Don Evans. Meals at the White House similarly began with

President Bush, or someone else he called on, asking a divine blessing. A visitor to the president's ranch at Crawford, early on in the presidency, was nevertheless struck by George W.'s efforts not to cause awkwardness to guests who were not of the Christian faith. One Jewish staffer found himself asked by the president to pray the blessing on the food in his own way and gracefully did so.

Jewish White House staffers certainly were quickly aware of the presence of a large corps of evangelical Christians filling important staff positions. National Security Advisor Condoleeza Rice, for example—the daughter of an African American Presbyterian pastor in Georgia—has spoken openly about her own Christian testimony. Her faith, rooted in her upbringing as the child of a pastor, took a backseat to her other life's activities, which included being a first-rate scholar of Soviet and Russian affairs, as well as a pianist of concert-level skills. That changed several years ago when she was approached by a stranger in a supermarket near Stanford University, where she rose to high academic and administrative rank. The stranger, also an African American, asked if Rice would play the piano in a forthcoming church picnic. She agreed, and found herself drawn back into the life of the Presbyterian church. Rice has given her testimony of a renewal of Christian faith at Washington-area churches and has also been a conspicuous participant at the annual Presidential Prayer Breakfast each year in late January or early February. The close relationship she has developed over the years with George W. and Laura Bush likely derives, at least in part, from their shared faith.

Within the White House, whose staff is spread out beyond the White House building into the adjacent Old Executive Office Building (OEOB), the incoming George W. Bush administration in 2001 made it clear that Bible study and prayer groups among staffers, on-campus, so to speak, would be encouraged. A senior White House staffer said late in 2003 he thought there were then seven separate Bible study or prayer-fellowship groups meeting every week in offices or meeting rooms around the White House-OEOB complex. Perhaps some two hundred of five hundred White House staffers, he said, participated one way or another in such meetings.

Rarely has an administration been so active and so open in encouraging Bible study and fellowship groups among its staff.

While Jews of many theological persuasions, from Reformed to Orthodox, have held high positions in the White House under George W., they have done so in the full realization that they work within a significantly Christianized administration. David Frum, an Orthodox Jew who was a speechwriter for President Bush in the first year of the new administration, discovered this early on. Frum recalled that literally the first words he heard on entering the White House to discuss his future job were, "Missed you at Bible study." They were not directed at him but at the man accompanying him into the building, chief speech-writer Michael Gerson. A graduate of Wheaton College, perhaps the preeminent private evangelical Christian university in the country, Gerson was a frequent participant in internal White House Christian programs. But Frum mistakenly thought that the comment had been directed at him, and it made him "twitch" with nervousness, he said, adding that it was "disconcerting to a non-Christian" like him.[6] But Frum got over his initial alarm and came to appreciate the evangelicals George W. had brought with him to help formulate and execute his policies. As he put it after several months of observation,

> The evangelicals in the Bush White House were its gentlest souls, the most patient, the least argumentative. They were numerous enough to set the tone of the White House, and the result was an office in which I seldom heard a voice raised in anger—and never witnessed a single one of those finger-jabbing confrontations you see in movies about the White House. The television show *The West Wing* might as well have been set aboard a Klingon starship for all it resembled life inside the Bush White House.[7]

George W., however, was well aware of the dilemma he faced in averring to his own Christian faith now that he was the president of all Americans, and not just the Republican Party presidential candidate, much less a contestant among other Republican presidential hopefuls for the party nomination. On the one hand, he had to placate the ardor of some of the conservative Christians in the United States enough to secure their continuing political support. On the other hand, he had to dissolve worries among Americans of different faiths—Jews and Muslims, to name only the most prominent groups—and American secularists of no religious faith at all, that he was not going to use the presidential office as a bully pulpit to bash Americans over the head with his own particular brand of Christian conservatism. In fact, the drumbeat of suspicion that George W. intended to break down the wall of separation between church and state, or perhaps already had succeeded in doing so, never entirely quieted down, despite ardent assertions by George W. that he had no intention of doing anything of the sort.

---

AS HAD BEEN THE CASE OF EVERY AMERICAN PRESIDENT since Eisenhower in the 1950s, George W. attended the annual midwinter convening in Washington of the Presidential Prayer Breakfast, a major event in the capital that is always held in the ballroom of the Washington Hilton Hotel at the end of January or in early February. With an attendance of some four-thousand to five-thousand men and women from every state of the Union, Christians from overseas, foreign government visitors, foreign diplomats living in the United States, and a large attendance of U.S. Senators and Representatives, the prayer breakfast is a massive operation. Its speakers have ranged from Mother Teresa (1993, with President Clinton) to virtually unknown Christian professionals whose lives have embodied core Christian values and solid altruistic work.

Every American president is expected to make a small speech as part of the Prayer Breakfast program, and all have done so. Reagan and Bush Senior tended to make the breakfasts sunny events, giving relatively brief, well-polished speeches with anecdotes from their own journeys of faith. Clinton one year introduced his remarks by saying that he and Hillary had been talking over what he should say just the night before, the implication being, getting the words for the occasion just right hadn't been an agonizing, months-long priority for him. But George W., mindful of the need for caution, delivered a carefully modulated expression of his own faith on his first appearance at the Washington Hilton event in February 2001. In fact, he sounded almost defensive about being there at all:

America's Constitution forbids a religious test for office, and that's the way it should be. An American President serves people of every faith, and serves some of no faith at all. Yet I have found my faith helps me in the service to people. Faith teaches humility. As Laura would say, I could use a dose occasionally.

This is a day when our nation recognizes a power above our power, an influence beyond our influence, a guiding wisdom far greater than our own. The American character, it's strong and confident; but we have never been reluctant to speak of our own dependence on providence.

Our country was founded by great and wise people who were fluent in the language of humility, praise and petition. Throughout our history, in danger and division, we have always turned to prayer. And our country has been delivered from many serious evils and wrongs because of that prayer.

We cannot presume to know every design of our Creator, or to assert a special claim on His favor. Yet, it is important to pause and recognize our help in ages past and our hope for years to come.[8]

George W. was clearly trying to set himself within an almost "civic religion" tradition of American presidential Christianity first demonstrated by President Eisenhower when, in expressing his own approval of faith, he had said, famously, "Faith is good for Americans, and I don't care what faith it is."[9]

George W.'s caution in his Prayer Breakfast remarks may have in part been a response to the harsh criticism, even ridicule, of his clumsy speaking style, his mispronunciations, and his malapropisms during the 2000 presidential campaign. In a way that amused his audience greatly, and that may have helped both disarm the irritation of his critics and soften his own embarrassment, he openly made fun of himself in an entertaining speech at the fifty-seventh annual dinner of the Radio-Television Correspondents' Association, also at the Hilton Hotel, on March 29, 2001. Referring to one of several books that have drawn wide attention to his verbal clumsiness, George W. said in self-mockery,

> Here's one from the book—and I actually said this. [Laughter] "I know the human being and fish can coexist peacefully." [Laughter] Now, that makes you stop and think. [Laughter and applause] Anyone can give you a coherent sentence, but something like this takes you into an entirely new dimension. [Laughter]
>
> I actually said this in New Hampshire: "I appreciate preservation. It's what you do when you run for President, you've got to preserve." [Laughter] I don't have the slightest idea what I was saying there. [Laughter and applause][10]

---

BUT WHERE GEORGE W. WAS SURE that he did know what he was talking about was the issue of "compassionate conservatism." In early 2001, George W. spoke and acted as though his primary task as president was to develop "compassionate conservatism" in such a way that his longterm goals of changing the direction of American culture could begin to take place. In February 2001, he appointed John Diiulio—a former member of the think tank Manhattan Institute for Policy Research—director of the newly created Office of Faith-Based Initiatives. George W.'s goal was as ambitious as it was simple: engage successful faith-based social programs in an overall plan to address America's toughest social problems, from teenage pregnancy to drug addiction and poverty. His concept, with which he had experimented with in Texas, was that the federal government should be able to provide financial funding and organizational support for institutions run by churches, synagogues, or mosques that seemed to have produced effective results in addressing certain social problems.

In a major speech in Dallas before the powerful National Association of Evangelicals, a grouping of national churches that do not belong to existing Protestant groups (the Southern Baptist Convention, for example, or the mainline Protestant National Council of Churches), Diiulio marshaled his arguments powerfully. He cited data by The Gallup Organization and other research groups that indicated very large majorities of Americans, both white and African American, believed that religion could help solve most or all current social problems in the United States. He pointed out that Charitable Choice, a law with strong bipartisan support signed by President Clinton in 1996 as part of the Republican-controlled Congress's efforts to pass welfare reform, had provided for federal funding of charitable institutions that were religious, as opposed to secular, in outlook. He also noted that the Charitable Choice law exempted religious institutions from being required to hire employees who did not share their core beliefs, even if the institutions received taxpayer funding. Such a precedent, Diiulio argued, could also be applied to the expansion of faith-based social services, with federal assistance, as envisaged by President Bush.[11]

From the outset, though, George W.'s faith-based initiatives ran into opposition from a variety of sources. Some conservative religious figures worried that churches, synagogues, and mosques might become corrupted by easy access to a public pork barrel. Ardent religion separationist groups, such as People for the American Way or Americans United for Separation of Church and State, feared that the president's ideas would lead to the emergence of religion as a factor in the distribution of government money. Some critics, including prominent gays, were alarmed that religious groups seeking federal financial help would continue to be able to express their opposition to gay sexual activity in hiring practices. Even some evangelical organizations were critical of the program as the Congress struggled in early 2001 to wrestle into shape a bill that would satisfy the widely varying views being expressed.

Jim Wallis, founding editor of *Sojourners*, a Washington-based evangelical journal that has been supportive of strong government support for social services, as well as critical of previous Republican administrations on many issues, including the first Gulf War of 1991 and Republican attitudes toward welfare was originally supportive of the faith-based program being fought in the Congress. But eventually Wallis soured on it, believing that the efforts to push forward faith-based initiatives were starving the funding of existing social welfare programs. In this respect, Wallis saw eye to eye with many secular advocates of broad government involvement in dealing with social problems. In July 2003, more than two years after Diiulio began his work, Wallis said,

> The good people are feeling betrayed, overwhelmed and stressed because they face this nightmare of increasing need and diminishing resources. We said from the start that the faith-based initiative can't substitute for good social policy. . . . The administration is breaking faith with the faith-based initiative by not providing resources.[12]

Diiulio himself, meanwhile, was regarded as abrasive and difficult to work with by some on Capitol Hill, and quirky, if not disloyal, by some in the White House with whom he had to deal. He resigned in August 2001, less than seven months into the job. His successor, Jim Towey, a much less prickly individual, had spent several years earlier in his career as the principal Washington-area coordinator for the Missionaries of Charity founded by Mother Teresa.

Towey attended an event at Christ Episcopal Church in Boston in the spring of 2003 to underline another part of the faith-based program, that of providing funding for the repair and preservation of historic religious structures. Christ Episcopal, also known as Old North Church, was made famous by the historic ride of American Revolutionary War hero Paul Revere. Interior Secretary Gale Norton, in May 2003, had announced that the federal government would provide three hundred and seventeen thousand dollars in aid for repair and restoration of the church. Other historic religious buildings eligible for such aid included Touro Synagogue in Newport, Rhode Island, and a historic Roman Catholic cathedral in Baltimore. Towey said of the federal decision to support repairs at Christ Episcopal, "The president's point here is, this isn't about funding churches. This is about saving a national treasure." Opponents complained that the buildings were still being used for religious purposes, thus implying state aid to functioning religious institutions.[13]

FOR MUCH OF GEORGE W.'S FIRST YEAR in the White House, efforts to get faith-based initiatives off the ground seemed to take up a great deal of the administration's energy. But away from the limelight, the president was also quietly trying to establish good relations with America's Jewish community, a political constituency that has traditionally tended to support Democratic candidates, sometimes overwhelmingly. In May 2001, he spoke to the American Jewish Committee and revealed a heart for Israel that may well have surprised some of his audience. He told them forthrightly,

> I am a Christian. But I believe with the psalmist, that the Lord God of Israel neither slumbers nor sleeps. Understanding my administration should not be difficult. We will speak up for our principles; we will stand up for our friends in the world. And one of the most important friends is the State of Israel. . . . It's a small country that has lived under the threat throughout its existence. At my first meeting of my National Security Council, I told them that a top foreign policy priority of my administration is the safety and security of Israel. (Applause.) My administration will be steadfast in supporting Israel against terrorism and violence, and in seeking the peace for which all Israelis pray.[14]

George W.'s support for Israel very quickly turned out to be far more than rhetoric. From the outset of his administration, the president continued to refuse to meet with Palestinian Authority president and PLO Chairman Yassir Arafat, reversing a trend that had brought the Palestinian leader to the White House more than twenty times during the Clinton administration. As George W. made clear in a meeting with Jewish leaders during the "Ten Days of Awe" surrounding the Jewish New Year holiday of Rosh Hashanah in 2003, if he disagreed with Israeli prime minister Ariel Sharon over actions taken by the Israeli government, he preferred to speak to Sharon privately rather than have United States officials voice displeasure in public.[15] This was a striking contrast, for example, to the behavior of the administration of George W.'s father when confronted by Israeli action that the Americans found irritating. Bush Senior's secretary of state, James Baker, found then Israeli premier Yitzhak Shamir's refusal to deal either directly or indirectly with the Palestinians after the first Gulf War in 1991 so irritating that at one press conference that year he publicly and ostentatiously announced the phone number of the White House switchboard. In effect, Baker wanted to make clear that he considered the Israelis to be the chief stumbling block to a Middle East peace settlement at that time.

But George W.'s open bond of friendship with Sharon clearly protected the Israeli premier from American diplomatic pressure when Israeli troops surrounded the Palestinian headquarters housing Arafat in Ramallah, West Bank, during dangerous Intifadeh (uprising) confrontations between Israelis and Palestinians in 2001 and 2002. When Israeli tanks surrounded Arafat's Ramallah headquarters in 2002, George W. spoke by phone to Sharon directly, according to Minnesota rabbi Jonathan Ginsburg. Bush complained to Sharon that while the United States was trying to "marginalize" Arafat, Israel's aggressive military posture was turning him into "a hero and martyr again."[16]

Was George W.'s supportive posture toward Israel influenced more by instinctive friendship with Sharon and reflexive support for a democratic ally of the United States, or by a much deeper sense of moral obligation emerging from George W.'s deep Christian faith and reverence for the Bible? There is no way of knowing for sure. But when I visited Israel in

October 2003, several Israelis told me, personally, that Bush was "the best American president Israel has ever had."[17] In June 2002, many Palestinians were angered, rather than heartened, by President Bush's announcement that the United States favored the establishment of a Palestinian state side-by-side with the State of Israel. George W.'s speech announcing this new initiative in American foreign policy—no previous American administration had ever publicly supported an independent Palestinian state—was qualified by a demand that Palestinians choose a new leader for themselves. In effect, Washington was saying that American support for a Palestinian state was conditional upon removing Arafat from power.

Rabbi Ginsburg recounted his meeting with President Bush, along with rabbis from the Reformed, Conservative, and Orthodox traditions of Judaism, with an enthusiasm befitting someone assumed to be supportive of the Republican Party. But other Jewish leaders have also come away from meetings with George W. almost enraptured by the sense of commitment to the defense of Israel and protection of Jews worldwide that George W. has often conveyed. At one meeting with rabbis in 2003, one participant said to a stunned George W., after hearing the president speak with zeal and eloquence about his concerns over various expressions of anti-Semitism worldwide, "Mr. President, I didn't vote for you, but if you had been president in 1938, I now think the Holocaust might not have happened."[18]

Israeli Premier Sharon was one of the first foreign visitors to meet with George W. in the new administration, arriving in Washington one month after his February 2001 election victory. It was a warm and upbeat reunion of two friends who had met under unusual circumstances.

---

LESS THAN A MONTH BEFORE THE MEETING, George W. took the important first step of getting acquainted with another foreign leader, British Prime Minister Tony Blair. Initial appearances suggested that the encounter for both men was cordial, friendly, but not especially buddy-

buddy. After all, Blair, a socialist and an assumed liberal in most social matters, had been very close to President Bush's predecessor and ideological nemesis, President Clinton. Blair often told friends how much he enjoyed Clinton's quick and sometimes brilliant intelligence, especially on political matters. The two men reportedly would speak for hours by phone on an early theme of the Blair government that came to power in 1998. He called it the "Third Way" of politics—a supposed middle ground between traditional and discredited, socialist thinking on the one hand, and brittle, ideological conservativism on the other.[19]

When Blair arrived in the United States in February 2001, he was given the unusual honor of a meeting with the president at Camp David, a privilege granted to few visiting foreign leaders. Their first press conference together nevertheless hinted at a certain stiffness, despite a surface cordiality. The president said that the two men had enjoyed "a couple of formal visits" and a walk around the Camp David property. A reporter asked what they had in common—suggesting more insightfully than he perhaps realized as possible areas of shared interest "religion, or sport, or music." George W. somewhat blithely said that they both used Colgate toothpaste, and they both like to work out in the Camp David gym.[20]

In fact, something else far more profound was taking place in this first encounter between the British and American leaders. Blair, who had become a Christian while an undergraduate at Oxford University in the 1960s, was learning firsthand that George W.'s Christian faith was real and unpretentious. Though there do not appear to have been shared times of prayer or Bible reading on this visit, they did say grace at the private dinner with only their wives present. In fact, George W. had made it clear that he wanted grace to be said before meals, no matter who the visitor was to the White House, Camp David, or the ranch at Crawford. This was the case, of course, with the Blairs' visit at Camp David. Because it was a private dinner of just the two couples, we don't know who actually said grace, but thanks was given for the meal, and perhaps at that very moment something took root in the relationship between the two men.

Blair apparently decided after this first visit that he could trust George W. at a deep level, and that feeling certainly was reciprocated. Two years later, when the United States was about to invade Iraq, the British prime minister was unequivocally on the American side, though at great risk to his own political future in Britain. He agreed with George W. on the perception of Iraq as a dangerous and unpredictable adversary in the Middle East, but it is hard to escape the sense that George W. Bush had transmitted to Tony Blair a backbone of conviction that grew out of his own Christian faith.

Blair, after all, had wrestled with many issues as a student before coming to his own Christian convictions as an adult. He had married a devout Roman Catholic woman with whom he frequently attended Roman Catholic Mass (though, not being formally received into the Catholic Church, he did not take Holy Communion there). Once the Iraq operation was under way, British TV journalists asked Blair point-blank whether Blair had prayed with Bush during his visits to the United States in 2003, but Blair either unconvincingly denied it or appeared momentarily flustered on-camera. When one British reporter asked Blair a question about religion, his hard-nosed communications director Alastair Campbell—later forced to resign in connection with the suicide of a British weapons scientist whose identity had been revealed to the British media by someone in the government—famously replied, "We don't do God." But to close observers of the White House and indeed of this special relationship between Britain and the United States, it appeared that Blair's own Christian faith was strangely fortified by his encounters with his counterpart across the Atlantic.

---

GEORGE W. FOCUSED MUCH OF HIS FOREIGN POLICY energy in the first year—before September 11, of course—on Mexico, whose president, Vicente Fox, he had already met while governor of Texas. There is no indication whether he and Fox shared any faith concepts or insights, but

in his intuitive manner, George W. seemed to attach high priority to relations with Mexico. Of course, resolving perennial Mexican-American
tensions over illegal immigrants would be one very satisfying fruit of good
bilateral relations. But what if Mexico also became available for oil exploration by American petroleum companies? George W. had none of the
sentimental feelings of affinity for the conservative Arab states that some
in his father's administration evinced. He would almost certainly favor
United States rapprochement with a neighbor that had so often previously expressed resentment of the "giant from the North."

In reality, Mexico had significantly larger petroleum reserves than the
United States and the capacity, if those reserves were skillfully developed,
to release all of North America from reliance on oil from the Middle East.
George W., even while coping with the continuing crisis in Iraq and in
Israeli-Palestinian affairs, pursued improved relations with Mexico in the
second half of his first four years in office with an alacrity that alarmed
many American conservatives. In particular, he advocated legalizing the
presence of Mexican workers in the United States who were technically
"illegal immigrants" but whose steady work performance and payment of
taxes had made them vital ingredients of American economic prosperity.
Did he have in mind the potential future benefits of American access to
Mexican petroleum? He wisely didn't say whether this was what he was
thinking, but it could have been.

---

IN A FAMOUS BUNGLING OF THE ENGLISH LANGUAGE on the
campaign trail in 2000, George W. once said that political adversaries and
critics sometimes "misunderestimated" him. He was surely right, and in
an odd way, the tendency of some observers to underrate his intelligence,
and particularly his diplomatic skills, turned strongly to his favor and, it
should be said, to that of the United States. Once again, the most striking
example was directly related to his faith.

In June 2001, George W. conducted his first lengthy meeting with the leader of major power—Russia's smart, disciplined, and perhaps overly authoritarian Vladimir Putin. The meeting lasted two hours in a castle in Slovenia, a pro-Western former Yugoslav republic now ardently pursuing membership in the European Union.

When the two men came out and addressed the media in a joint news conference, George W. sounded to some critics not just sentimental about Putin but downright naive about the former KGB officer in East Germany. "I looked the man in the eye," the president told the dumbfounded media, "and I found him to be very straightforward and trustworthy. We had a very good dialogue. I was able to get a sense of his soul."[21] Television commentator Chris Matthews mocked the president for asserting powers of perception that not even Superman possessed.[22]

There was much more to George W.'s perceptions than was known at the time, though. During a warmup conversation between the two men before substantive discussions on Russian American bilateral and global viewpoints, Putin revealed that he wore around his neck a Russian Orthodox crucifix given to him by his mother. Moreover, he said, there was an interesting story behind it. A fire in his office had once destroyed many of his personal possessions, but, Putin told George W., he had sent a fireman back to search one more time for the crucifix, which was so important to him. The fireman obeyed and returned with the recovered crucifix, which Putin said he wore constantly. George W. then made a comment that I have heard reported in different versions, the gist of it being, "Then you are close to eternal life."

In effect, George W. responded to something in Putin, some glimmer of childhood faith that had caused the stern Russian leader to trust the American president, by sharing this very personal story, on an emotional level—and on the face of it, in a rather unexpected way. This highly personal affinity quickly bore political fruit. Five months later, at the start of the Afghan war, U.S. bombers and transport aircraft sought permission to overfly Russia en route to newly established anti-Taliban bases in the Central Asian republics of Uzbekistan and Tajikistan. Putin overruled his own military advisors by agreeing to the request and not matching

American military alert status with a similar order to his own military.

In December 2001, the United States unilaterally pulled out of the Anti-Ballistic Missile Treaty, the important U.S.-Soviet agreement of 1973 that had restrained both Moscow and Washington from developing defenses against ballistic missiles. Though not pleased with the U.S. decision, Putin seemed to know, again intuitively, that the move was not motivated by an American desire to secure a strategic nuclear advantage over Russia. Rather, it was meant to develop what Washington hoped would eventually be effective defenses against possible missile attack from rogue regimes like North Korea.

How did Putin know he could trust George W. Bush? After all, he must have heard protests from his own more "realistic" Russian analysts pointing out, perhaps, that Bush was an archconservative tool of American big business and an ideological foe of Russian greatness. But something had clicked between Putin and Bush. Almost certainly, George W.'s faith and his warm response to Putin's shy acknowledgment of his own faith played a major role.

Conversations with senior White House officials make it clear that George W. is perfectly aware of Putin's apparent drive to gather even more domestic political power into his own hands. "He knows what Putin is up to," said an official familiar with the president's calculus. The implication: if Putin evolved from political authoritarianism to dictatorship or, perhaps, bullying his neighbors, the faith connection would be eclipsed by altogether different calculations of the Russian president's purposes.

The Putin incident was not the only one in which George W.'s Christian faith seems to have played a role in establishing a powerful relationship and friendship. But it was, in some ways, the most startling.

# 8

## A Nation Deeply Wounded

*Faith shows us the reality of good, and the reality of evil. It is
always, and everywhere, wrong to target and kill the innocent . . .
to be cruel and hateful, to enslave and oppress. It is always, and
everywhere, right to be kind and just, to protect the lives of others,
and to lay down your life for a friend.*

—George W. Bush

David frum—the Canadian-born Orthodox Jew and speechwriter—
found himself admiring George W.'s leadership, in spite of inherent
cultural suspicions of the Texan. Frum summed up the Vladimir Putin
episode this way:

> Bush was not a lightweight. He was, rather, a very unfamiliar type of
> heavyweight. Words often failed him, his memory sometimes betrayed
> him, but his vision was large and clear. And when he perceived new possi-
> bilities, he had the courage to act on them—a much less common virtue in
> politics than one might suppose.[1]

An interesting example of such possibilities occurred during George
W.'s visit to China in early 2002. His first year in office had been overshadowed by the worrisome incident of the collision of a U.S. reconnais-
sance aircraft with a Chinese fighter over the South China Sea. Shortly
after the issue was resolved, with compensation to the Chinese and the
return in sections of the damaged American aircraft, the president told an
interviewer that the United States would come to Taiwan's aid if the

island were attacked by Beijing and would provide "whatever it takes to help Taiwan defend itself."[2] This certainly seemed like a departure from the deliberate policy of "strategic ambiguity" about Taiwan that American administrations from Nixon's onward had used as their guideline for dealing with China on the Taiwan issue. The policy had previously been to give no clear sign that the United States would intervene to rescue Taiwan from Mainland attack but no clear sign that it would not either.

George W.'s seemingly pro-Taiwan posture was more than counterbalanced in December 2003 when Chinese premier Wen Jiabao made his first visit to Washington. With Wen standing beside him, George W. said that the United States did not support a referendum that the government of Taiwan was preparing for its citizens at the time of forthcoming national elections in March 2004. Beijing had declared the referendum to be politically provocative and suggestive of further moves by Taiwan to nudge itself toward total independence from China. Many conservatives on Capitol Hill criticized George W. for this statement, arguing that it appeared to show the United States kowtowing to Chinese bullying of Taiwan.

In early 2002, though—between the American spy plane incident in early 2001 and Wen Jiabao's visit to Washington in December 2003— George W. had made his own first presidential visit to Beijing. There he had spoken out forthrightly on an issue directly connected to his own Christian faith, that of religious freedom in China. Speaking to students at Beijing's elite Qinghua University, George W. ringingly asserted the virtues of religious freedom, not just in abstract terms, but as profoundly valuable to China herself. He is also reported to have shared his faith directly with China's outgoing president, Jiang Zemin, on this and on other occasions when the two met.

George W.'s concern about global religious freedom caused him to be highly responsive to the concerns of religious freedom activists in Washington about the suppression of Christian freedom around the world. The vicious cruelties toward all of its citizens, and especially those of Christian faith, on the part of the North Korean regime of Kim Il Jong angered him and touched him deeply. He told one group of human rights activists in Washington that listening to their concerns helped him understand how profoundly important the presidency could be in championing the cause of the afflicted and persecuted around the world. Though not widely read in Christian history at the outset of his presidency, George W. became acquainted with the examples of policy waged on behalf of the powerless by such an outstanding early nineteenth century British statesmen as Wilber Wilberforce. He continued, meanwhile, to be open in various ways about his own personal faith during visits of other national leaders to Washington. He reportedly spent several minutes in the White House praying with Macedonia's president Boris Trajkowski during Trajkowski's visit in 2001.[3]

---

SOME OF THE LEAST KNOWN, though in many ways most telling, illustrations of George W.'s faith have come from within the White House itself. One incident I heard about from two sources, independent of each other. When a White House courier once entered the Oval Office unannounced to make a very important delivery, there was no sign of the president. Only his shoes were protruding from behind his desk. The president of the United States was lying prostrate on the floor in prayer.

George W. has not been bashful about speaking with various interviewers about his prayer life. During a September 2003 interview with Brit Hume of Fox News, George W. said, "Well, I pray daily, and I pray in all kinds of places. I mean, I pray in bed, I pray in the Oval Office. I pray a lot . . . as the Spirit moves me. And faith is an integral part of my life."[4] At the first National Prayer Breakfast he attended, just twelve days after his inauguration, Bush spoke about the role of prayer in America's history:

> Our country was founded by great and wise people, who were fluent in the language of humility, praise and petition. Throughout our history, in danger and division, we have always turned to prayer. And our country has been delivered from many serious evils and wrongs because of that prayer.[5]

More than a year later, at the annual Hispanic National Prayer Breakfast in Washington, D.C., George W. also expressed his concept of prayer as a national tradition in a form that he has since repeated in different forums many times. "Throughout our history," he said, "Americans of faith have always turned to prayer—for wisdom, prayer for resolve, prayers for compassion and strength, prayers for commitment to justice and for a spirit of forgiveness."[6]

An observation of the George W. Bush White House as a hotbed of prayer came from an unlikely source—British Broadcasting Corporation correspondent Justin Webb: "Nobody spends more time on his knees than George W. Bush," he reported from Washington. "The Bush administration hums to the sound of prayer. Prayer meetings take place day and night. It's not uncommon to see White House functionaries hurrying down corridors carrying Bibles."[7]

George W., of course, does not confine his practice of an active Christian faith to prayer alone. His daily devotional activities include reading from the *The One Year Bible* (which divides the Bible text into 365 passages so the reader can complete the entire Bible in a year), and other, more traditional Bibles, along with daily passages from devotional books. His favorite authors include Oswald Chambers, who wrote *My Utmost for His Highest*; Charles Stanley, a well-known Southern Baptist teacher and speaker; and even, occasionally, Charles Spurgeon, the famous English Baptist evangelist whose preaching led to the conversion of thousands of members of London's working class in the second half of the nineteenth century.[8]

---

ALL OF THIS FAITH-BASED INPUT TO BUSH'S LIFE had begun to change the way he behaved and thought from at least the second half of the 1980s. Bush friend Mercer Reynolds said he began to notice major changes in Bush by the late 1980s. But Rev. James Robison, meeting George W. for the first time in 1992, was still not very impressed by what he saw at that time, at least in terms of Christian maturity. Robison acknowledges, however, that the Bush he met as governor of Texas for the second term was a significantly more mature person than the man he had met just a few years earlier.

Part of the maturity of Bush's faith is expressed in the way he deals with social issues in the White House. He is conservative, but not right-wing in a predictable, brittle way. On the issue of gays, for example, he has repeatedly expressed his view that marriage is an institution designed by God to be between a man and a woman. But he has not spoken out against gay sexual activity, as many American evangelicals often do. He has, in fact, been studiously quiet—some conservatives, including evangelical Christians, would say too quiet—on whether local legislatures should or should not pass laws allowing for civil unions between gays. "I am mindful that we're all sinners, and I caution those who may try to take the speck out of their neighbor's eye when they have a log in their own" he said at one point, referring to Jesus's warning in Matthew 7:3. Then he added, "I think it's very important for our society to respect each individual, to welcome those with good hearts, to be a welcoming country."[9] *National Review* editor Rich Lowry, not entirely happy with George W.'s apparent fudging on many issues dear to American conservatives, observed,

> What Reagan did for defense and economic conservatives, Bush may be doing for religious conservatives. Reagan believed everything Barry Goldwater believed, but gave it a more optimistic tinge. [George W.] Bush represents a similar makeover for the religious right, the same basic convictions but in a more palatable form.[10]

President Bush appointed Michael Guest, an openly gay State Department official, to be ambassador to Romania and Dr. Joe O'Neill, also gay, to head the White House office on AIDS. He also did not stand in the way of other talented gays assuming significant positions in the administration.

AS THE FIRST MONTHS OF GEORGE W.'S ADMINISTRATION slid by, his approval rating was quite high, but he clearly did not seem to have made a major mark in the American consciousness of his leadership at the national level. The faith-based initiatives seemed to have become mired in wrangling on Capitol Hill, where the U.S. Senate was now back in the hands of Democrats, thanks to the defection to the Democrats of Republican Senator James Jeffords of Vermont.

While on a ranch vacation in Crawford, Texas, in August 2001, George W. made a major speech on the issue of stem cells. Research from stem cells found in human embryos had been declared by some scientists to hold great promise in finding a cure for some of America's still terrifying list of untreatable diseases, such as Alzheimer's, infant diabetes, and various forms of muscular paralysis. The problem was, to obtain such embryos, abortions and the destruction of infant life would be necessary. George W. was lobbied both publicly, by the media, and privately, by experts and ethicists he consulted from the White House about the pros and cons of stem cell research. Pro-stem cell research lobbyists believed that stem cell research might well unlock the thorniest problems confronting the medical community. Pro-life activists believed that allowing stem cell research to continue might lead to a crescendo of abortions across the nation, perhaps a horrible new market of embryos for sale.

In his televised speech articulating his decision on how to proceed, George W. demonstrated the wisdom of Solomon. On the one hand, he was as vigorously pro-life as any previous president had been publicly. He said, "I also believe human life is a sacred gift from our Creator. I worry about a culture that devalues life and believe, as your president, I have an important obligation to foster and encourage respect for life in America and throughout the world." On the other hand, George W. said, research would continue to be permitted on stem cells already taken from aborted fetuses, and the federal government would spend generously to support more research on adult stem cells, that is, those taken from a patient's own body.[11] In some ways, this approach satisfied neither side. Pro-life Roman Catholics criticized it as still leaving an open door to the endorsement of abortion (since it didn't close the door to research upon already aborted fetuses). Pro-science lobbyists thought that George W. had surrendered to the clamor of religious conservatives or "pro-life purists."

---

THE SUMMER OF 2001 HAD JUST ENDED, and George W.'s polls were slowly climbing, even though the elite media seemed to view him as an amiable bumbler in international affairs and not a particularly effective leader on the domestic scene. George W. had ended his vacation and, on the morning of September 11 was trying to promote an initiative for education reform by visiting Emma E. Booker Elementary School in Sarasota, Florida. It was while he was sitting among a class of grade-schoolers, reading aloud to them from a school textbook, that George W. Bush was confronted with the most serious crisis to befall the United States in decades. Both still and video cameras caught the stunned, shocked, almost bewildered expression on his face as White House Chief of Staff Andrew Card whispered in his ear that two civilian airliners had crashed into the twin towers of the World Trade Center in New York City. What was worse, they were obviously part of a deliberate enemy attack upon the United States.

The next few hours seemed as chaotic as they were incomprehensible to many Americans. Who had done the heinous deed, and why? Where was the president of the United States? What was he doing flying around the country in Air Force One, rather than returning to Washington to deal with the crisis?

As became clear eventually, the decision not to fly George W. back to Washington immediately was based on a report received by the Secret Service that the presidential aircraft might become the next target. In fact, it was the president who insisted toward the end of the day that he would no longer stay away from the nation's capital, even if there still were direct threats to the presidential plane.

George W.'s first words to the nation and the world about the attack were regarded by many people as less than adequate. They expressed grief and sympathy for the relatives of victims of the attacks, but not what most Americans wanted to hear—anger, outrage, determination to respond adequately. It was a new Pearl Harbor, and the rhetoric needed to match the horror and magnitude of the deed. "This is a day when Americans from every walk of life unite in our resolve for justice and peace," the president said into the camera. The words, in the view of then White House speech-writer David Frum, were "not those of a war speech. It was a hastily devised compassionate conservatism speech."[12]

Many people agreed. Americans were watching their commander-in-chief to see if he could summon the intuitive connection with ordinary Americans that Ronald Reagan seemed to have possessed or, before him, John F. Kennedy during the Cuban missile crisis in 1962 or, two decades before that, Franklin Delano Roosevelt, with his effulgent characterization of the attack on Pearl Harbor as "A day that will live in infamy."

---

AMERICANS DIDN'T HAVE TO WAIT LONG for a new, strikingly more focused, yet calm, patient, and presidential George W. Bush to emerge. The first clear indication that George W. Bush just might be the right leader for an America experiencing the most violent attack upon its soil since Pearl Harbor was a memorial service in the Washington National Cathedral on September 14. Presiding over a multifaith service that seemed to some dangerously close to a politically correct version of the American religious scene with Protestants, Catholics, and Muslim Imams all playing a role, George W. projected what many thought was an impressive level of calm and determination, devoid of any clamor for revenge for the attacks. Frum, along with Gerson and others, recalled receiving speechwriting instructions from Bush that were quite specific: "He [Bush] made it clear to his writers that he would pronounce no words of vengefulness or anger. When he spoke off the cuff, he again and again paraphrased the biblical commandment of Romans 12:21: 'Be not overcome by evil, but overcome evil with good.'"[13]

Billy Graham, depicted in the 1990s on a cover of *Time* magazine as "the lion in winter," and now a wizened emblem of Protestant rigor, delivered a finely honed message that contained, of course, pure nuggets of the Christian salvation message. It was George W.'s task to sum up the national grief and national sense of self in the face of this wicked adversity. He did it brilliantly, saying, "God's signs are not always the ones we look for. We learn in tragedy that his purposes are not always our own. Yet the prayers of private suffering, whether in our homes or in this great cathedral, are known and heard, and understood." The cadences were measured, calming. Then came a paraphrase of one of the best-loved verses in the entire New Testament, Romans 8:28:

As we have been assured, "Neither death nor life, nor angels nor principalities nor powers, nor things present nor things to come, nor height nor depth, can separate us from God's love." May He bless the souls of the departed. May He comfort our own. And may He always guide our country. God bless America.[14]

Speechwriter Frum, who had given his ticket to the event to someone else, in order to get a better view of the proceedings on TV, wrote, "That service was the first time the nation saw a new Bush. A few hours later came the second—and this time, the encounter was entirely unscripted."[15] Frum was referring to George W.'s visit to ground zero of the World Trade Center destruction in Manhattan and his astonishing address to fire and rescue workers using a worker's bullhorn. In what will surely go down in United States history as one of the great exchanges between a leader and the led, as the president tried to speak through a bullhorn that did not properly amplify his words, some firemen shouted at him, perched on a wrecked fire truck, "We can't hear you!"

George W. pulled the bullhorn away from his face and shouted back, "Well, I can hear *you*. I can *hear* you. The rest of the world hears you. And the people who knocked these buildings down will hear all of us soon."[16] In the space of a few hours, a seemingly hesitant, almost bewildered president had changed into a self-confident, dynamic, popular leader of a nation deeply wounded and surprised by the hatred launched against it three mornings earlier.

---

THE PRESIDENT WAS QUICKLY MADE AWARE of some of the vengeful attacks made by outraged Americans against a few Muslims in their midst, and sometimes against non-Muslims who just happened to be wearing turbans. He responded conspicuously and quickly. Making it clear to everyone that he regarded himself as a president of all faiths of the United States, not just of Christianity, George W. visited the Islamic Center of Washington, D.C., to reassure frightened and bewildered American and foreign Muslims in the nation's capital. "The face of terror is not the true faith of Islam," he told them. "That's not what Islam is all about. Islam is peace. These terrorists don't represent peace. They represent evil and war."[17]

Several observers and analysts criticized this formulation, noting that Islam, for all of its outstanding cultural achievements hundreds of years ago, has never abandoned an aggressive militancy in its worldwide expansion. This militancy, they noted, can be discerned in the text of the Koran itself and in the writings of major Koranic scholars over the centuries. But in retrospect, George W.'s reaching out to American Muslims at this critical time was surely the "Christian" thing to do. Though some American Muslims do seem to have applauded the September 11 attacks, the overwhelming majority did not. It would have been profoundly unfair if they, innocent of any wrongdoing, had been singled out by angry and outraged Americans simply because Muslim co-religionists from overseas—or even their coreligionists who were American citizens—had masterminded the terrorist attacks.

The president's visit to the Washington, D.C., mosque was gratefully noted by many American Muslim leaders, and it may well have headed off further acts of vengeance by Americans lashing out at people who *resembled* those who had done the heinous deed. Many Muslims noted that George W. Bush received far more Muslim votes in the 2000 election than his Democratic rival Vice President Al Gore. Despite what some observers might have expected, many American Muslims felt *more* comfortable having a president in the White House with strong religious faith, even if it were Christian, than with someone of more secular perspective. Said Khaled Saffuri, president of the Islamic Free Market Institute Foundation, "I have met with President Bush several times. I respect his religious belief, and he doesn't try to impose it on anyone. I think Muslim religious people would prefer to have someone in the White House who fears God."[18]

In the journalistic aftermath of September 11, several prominent Protestant evangelical leaders articulated in public a point that someone certainly needed to make: Islam unquestionably has an important tradition within it that supports the use of violence in the cause of advancing the faith. These evangelical leaders included Billy Graham's son, Franklin, Pat Robertson, and Jerry Falwell. In effect, their sharp criticism of Islam as the ideological source of violence implicitly rebuked George W. for what many regarded as a naïve misunderstanding of Islam when he said, "Islam is peace."

George W. probably acted on instinct in saying that. Whatever he may have felt about the true nature of Islam in the privacy of close Christian fellowship, he could not, as president of the United States, publicly endorse a Christian theological view of the nature of any other faith in America. When he was in London on a state visit late in 2003, his response to a somewhat tricky question from a journalist was equally sound. Britain's frequently aggressive and irreverent reporters were eager to trip up the American president if they could. Some Christians argued that Islam's God was not the same as the Christian God, said a British reporter smoothly as a preface to his question. What were President Bush's views? "I believe we worship the same God," George W. replied.

Again, it was the only way he could have responded, given the setting, even if many Christian observers of Islam would argue that the Islamic concept of the Almighty was simply incompatible with the Christian view of God. "The president is not the theologian-in-chief," commented one Washington wag. Had George W. tried to explain what he might privately have thought were indeed crucial faith differences between Islam and Christianity, he would, in effect, have been using his office of chief executive of the U.S. government to make religious pronouncements. A clearer breach in the wall of separation between church and state could hardly have been envisaged.

In fact, even before his London trip in November 2003, George W. had already broadened his concept of "faith" to go well beyond Christianity and Judaism. Some evangelical Protestants might well have wondered if his public pronouncements on what he regarded as a valid "faith" were still compatible with normative Protestant Christian theology. Speaking about his faith-based concepts at Houston's Power Center in August 2003, in the presence of Rev. Kirbyjon Caldwell, George W. explained,

> I don't talk about a particular faith. I believe the Lord can work through many faiths, whether it be the Christian faith, the Jewish faith, Muslim faith, Hindu faith. When I speak of faith, I speak of all faiths, because there is a universal call, and that main universal call is to love your neighbor. It extends throughout all faith.[19]

In an ironic way, by taking this view of "faith," as opposed to the evangelical Christian view that he had adopted in the 1980s that a person could come to God only through Christ, George W. appeared to be aligning himself with a broader, seemingly more indulgent concept of God's grace that had characterized Barbara Bush at the time her son was going through his own faith reawakening. Was this the case, or were political pressures on George W. to sound more inclusive in the American faith community creating this impression? There is, of course, no clear answer to this question, but the evidence of conversations with those Christians who stayed in close touch with George W. for several years is that George W. has not altered his orthodox Protestant view of the requirement of faith in Christ for Christian redemption and salvation. What he appears to have made more inclusive is his definition of what "faith" means. His elaboration turns faith into something of a generic belief in the virtues of all religions, tinged by the need for everyone to adopt the golden rule.

---

THE ONE THING THAT DID SEEM TO BECOME CLEARER in George W.'s mind after September 11 was the concept of "evil" and "evildoers." Al Qaeda, the Taliban, and then, increasingly, Saddam Hussein, were lumped into a category of wickedness that George W. always hinted was a moral absolute. At the Presidential Prayer Breakfast in Washington, D.C., on February 7, 2003, George W. seemed to envisage faith—in effect, any religious faith—as providing people with an ability to discern good from evil. He spoke enthusiastically of the overall absence of bigotry on the part of most Americans, despite some isolated anti-Muslim expressions here and there. This was also a product, he said, of the faith of many Americans. Then he added this:

> At the same time, faith shows us the reality of good, and the reality of evil. Some acts and choices in this world have eternal consequences. It is always, and everywhere, wrong to target and kill the innocent. It is always, and everywhere, wrong to be cruel and hateful, to enslave and oppress. It is always, and everywhere, right to be kind and just, to protect the lives of others, and to lay down your life for a friend.[20]

Already gelling in George W.'s mind was a formulation that would categorize the world's most vicious and potentially dangerous regimes. The Taliban had been overthrown in Afghanistan in November 2001, but there was already a strong current within the administration, especially the Department of Defense, that wanted to wreak havoc upon Iraq. After all, Iraq had invaded Kuwait in 1990; it had attempted to assassinate a president of the United States, Bush Senior, during his visit there in 1993; and it had a documented history of having produced and used against foreign foes, and even its own people, weapons of mass destruction. At the same time, a powerful, self-isolated nation in East Asia, North Korea, was in the process of trying to develop nuclear weapons, despite a commitment to the United States and the world community in 1994 that it would not do so.

As George W.'s speechwriters prepared for his key State of the Union address in 2002, they came up with a phrase that was to ricochet around the world: "axis of evil." President Bush used it to refer specifically to Iraq, Iran, and North Korea. In the speech, George W. told the assembled members of the House and Senate,

> States like these [Iraq, Iran, North Korea], and their terrorist allies, constitute an axis of evil, arming to threaten the peace of the world. By seeking weapons of mass destruction, these regimes pose a grave and growing danger. They could provide these arms to terrorists, giving them the means to match their hatred. They could attack our allies or attempt to blackmail the United States. In any of these cases, the price of indifference would be catastrophic.
>
> We'll be deliberate, yet time is not on our side. I will not wait on events, while dangers gather. I will not stand by, as peril draws closer and closer. The United States of America will not permit the world's most dangerous regimes to threaten us with the world's most destructive weapons.[21]

In effect, by labeling the regime in Iraq as part of the "axis of evil," and by focusing attention on its capacity and apparent intention to produce weapons of mass destruction, George W. Bush was serving notice that a ticking clock had been started for Iraq.

Throughout much of 2002, U.S. diplomacy strenuously sought to engage the United Nations in condemning Iraq and passing a Security

Council resolution that would compel Iraq to admit inspectors and reveal the workings of its weapons program. But when it became clear that the French, Germans, and Russians were increasingly resistant to the use of force against Iraq, George W. found himself drawn closer and closer to the one European ally upon whom he could rely—British Prime Minister Tony Blair.

The two men met frequently—at Camp David, in the Azores, in Washington—and each time, they got to know each other better and found themselves in increasing agreement. During the tense month leading up to the American-British attack upon Iraq in March 2003, they came to know each other so well that something of a division of labor seemed to emerge. Blair, who is charming, intellectually supple, and rhetorically gifted, would provide the world with the best-argued reasoning for an American-British attack upon the Saddam Hussein regime. In effect, he would be the "good cop." George W., who is blunt, feisty, and not as verbally gifted, would be the "bad cop," the giver of terse ultimatums, the this-is-the-way-it's-going-to-be guy on the team.

It is more than probable that Blair and George W. sometimes prayed together during their meetings in late 2002 and early 2003. Neither man has convincingly confirmed or denied this. But it is revealing that, when President Bush visited London in late 2003 and was questioned about his friendship with Blair, a journalist asked George W. if the reason he and Blair got on so well was the fact that both men shared strong faith, President Bush replied, "I think so. Tony is a man of strong faith. You know, the key to my relationship with Tony is he tells the truth, and he tells you what he thinks, and when he says he's going to do something, he's going to do it. I trust him, therefore."[22]

By the time of that meeting in November 2003, British and American troops had been in Iraq since March. No weapons of mass destruction had been found, though George W. expressed confidence whenever asked that at some point they would be. Less publicly, during the seven months after the defeat of the Saddam Hussein regime in Iraq, George W. had expressed to close Christian friends from Texas his quiet confidence that Saddam himself would sooner or later be captured, even though for months he successfully eluded every dragnet arranged for him by United States forces. Doubtless he was relying more than ever on frequent moments of prayer throughout the day and his morning and evening Bible and devotional readings. Those close to George W. during the 2001–2003 period said that he grew in strength, depth, calmness, and steadiness as he dealt with the post-September 11 challenges to the United States.

---

GEORGE W. EXPRESSED HIS FAITH in the foreign affairs domain in two other ways during 2003:

- His determination to provide massive U.S. funding for programs to control AIDS in Africa, and
- His opening a new front in what was now being dubbed the "Bush Doctrine" of American foreign policy, namely, determined efforts to push the Arab Muslim Middle East toward democracy.

George W. announced in his 2003 State of the Union address that he would request from Congress fifteen billion dollars more over the next five years to fight AIDS in Africa. The president had expressed concern about Africa's situation several times previously, but the size of the funding he said he would request surprised almost everyone. Almost certainly, George W. was responding to a call of his conscience as a professed Christian, to make some leadership gesture that would draw attention to the plight of AIDS victims in the whole of Africa. While visiting there in July 2003, George W. spoke at an AIDS clinic in Uganda, where government-religious group cooperation on stressing abstinence has had a dramatic effect on lowering the number of HIV cases: "I believe God has called us into action. We have a responsibility to help a neighbor in need, a brother and sister in crisis." Commentator William McKenzie in the *Dallas Morning News* said that those words put Bush in the "duty-obligation" wing of Protestantism "whose roots run past Wesley [the founder of Methodism] to Reformation leaders like John Calvin. I'm not saying Mr. Bush sees himself in that light. I doubt he spends much time studying various theologians. His is a practical, instinctive faith."[23]

Though George W.'s critics among liberals paid little or no attention to the Africa announcement, it struck some observers as a radical and unusual initiative for a conservative Republican president. "Unradical son George W. Bush isn't the fire-breathing reactionary liberals love to hate," was the headline of a column in the *Boston Globe* by George Mason Law School professor Peter Berkowitz. In an interview with Peggy Noonan for *Ladies' Home Journal*, George W. explained, "You shouldn't fear a religious person. The Bible talks about love and compassion. . . . That's really behind my passion on the AIDS policy, for example."[24]

There was growing passion also behind his conviction, first voiced in his speech to a joint session of Congress in early 2003, that freedom is not something the United States or any particular government bestows on people, but it's something from God himself. "The liberty we prize," he said in that speech, "is not America's gift to the world; it is God's gift to humanity."

In Europe, there was the usual spluttering in some newspapers about George W.'s being obsessive about religion, about his conducting foreign policy through the lens of theology. But it turned out that this concept of liberty as a divine gift was to play a growing role in George W.'s elaboration of his policy of encouraging democracy in the Middle East. It is too early to say at this writing, early in 2004, that Bush's Middle East democracy push has become one of the most far-reaching of his administration's foreign policy strategies, but by late in 2003 it began to look as if this would be the case.

George W. articulated his concept of democracy in detail and with some lucidity during his visit to London in November 2003. He was met by large numbers of Britons demonstrating in opposition to the war in Iraq. Some of the British press also exhibited its usual snobbery about American presidents for their, at times, grammatically challenged speech. But in a well-argued, well-articulated address in the Royal Banqueting House of London's Whitehall Palace, George W. advanced his pro-freedom arguments in several ways. He said, speaking of the United States and his host country, Britain:

> The deepest beliefs of our nations set the direction of our foreign policy. We value our own civil rights, so we stand for the human rights of others. We affirm the God-given dignity of every person, so we are moved to action by poverty and oppression and famine and disease. The United States and Great Britain share a mission in the world beyond the balance of power or the simple pursuit of interest. We seek the advance of freedom and the peace that freedom brings. Together our nations are standing and sacrificing for this high goal in a distant land at this very hour. And America honors the idealism and the bravery of the sons and daughters of Britain.[25]

George W. then added a closely woven argument to explain his administration's current push to try to move the Middle East toward democratic institutions and practices as quickly as possible.

> And by advancing freedom in the greater Middle East, we help end a cycle of dictatorship and radicalism that brings millions of people to misery and brings danger to our own people.
>
> The stakes in that region could not be higher. If the Middle East remains a place where freedom does not flourish, it will remain a place of stagnation and anger and violence for export. And as we saw in the ruins of two towers, no distance on the map will protect our lives and way of life. If the greater Middle East joins the democratic revolution that has reached much of the world, the lives of millions in that region will be bettered, and a trend of conflict and fear will be ended at its source.
>
> The movement of history will not come about quickly. Because of our own democratic development—the fact that it was gradual and, at times, turbulent—we must be patient with others. And the Middle East countries have some distance to travel.
>
> Now we're pursuing a different course . . . a forward strategy of freedom in the Middle East. We will consistently challenge the enemies of reform

and confront the allies of terror. We will expect a higher standard from our friends in the region, and we will meet our responsibilities in Afghanistan and in Iraq by finishing the work of democracy we have begun.[26]

In an interview before he left London for Washington with the British tabloid newspaper, the *Sun*, often very critical of Tony Blair and certainly of the United States, George W. expressed again his thoughts on the origins of freedom: "There are hundreds of reformers that are desperate for freedom. Freedom . . . is not America's gift to the world, or Great Britain's gift to the world; freedom is the Almighty's gift to everybody who lives in the world."[27]

George W. also took issue in this interview, as he has done many times elsewhere, with what he regards as an elitist arrogance about freedom—the erroneous assertion of some that certain ethnic, community, or cultural groups are inherently incapable of either appreciating freedom or of living it out.

They [the elitists] may say, well, you can't possibly expect a country like Iraq to be free—and then we'd have an interesting, philosophical debate, because I believe freedom exists in the heart of every single human being. It may take longer for people to accept freedom, if they've been tortured and brutalized like Saddam Hussein did.[28]

George W.'s view of freedom as a desire inherent to the human nature was not, technically, a theological position. Yet it clearly derived from his understanding of the human condition, sinful in every case, and of God's plan to redeem and change humanity. This process, in George W.'s understanding, would come through both personal faith—preferably Christian, in his view—and through eliminating the cruel obstacles to the enjoyment of freedom in society and in people's lives in general. Other presidents, as we shall see, thought deeply about the role of government in changing the conditions of ordinary men and women. Few, however, derived their understanding of it so inherently from their own Christian experience and understanding.

# 9

## Faith: Our Heritage, Our Hope

*No nation has ever yet existed or been governed without religion.*
*Nor can be. The Christian religion is the best religion . . . and I . . .*
*am bound to give it the sanction of my example.*

—Thomas Jefferson

During the presidential race of 2000, the Pew Research Foundation, aware of the controversy that had swirled around the candidacy of George W. Bush because of his forthright expression of Christian faith in the primaries, conducted a poll to discern what Americans thought of presidential aspirants with strong religious convictions. The poll found that a whopping 70 percent want their president to be "strongly religious," though some 50 percent also said they felt uncomfortable if presidential faith were expressed in public too much. Polls during the presidency of George W. have shown that some 58 percent of Americans think that his public religiosity is "about right." Interestingly, those who think the president isn't sufficiently expressive of his faith outnumber by two to one those who think he is too much so.

Europeans and other overseas visitors are often amazed by the religiosity of the American people. It baffles them that, ever since polling began, upwards of 90 percent of Americans have expressed belief in God or at least in some "higher power" directing their lives. They're amazed that on any given Sunday, one-third of the entire American population is likely to be attending church. Over the years polls have found that 70–80 percent of Americans consider themselves Christian. More precise questions to determine how many Christians consider themselves "evangelical" come up with figures of between 25 and 40 percent.

"Evangelical" is a hard term to define. Questions concerning whether people are "evangelical" often focus on whether they believe the Bible to be God's Word, perhaps whether it is "inerrant"—another complicated term—and whether they believe Christians should make a personal commitment of faith, in prayer, to Jesus Christ as their Savior and Lord.

Yet America's mainstream print newspapers, magazines, and journals do not reflect much of the religiosity of the American heartland. Nor does popular entertainment convey the impression of a religious America. Hollywood, media elites, academic centers, and major financial foundations are, for the most part, dominated by people who have given up on organized religion, or at least on Christianity. As sociologist Peter Berger once put it, "America is a nation of Indians [that is, people eager for religious expression] governed by an elite of Swedes [that is, sophisticated secular intellectuals who think religion is probably all bunk]."[1] Those who occupy the cultural rooftops of the nation, for the most part, appear to be secular in orientation, while the ordinary folk of America continue steadily along their way, going to church, giving to charities, and continuing to pay attention to such seemingly outmoded notions as the Ten Commandments or the Sermon on the Mount.

---

THE ELECTION OF 2000 seemed to paint this cultural dichotomy literally in vivid colors. When election analysts colored those counties that had voted for George W. Bush red, and those that had voted for Vice President Al Gore blue, an interesting pattern emerged. The red counties were indeed in the geographic heartland of the nation, while the blue counties were clustered in and around the large cities of the East and West Coasts and parts of the Midwest. Various commentators have made sometimes entertaining comments on this apparent national divide. "Red" Americans, for example, are more likely to listen to country music or watch NASCAR. "Blue" Americans are more likely to know who slept with whom in the latest episode of TV's *Sex and the City*.

Serious-minded pollsters, meanwhile, picked up on something even more curious: "Red" America was strikingly more churchgoing than "blue" America. More specifically, those Americans who attended church almost every Sunday were twice as likely to have voted for George W. Bush as those who resolutely stayed home and read the Sunday newspapers—those, in fact, who seldom or never went to church or synagogue. The phenomenon of support for, or antipathy toward, religion in the United States has become part of the discussion of America's "culture wars."

It has probably been true since large urban centers began to emerge in the newly prosperous American colonies that urban dwellers, on the whole better educated than their rural or small-town compatriots, were more open to new ideas filtering into the country from overseas or sometimes spontaneously coming to life within America itself. But what has also been true is that, despite an urban-rural dichotomy, no doubt intensified in our own era, every observant foreign visitor to the United States from the early nineteenth century onward has been struck by the role that religion plays in American life.

It is impossible to consider this issue at all without first going to Alexis de Tocqueville, whose 1835 book *Democracy in America* first vividly recounted how powerfully the faith habits of ordinary Americans affected the way they lived, related to each other in community, and lived out the political realities of republican government. De Tocqueville wrote,

> There is no country in the world where the Christian religion retains a greater influence over the souls of men than in America; and there can be no greater proof of its utility, and of its conformity to human nature, than that its influence is most powerfully felt over the most enlightened and free nation of the earth.[2]

De Tocqueville is quoted so frequently on America's religious foundation that some analysts may suspect that he was eccentric in his observations. But in 1833 another Frenchman, Achille Murat, made nearly identical observations:

> There is no country in which the people are so religious as in the United States; to the eyes of a foreigner they even appear to be too much so. The great number of religious societies existing in the United States is truly surprising: there are some of them to distribute the Bible; to distribute tracts; to encourage religious journals; to convert, civilize, educate the savages; to marry the preachers; to take care of their widows and orphans; to preach, extend, purify, preserve, reform the faith; to build chapels, endow congregations, support seminaries; catechize and convert sailors, Negroes, and loose women.[3]

---

OF COURSE, SUCH SENTIMENTS TODAY sound paternalistic and in some measure condescending. But such sentiments existed at the founding of the United States, and they have been a constant theme running through the presidency from the very beginning. The argument over how Christian (as opposed to deist, agnostic, Unitarian, and so forth) were America's founders will no doubt continue as long as historians study the early decades of the United States. But that virtually *all* of the founders thought that America's establishment was closely connected with a biblical view of the world and that Christianity, whether or not individuals believed its faith tenets, was something they approved of, is plain to anyone who is not utterly prejudiced against religious faith in any form. Noah Webster (1758–1843), whose name has been linked to an outstanding dictionary of the English language for the past two centuries, declared emphatically that the Bible was "the most republican book in the world."[4] He also said, "Our citizens should early understand that the genuine source of correct republican principles is the Bible, particularly the New Testament, or the Christian religion."[5]

Of the fifty-six signatories of the Declaration of Independence, some were deists, perhaps even agnostics as the term is today understood, but the overwhelming majority of them were Christian—believers in the classic doctrines of Christianity and, in most cases, active members of one church or another. Many of them had studied under John Witherspoon, scholar, preacher and president of Princeton, who has been described as "the most influential academic in American history."[6] Witherspoon's students included a U.S. president, twenty-eight U.S. Senators, three Supreme Court justices, three attorneys general, a secretary of state, two high-ranking U.S. diplomatic envoys, and scores of officers in the Continental Army.[7]

Witherspoon delivered one of the most famous, and certainly the most influential, sermon in American history on May 17, 1776, in which he sided with the colonialists against Great Britain's King George III, citing the biblical conflicts between the people of Israel and the kings ruling over them. Perhaps the most important theme of Witherspoon's sermon, which was reprinted and distributed to hundreds of Presbyterian churches throughout the colonies, was that of "the doctrine of divine providence." God's purposes in providence, Witherspoon said, were worked out through natural disasters, wars, political struggles, and all kinds of other vicissitudes of life affecting—and often afflicting—both individuals and nations. The way the struggle against British tyranny was proceeding, Witherspoon argued, showed that providence was moving in favor of the American struggle for freedom. And centuries before George W. Bush came on the scene, Witherspoon was elaborating the notion that freedom comes from the hand of God.

As Michael Novak puts it in his brilliant analysis of the theological and philosophical core of the American struggle for independence, *On Two Wings: Humble Faith and Common Sense at the American Founding*, "Witherspoon's underlying argument is that liberty is God's gift and all of creation has been contrived so that it will sweetly, freely, even out of darkness and despair, come to fruition."[8] In Witherspoon's own words,

So in times of difficulty and trial, it is in the man of piety and inward principle, that we may expect to find the uncorrupted patriot, the useful citizen,
and the invincible soldier. God grant that in America true religion and civil
liberty may be inseparable, and that the unjust attempts to destroy the one,
may in the issue tend to the support and establishment of both.[9]

Novak notes that, rather than citing from the New Testament, which
Christian clergy might have been expected to do in support of the new
American cause, the argumentation that the colonialists were cooperating
with providence in defying the British came mainly from the Old
Testament—the Hebrew Bible—and its concepts of a people covenanted
with God. According to Novak, some three-fifths of the scriptural texts
employed in Revolutionary War-era sermons justifying the revolt of the
colonies were derived from the Old Testament.[10]

Lest it be thought, however, that it was only the Protestant clergy who
were drawing the connection between the ways of providence and of
freedom, Thomas Jefferson himself can be quoted. He wrote, "And can the
liberties of a nation be thought secure when we have removed their only
firm basis, a conviction in the minds of the people that these liberties are the
gift of God? That they are not violated but with his wrath?"[11] Jefferson was
not a Christian, but a deist. Yet in all of his writings, his understanding of
how God worked in the affairs of men seemed to closely parallel the views of
orthodox Protestant Christian clergymen like Witherspoon.

There were good reasons for the reluctance of the founders to employ
Christian terminology in their writings about providence. For instance,
they preferred to refer to God as the Creator, the Lawgiver, the Judge,
Providence, the Invisible Hand, the Supreme Being. This is precisely
because there were great fears that internal theological squabbles among
Christian denominations would undermine the grander notion that the
Almighty, in spite of the follies of those who claimed to be his followers,
wanted Americans to work in unity with each other. This was equally
true for men like Witherspoon, whose Christianity was emphatically in
the Protestant, Puritan tradition; men like Jefferson, who weren't

orthodox Christians at all; and Unitarians, who fell somewhere in the middle—men like John Adams and John Quincy Adams.

---

THE LATE EIGHTEENTH CENTURY in America was a time when many of the notions of the European Enlightenment won broad acceptance among educated people. But it was also the era of the aftermath of the First Great Awakening—that explosion of evangelical zeal that swept through much of New England in the late 1730s in the wake of preaching by visiting Englishman George Whitefield and the native-born Jonathan Edwards. Despite the struggles between intelligentsia and clergy in Europe, Enlightenment thinking and Christian conviction appeared to coexist rather equitably in the American colonies.

It was thus that the Continental Congress, in the difficult months following the Declaration of Independence in July 1776, decreed a day of fasting and repentance for the colonies on December 11, 1776. "It becomes all public bodies," the decree read, "as well as private persons, to reverence the Providence of God, and look up to him as the supreme disposer of all events, and the arbiter of the fate of nations."[12]

The father of the nation, George Washington, was rather aloof in his public expressions of faith. He attended an Episcopal church in northern Virginia, but he never took communion in it. He certainly rejected the Calvinist notion, which Witherspoon and, before him, Jonathan Edwards, espoused, of the fallen nature of mankind. Washington believed in the inherent goodness of people, not at all a Christian notion. Yet he believed firmly in Christian notions of ethics and morality. As commander of the Continental Army, he forbade profanity or drunkenness, and he ordered his army officers to begin each day by reading prayers to their units. In July 1776, he issued an order to his officers to procure chaplains for their units.

He displayed sympathy to all Christian denominations, conducting a correspondence with leaders of many different Protestant groups and urging them to get along with each other. In the army, he tried to curtail expressions of anti-Catholicism, a common phenomenon in that era.

Yet there were suspicions of George Washington among many devout Protestants of the day, both laity and clergy. Was he a deist? Or, heaven forbid, was he an atheist? Why did he not say clearly what he himself believed about the Christian gospel? No one could deny his selfless patriotism and his solemn integrity in turning down rewards and honors for his leadership of the fledgling nation that, in other nations, might have amounted to kingship, or at least dictatorship.

Thus, when the first president of the United States was to be inaugurated at Federal Hall in New York City on April 30, 1789, many wondered how he would deal with the question of taking the oath of office. They need not have. Washington placed his right hand on the Bible, swore to "faithfully execute the office of president of the United States," then added the unexpected and unscripted words, "I swear, so help me God." Next, he bent over and kissed the Bible. Washington may have been no communicant in the Episcopal church, much less a Calvinist, but he understood the importance of symbolic allegiance to Christian forms and standards.

But Washington's behavior at his inauguration was more than just show. As he made clear in his inaugural address, he believed that the United States had a formal contract with destiny. Washington believed absolutely in a God who created the world and held its future in his hands. He felt that Americans, more than the people of any other nation, ought to be in a position to recognize this.

> I am sure there never was a people who had more reason to acknowledge a divine interposition in their affairs than those of the United States; and I should be pained to believe that they have forgotten that agency, which was so often manifested during our Revolution, or that they failed to consider the omnipotence of that God who is alone able to protect them.[13]

Again, Washington was expressing this view because he knew that his co-conspirators against the British shared it almost to a man. His conviction that religious faith—and he clearly understood this to be Christian—was essential to the future harmony of America was clearly stated in this much-quoted passage from what has become known as his "farewell address," which though widely distributed was never delivered. Washington wrote,

> Of all the dispositions and habits which lead to political prosperity, religion and morality are indispensable supports. . . . let us with caution indulge the supposition that morality can be maintained without religion. Whatever may be conceded to the influence of refined education on minds of peculiar structure, reason and experience both forbid us to expect that national morality can prevail in exclusion of religious principle.[14]

THOUGH THOMAS JEFFERSON, the true Renaissance man of the American Revolution, did not express himself in such a forthright manner on this subject, he certainly seems to have shared Washington's views on the usefulness of religion. Although his distaste for traditional Christian doctrine was strong, he also permitted the Capitol to be used every Sunday for the largest church service in the country.

In an incident written down by hand and now kept in the Library of Congress, the Rev. Ethan Allen told the story of how a friend of Jefferson encountered the then president out walking one Sunday morning with a large red prayer book tucked under his arm. The friend asked where he was going.

"To church, Sir."

"You going to church, Mr. Jefferson? You do not believe a word of it."

"Sir, no nation has ever yet existed or been governed without religion. Nor can be. The Christian religion is the best religion that has ever been given to man and I, as chief Magistrate of this nation, am bound to give it the sanction of my example. Good morning, Sir."[15]

It is interesting that Jefferson did not deny the accusation that he was not a believer in Christianity. He was accused of being everything from an atheist to a deist, but he liked to speak of himself as a Christian. He often said that he objected to "the corruptions of Christianity" and insisted that he, rather than others, understood the faith correctly. In 1815, after leaving the White House, he published *The Life and Morals of Jesus of Nazareth (The Jefferson Bible)*, a combination of his presidential jottings and a rearrangement of the Gospel texts from which anything supernatural or miraculous has been excised.

---

JEFFERSON WAS NOT THE ONLY UNORTHODOX CHRISTIAN, deist, or perhaps Unitarian believer in God who held a high view of the utilitarian value of Christianity. James Madison, president from 1809 to 1817, coauthor of the Federalist Papers and great champion of religious liberty (starting in his own state of Virginia), was a churchgoing Episcopalian who nevertheless was known for his skepticism about traditional Christian doctrines. Yet even Madison, at his inauguration in 1809, said he believed that "the power of Almighty God regulates the destiny of nations." His cousin, an Episcopal bishop, noted that "Madison's religious feelings died a quick death [when he was still a young man]."[16]

Even Benjamin Franklin, America's great inventor, champion of the common man, and unorthodox thinker in general (and certainly not an evangelical Christian of any variety), wrote, "Only a virtuous people are capable of freedom. As nations become corrupt and vicious, they have more need of masters."[17]

America's second president, John Adams, was not a deist, but either a Unitarian or something of a self-described generic, nondenominational Christian. As he said, "Ask me not whether I am Catholic or Protestant, Calvinistic or Arminian. As far as they are Christians, I wish to be a fellow disciple with them all.")[18] He had studied at Harvard initially for full-time Christian ministry, but, after finding doubts creeping into his convictions, he switched to law.

Adams has been much quoted for his view that it would be very difficult for the United States to sustain free institutions unless the ethical behavior of its citizens was guided by Christian principles. He wrote, "We have no government armed with the power capable of contending with human passions unbridled by morality and religion. . . . Our Constitution was made only for a moral and religious people. It is wholly inadequate to the government of any other."[19]

Adams, the first president to occupy the White House, ordered this prayer inscribed in the formal dining room:

> I Pray Heaven to Bestow
> the Best of Blessings on
> THIS HOUSE
> And on All that shall hereafter
> Inhabit it. May none but Honest
> And Wise Men ever rule under this Roof!

Adams died on the very same day as Thomas Jefferson, July 4, 1826, exactly a half century after the signing of the Declaration of Independence that Jefferson had composed.

His son, John Quincy Adams, president from 1825 to 1829, did not attend church regularly in Washington because, he complained, there was no church of his denomination, the Independent Congregationalists. He has been designated in some accounts as a Unitarian, along with his father, but if so, it was of a variety that sailed close to Protestant orthodoxy.

John Quincy read three chapters of the Bible every day—approximately the same number of chapters as George W. reads when following *The One Year Bible*—and every night before going to sleep recited a childhood prayer that his mother had taught him:

> Now I lay me down to sleep.
> I pray the Lord my soul to keep;

If I should die before I wake,
I pray the Lord my soul to take.[20]

The successor to President John Quincy Adams was Andrew Jackson—another diligent daily Bible reader who also read three to five chapters daily. Jackson went through a deep awakening of his Christian faith late in life, announced that he was forgiving all his enemies, and on his deathbed spoke in the language of Protestant pietism: "Death has no terror for me . . . . What are my sufferings compared to those of the Blessed Savior? I am ready to depart when called."[21]

Throughout the nineteenth century until Abraham Lincoln, all the presidents professed some form of Christian faith, though not all were church members. Some were more devout than others, reading the Bible and praying daily, and, in the case of James Knox Polk (1845–1849), were even Calvinistic to the point of not permitting any work to be done in the White House on Sundays.

Despite devotion to his wife's Presbyterianism, Polk demonstrated what many American presidents have done, namely, showing special loyalty to clergy who performed important pastoral roles of encouragement in their lives. And despite his Presbyterian background, Polk became much more sympathetic to Methodism through the friendship and preaching of Rev. John B. McFerrin. A week before his death, Polk was formally received into the Methodist Church. He, William McKinley, and George W. Bush are the only Methodist American presidents.

---

ABRAHAM LINCOLN'S FAITH HAS BEEN a great conundrum for many historians. This towering American hero was not, in his adult life, a member of any particular church and, indeed, was inherently skeptical toward the various theological assertions of different American Christian traditions. "I cannot without mental reservations," he once said, "assent to long and complicated creeds and catechisms."[22] Yet paradoxically, Lincoln was steeped in the language and the lore of the Bible (as well as of Shakespeare) and remembered fondly the Christian moral instruction of his mother, Nancy Hanks Lincoln.

One reason that Lincoln refrained from attaching himself to any church on assuming the presidency was his desire to avoid any denominational endorsement that might bring even greater division to a nation already radically split over the issue of slavery. He nevertheless attended services at St. John's Episcopal Church, Lafayette Square, on the morning of his inauguration, as did several of his successors, including George W. Bush. He also liked to slip into the study of Presbyterian pastor Rev. Phineas Gurley during midweek prayer meetings at New York Avenue Presbyterian Church. With the door to the sanctuary open, he could hear what was said but avoid being seen and perhaps fussed over.

Lincoln always prayed standing up. When once asked by a parishioner at the Presbyterian church why he did, he replied, "When my generals visit the White House, they stand when their commander-in-chief enters the Oval Office. Isn't it proper, then, that I stand for my commander-in-chief?"[23]

Gurley was not just a friend and pastoral counselor to Lincoln, he was an intercessory prayer warrior. "I have been driven many times to my knees in prayer," Lincoln said, speaking figuratively, not literally, "by the overwhelming conviction that I had nowhere else to go. My wisdom, and all that about, seemed insufficient for the day."[24]

It is in many ways Lincoln's profound humility, his unwillingness ever to be triumphalistic about his Christian faith, that has rendered him so attractive to nearly all cultures and ages. He is often quoted for his retort to the earnest pastor who expressed the hope that the Lord would be on the side of the Union. Lincoln's reply: "I am not concerned about that, for I know that the Lord is *always* on the side of the *right*. But it is my constant anxiety and prayer that I and the nation should be on the *Lord's* side."[25] His second inaugural address, immortalized in a stone engraving at the Lincoln Memorial in Washington, D.C., is steeped not just in biblical references, but in a profoundly Christian view of life. Speaking of the practice of slavery that had nearly destroyed the nation, Lincoln said of men both black and white, master and slave:

> Both read the same Bible and prayed to the same God and each invoked His aid against the other. It may seem strange that any men should dare to ask a just God's assistance in wringing their bread from the sweat of other men's faces, but let us judge not, that we be not judged. The prayers of both could not be answered. That of neither has been answered fully. The Almighty has His own purposes. Woe unto the world because of offenses; for it must needs be that offenses come, but woe to that man by whom the offense cometh.

Lincoln also took up in his second inaugural address the theme of providence (that is, God's purposes) in the outworkings of American history that Witherspoon less than a century earlier had first so fully introduced. He said,

> If we shall suppose that American slavery is one of those offenses which, in the providence of God, must needs come, but which, having continued through His appointed time, He now wills to remove, and that He gives to both North and South this terrible war as the woe due to those by whom the offense came, shall we discern therein any departure from those divine attributes which the believers in a living God always ascribe to Him? Fondly do we hope, fervently do we pray, that this mighty scourge of war may speedily pass away. Yet, if God wills that it continue until all the wealth piled by the bondsman's two hundred and fifty years of unrequited toil shall be sunk, and until every drop of blood drawn with the lash shall be paid by another drawn with the sword, as was said three thousand years ago, so still it must be said "the judgments of the Lord are true and righteous altogether."

Finally, of course, comes the ringing call to basic human decency toward the almost conquered foes, the Confederate forces still fighting:

With malice toward none, with charity for all, with firmness in the right as God gives us to see the right, let us strive on to finish the work we are in, to bind up the nation's wounds, to care for him who shall have borne the battle and for his widow and his orphan, to do all which may achieve and cherish a just and lasting peace among ourselves and with all nations.[26]

Some have argued that Lincoln was not, in fact, a Christian believer at all, but his own words belie this. His antipathy to creedal formulations certainly kept him a safe distance from most of the churches of his day, except for the Presbyterian church in Washington with whose pastor he was a close prayer friend. He was also rather specifically disobedient to all Christian traditions in inviting a spiritual medium into the White House in 1863 so that his wife, Mary Todd Lincoln, could supposedly get in touch with a dead relative. (Lincoln quipped later that the eerie voices heard in the room "sounded very much like the babbling of my cabinet.")[27]

But Lincoln seemed to have had a profound experience at Gettysburg when he toured the battlefield after the great July 1863 slaughter of sixty thousand soldiers in battle, some intimation of the Almighty's deep purposes in that terrible cauldron of Civil War suffering. Not long before his death by an assassin's bullet in April 1865, he told a pastor from Illinois, "When I left Springfield [to come to Washington for the inauguration of 1861], I asked the people to pray for me. I was not a Christian. When I buried my son [Willie, who died as a child], the severest trial of my life, I was not a Christian. But when I went to Gettysburg and saw the graves of thousands of our soldiers, I then and there gave my heart to Christ. I can now say I do love the Savior."[28]

What Lincoln's particular Christian theology may have been in that brief period between his walk through the fields of Gettysburg and his death less than two years later, is not important. It is, of course, significant that he signed the Thanksgiving Proclamation late in 1863, thus perpetuating in American history a celebration originally concocted by the early Puritans. But the Gettysburg Address itself, memorized and beloved by generations of Americans and foreigners alike, is especially important in showing what Lincoln thought to be America's purposes in the context of world history. Even the former president of China, Jiang Zemin, has memorized the entire Gettysburg Address in English and enjoys reciting it to Americans. The concluding sentence of the address makes it clear that Lincoln deemed it vital for America to remain "under God," obedient to the purposes of God's providence, as he might have put it, and that it remain a beacon light for freedom everywhere else in the world:

> It is for us the living, rather, to be dedicated here to the unfinished work which they who fought here have thus far so nobly advanced. It is rather for us to be here dedicated to the great task remaining before us—that from these honored dead we take increased devotion to that cause for which they gave the last full measure of devotion—that we here highly resolve that these dead shall not have died in vain—that this nation, under God, shall have a new birth of freedom and that government of the people, by the people, for the people shall not perish from the earth.

Many have noted that Lincoln's death occurred on Good Friday, as though it were a kind of Christian atonement for the suffering that white Europeans and Americans had imposed upon African Americans. At Ford's Theater, where John Wilkes Booth was lying in wait, Lincoln arrived late for the play and was leaning forward to whisper to his wife. According to one account, "He told her that the war was over and that he would like now to take her for a tour of the East. They would visit Palestine—would see Gethsemane and Calvary—would walk the streets of Jeru—" and then a shot rang out, and Lincoln's life was snuffed out.[29]

---

AFTER LINCOLN, THE WHITE HOUSE WAS OCCUPIED by an assortment of faiths and nonfaiths. Rutherford Hayes (1877–1881) was one of the first American presidents to make a public point about his Christian life. He attended the Foundry Methodist Church in Washington, D.C. (as President

Bill Clinton was to do during his presidency in the 1990s), and his wife presided over a White House from which tobacco, alcohol, and card-playing were banned. ("Lemonade Lucy," was what some wags dubbed her.)

The next two American presidents to be assassinated in office, James Garfield in 1881 and William McKinley in 1901, both were devout Christian believers. McKinley said in 1899, "My belief embraces the divinity of Christ and a recognition of Christianity as the mightiest factor in the world's civilization." McKinley was a fervent Methodist. After he was shot and his assailant was being dragged off, he said, "Be easy with him, boys." On awakening for the last time before his death, he said, "Good-bye all, good-bye. It is God's will. His will, not ours, be done."[30]

McKinley's vice president and successor, the authentic American hero Theodore Roosevelt, was what has been described as a "muscular Christian," a manly man who certainly wouldn't have passed muster with evangelicals of his day or today, because he rejected the doctrine of justification by faith and solidly promoted a works-based righteousness. "I believe," he said, "in the Gospel of works as put down in the Epistle of James—'Be ye doers of the word, and not hearers only.'"[31] But Roosevelt was a strong believer in church attendance and when in Washington, D.C., attended Grace Reformed Church on 15th and G Street, N.W.

By the time Roosevelt left office, Americans, perhaps momentarily tired of any religious pronouncements from the White House, elected Howard Taft over the outspoken fundamentalist Christian William Jennings Bryan (later to be involved in the 1925 Scopes trial in Tennessee over the issue of the teaching of Darwin's theory of evolution). Taft was an unequivocal Unitarian. "I believe in God," he said. "I do not believe in the divinity of Christ, and there are other of the postulates of the orthodox creed to which I cannot subscribe."[32]

Yet in Taft's successor, Woodrow Wilson, former president of Princeton University and a devout Presbyterian, the pendulum swung back to more traditional notions of America's global destiny under God. Wilson could be succinct when he wanted, which might not have been very often. "I believe in divine providence," the serious Calvinist said. "If I did not, I would go crazy."[33] He made many strong statements about his belief that the United States was a Christian nation.

Franklin Delano Roosevelt was not an especially religious-minded man, yet he nonetheless concluded his inaugural address in 1933 with a prayer: "In this dedication of a nation we humbly ask the blessing of God. May he protect each and every one of us. May he guide me in the days to come." Roosevelt read the Bible often and, undoubtedly, turned to prayer many times during the ordeal of the Depression and World War II.[34]

Roosevelt's vice president and successor, Harry Truman, was a blunt-spoken Baptist, who had little time for religious display, but who nevertheless carried around with him in his pocket his personal printed prayer. This began, "Almighty and everlasting God, creator of heaven and earth and the universe, help me to be, to think, to act what is right, because it is right. Make me truthful, honest, and honorable in all things."[35] It was Truman who in 1952 signed a joint resolution of Congress creating the National Day of Prayer. This became law in 1988 under President Reagan.

---

THE CONGRESS, BOTH HOUSE AND SENATE, in the 1950s reflected a conservative Protestantism that was influential over the United States after World War II. Under Eisenhower, the United States Congress confirmed the phrase "one nation under God" in the Pledge of Allegiance to the flag and the words "In God we trust" on the nation's coinage.

The 1950s have often been excoriated as a time when Americans were conformist and unimaginative, when the fear of global Communism or of nuclear war made life for many pinched and fearful. But it was also the last period in American history when mainline Protestant denominations remained evangelical, or at least orthodox in theological outlook.

Even so, the nation was ready for a change in 1960, when it elected John F. Kennedy rather than the experienced but not especially exciting political figure Richard M. Nixon. Kennedy offered not only intelligence, freshness, youth, and wit to a perhaps somewhat jaded nation, but also the distinctly novel experience of a chief executive who was Roman Catholic.

American Protestant leaders—Norman Vincent Peale among them—expressed loud concerns before the 1960 election that, if Kennedy were elected, the Vatican would be directing the affairs of the nation. Obviously, their worries were not well founded. Kennedy's Catholicism may have been genuine, but it did not insulate his life from carnal temptations—to which he readily succumbed—while in the White House, nor did it translate into a view of the existence of evil compatible with a Christian world-view.

In some ways, Kennedy may have been the first American president whose world-view was essentially secular and humanist: there was no such thing as evil, and whatever task there was to accomplish in the world could be accomplished through appealing to broad human ideals and through strength and dedication.

Kennedy's rhetoric was appealing to an age that wanted to believe man was indeed the measure of all things and that whatever people believed possible could, in fact, be accomplished. In the interesting book by Peter Kreeft, *Between Heaven and Hell,* there is an imaginary conversation between Kennedy and two prominent world literary figures who died on the day that he was assassinated. They were C. S. Lewis, the gifted British Christian writer, and Aldous Huxley, the British novelist who dabbled prominently in hallucinogenic substances and in Hindu and New Age cosmology. In Kreeft's book, Kennedy comes across as practical and down-to-earth but lacking insight into anything spiritual.

By the time of Kennedy's assassination in November 1963, America was struggling to come to terms with a host of complex and sometimes conflicting ideas. In retrospect, the best endeavor to come out of the early 1960s was the moral crusade led by Martin Luther King Jr. to extend civil rights to African Americans. That crusade struck a chord with a majority of Americans, who readily elected as president in 1964 a leader, Lyndon Baines Johnson, who was committed to continuing the implementation of those rights that Kennedy had endorsed.

But civil rights protests morphed into black power demonstrations, and antiwar marches morphed into more nihilistic, even more sinister, calls for the overturning of core institutions of American life. The sexual revolution, experimentation with drugs, and New Age perceptions of reality rent the fabric of American culture perhaps more thoroughly than in any previous period of national upheaval.

---

WHEN THE WHITE HOUSE WAS OCCUPIED ONCE MORE by a leader who clearly rejected this outlook, Richard Nixon, there might, perhaps, have been an opportunity to rethink the concepts of America and providence with which every generation in American history had been faced. But Nixon, despite his friendship with evangelist Billy Graham, was a conflicted and complex man. His Quaker background was not reflected in any worship association during his presidency, with the Society of Friends, either in Washington, D.C., or elsewhere in the nation.

Even with major foreign policy achievements, Nixon's presidency was overshadowed by the disgrace of Watergate. More troublingly, the failure of the nation's Christian leaders to speak powerfully into this collapse of presidential integrity raised disturbing questions about the effectiveness of the Protestant Christian church as a witness in public life in America. If Nixon's evangelical Christian friends couldn't stop him from doing what he did, what was the point of their being friends with him?

By the late 1970s, the Jesus Movement had penetrated deeply into the culture, bringing to power, no doubt with the help of evangelical Christians, a Southern Baptist Democrat, who spoke openly and unapologetically about being "born again." Crusty Washington reporters were sent scurrying to their telephones to learn from distant relatives in America's heartland what that term meant. Carter was unquestionably sincere in his faith. He taught Sunday school at a Baptist church in Washington, D.C., did not drink alcohol at official receptions, and was given the Secret

Service code name "Deacon." In 1987, looking back upon his presidency, he told an interviewer,

> The country at that time was searching for someone who would publicly profess a commitment to truth and integrity and the adherence to moral values—concerning peace, human rights, the alleviation of suffering—and I put forward these concepts, which are very deeply ingrained in my own character and motivations.[36]

Carter's assessment of the mood of the country in 1976, the year of his election, was surely correct: after the debacle of Watergate, Americans were happy to elect someone to the White House who publicly sought to abide by standards of morality and truth.

But by 1980, both the United States and the world had moved on. Carter did not seem able to respond effectively to crises, such as the taking of American hostages in Iran in 1978, and the apparent breakout of the Soviet Union when it invaded Afghanistan in 1979. He also projected the image of someone weighed down by moral questions—the petroleum crisis in America of 1979 was "the moral equivalent of war," he said.

In the election year 1980, Americans once again swung back to someone who projected a sunny belief in America's positive destiny and who also was, it seemed, a definite Christian believer—Ronald Reagan. "I've always believed that there is a certain divine scheme of things," Reagan said. "I'm not quite able to explain how my election happened or why I'm here, apart from believing it is a part of God's plan for me."

Reagan, though he did not attend church while in the White House—and took criticism for this from evangelical supporters—somehow recaptured for many Americans the belief that the purposes of providence were still being worked out through the destiny of the United States. But he identified strongly with evangelical Protestantism and, as new studies of his life are making clear, was animated by his spiritual convictions more than by anything else to denounce the repressive nature of Communism.

Nothing illustrated this more vividly than his reaction after the assassination attempt against him in 1981. His closest clergy friend, Rev. Don Moomaw, a former football player, asked Reagan as he was recovering from the bullet wound whether he was right with God. When Reagan said that he was, Moomaw asked him how he knew. "I have a Savior," Reagan replied, which is the perfect answer for an evangelical Christian.[37]

Reagan believed that America had a continuing and vital destiny in the world and that those who occupied the White House were bit players in a divine drama. It certainly fit with his own experience as an actor in Hollywood. In Berlin in the 1980s, he used a figure of speech that has resonated in American history since the words were first uttered by Massachusetts Governor John Winthrop in 1640:

For we must consider that we shall be as a City upon a hill. The eyes of all people are upon us. So that if we shall deal falsely with our God in this task we have undertaken, and so cause Him to withdraw His present help from us, we shall be made a story and a byword throughout the world.[38]

---

REAGAN'S VIEW WAS NOT ARTICULATED by President George H. W. Bush when he succeeded Reagan in 1988. Indeed, some have argued that Bush Senior's defeat in 1992 resulted from his failure to convey to the American people any sort of "vision" for their future. "The vision thing" became—surely unfairly—a mocking commentary on Bush Senior's overall reticence to speak in bold, uplifting rhetoric.

Undoubtedly, Bush Senior was conscious of the need for prayer and the need for firm pastoral support. When he was preparing to launch the Gulf War in January 1991, he invited Rev. Billy Graham to the White House to pray before Bush made the official announcement that hostilities to liberate Iraq had been set in motion. Graham stayed at the White

House several times during the Bush Senior presidency, continuing a personal friendship with the Bushes that went back many years.

---

BILL CLINTON CAME INTO OFFICE IN 1993, riding, to some extent, on the metaphor of "hope." He was originally from Hope, Arkansas, and in his election campaign he played heavily on this theme: the man from Hope bringing hope to America. Clinton was a Southern Baptist, who nevertheless attended Foundry Methodist Church in Washington, D.C., a Protestant church with a more liberal political perspective than most Southern Baptist churches, either in Washington, D.C., or elsewhere.

Paradoxically, in light of the scandal in his second term of his White House dalliance with intern Monica Lewinsky, Clinton was well-versed in the Bible, in Christian theology, and in the nuances of many moral positions from a Christian perspective. He was comfortable with evangelical Christian rhetoric and seemed especially at home in African American churches. Despite his being a Democrat and on some issues clearly liberal, he made a big effort to reach out to America's conservative evangelicals. Rich Cizik, vice president of the Washington-based National Association of Evangelicals, says that he has at least eight photographs of meetings with President Clinton during Clinton's two terms in office, but he has yet to have a single meeting with President George W. Bush.

There are a number of possible explanations for this. While George W. has indeed met several times with prominent evangelical leaders, such as Charles Colson of Prison Fellowship, James Dobson of Focus on the Family, and Pat Robertson of CBN's *The 700 Club*, he has not been nearly as active as Clinton was in cultivating potential supporters. It could be that such supporters are so unlikely to vote against him that it is not worth the effort to be constantly extending a public hand to them.

But there may be other, more subtle explanations for George W.'s care not to be seen too often with conservative evangelicals. For one thing, it is not in his interest to be presumed as being in the pocket of "the Christian right." For another, George W. in fact belongs to a mainstream Protestant denomination. He could easily have joined an independent evangelical church at any time. But he didn't. It is probable that he finds himself far more comfortable with a fluid, generic interpretation of the Christian faith than a sharply stamped version of it.

One close observer of George W.'s spirituality has an even simpler explanation. Alluding to the concept of "mere Christianity" written about by the late British writer, C. S. Lewis (Lewis's book *Mere Christianity*, has sold millions of copies in multiple languages), this observer says, "I think he is the first 'mere Christian' in the White House. I think he believes the essentials and has no interest in the inessentials."[39] This observer's point: unlike every previous president who took his faith seriously, George W. has no real interest in strong denominational allegiance. Even his church-going reflects that: to St. John's Episcopal Church in Lafayette Square when he is in Washington, D.C., to the chapel of Camp David (whose chaplain is rotated through from different denominational clergy representatives in the U.S. Marine Corps) when at the presidential retreat, to wherever he happens to be where worship can be conducted without too much disruption for security reasons when on the road.

George W. also has a handful of clergy friends, who do not even belong to the same denomination as he does, with whom he keeps in touch by phone and through their visits to the White House, Camp David, or the ranch at Crawford, Texas.

Those who have observed George W. close-up both before and after the September 11 events say that he is calmer, steadier, less given to pranks than before. Karen Hughes recalled

his incredible strength throughout it all and his incredible lack of fear for himself. He was very steady and very resolute. It was a time for people to confront their mortality. Every day we were told there could be another attack, perhaps on the White House. He knew that life is "a temporary assignment." He became more aware of this after 9/11. He has always been disciplined, but now he became more so. He was very, very determined.[40]

But that resolute manner and George W.'s frequent use of the term "evil" and "evildoers," comforting though it was to many Americans, has been disconcerting to others. "He's the most recklessly religious president we've seen," says Annie Laurie Gaylor, editor of *Freethought Today*, the publication of the Freedom from Religion Foundation, in Madison, Wisconsin. "He's on a religious mission, and you can't divorce religion from his militarism. He believes in fighting righteous war."[41] In fact, though George W. has indeed used the term "evil" for some of the regimes he believes have been deeply oppressive of their own people, as well as supportive of terrorism and threatening to the United States, he has never employed the phrase "righteous war" to describe U.S. military action against any opponent.

Strangely perhaps, George W.'s faith has been criticized from some sectors that might have been assumed to support him. Fr. John McCloskey, director of the Catholic Information Office in Washington, D.C., describes the president as "a totally unformed Christian," whose faith is "shallow." McCloskey's reasoning: a serious Christian would have read St. Thomas Aquinas or would be informed about the significance of the Council of Chalcedon and other important events in Christian history. But another Roman Catholic, Deal Hudson, editor of *Crisis* Magazine, has a different view. He says, "Every person whom I have ever taken to meet the president has been won over. What wins people over is the simplicity of his faith and the lack of grandiose claims about it. George W. Bush occupies a niche between the mainstream and the evangelical right."[42]

Popular Christian singer Michael W. Smith has a similar perspective:

The president's faith is what grounds him. It's his stabilizing force in times of crisis. He's essentially the same man in good times and bad: calm, confident, focused. He credits his relationship with God for sustaining him and enabling him to be optimistic. He sees freedom as a God-given right of every human being and America as the world leader in bringing that freedom to oppressed people. I like it that what really pushes his button is that he would like to be known as someone who inspired people to do their very best. He thinks that it isn't all that important to grow up through company ranks and become chairman if that doesn't bring you peace. I love it that we have a lot in common there. We can sit for hours and talk about how to change the world.[43]

If George W. Bush indeed can sit for periods of relaxing conversation with a musician who is not connected with any aspect of politics or governance, that may confirm the observer's judgment of George W. Bush as the first "mere Christian" to occupy the White House. That, surely, is reassuring to many ordinary American Christians, who would like their president to be, well, a bit like them. But of course, Americans, whether Christian or not, do not want their national leader to be "just like them." They want him to be special, to lead the country in the direction of peace and prosperity and of leadership that will benefit not just the people of the United States, but of the entire world.

---

THIS IS NOT THE PLACE to make sweeping judgments about the effectiveness of the presidency of George W. Bush. After all, we have been focusing on his faith and trying to set it in the context not only of his own personal development but of faith precedents in the leadership of the United States over a period of more than two centuries. Besides, American people will have an opportunity to have their voices heard at the polling booths in November 2004.

Naturally, some of those who have been close to George W. from a faith perspective already deeply admire him and his conduct in the American presidency. Evangelist James Robison says, "I think this man's destined to be one of the great presidents in American history. I don't think there's any doubt about it. I think he will have taken a very firm stand for the direction in which we must move and for the principles upon which we must build."[44]

Whether or not George Bush is a great president is something history will take its time to ascertain. On the question of how good a Christian he is and how honorable his conduct has been, the ultimate judge, of course, will be the Almighty. But to a remarkable degree George W. Bush, independent of his qualities and shortcomings, has made his personal faith, his Christian faith, and yes, even his own version of Methodism, the lodestar of his course as national leader. That in itself is a remarkable act of faith.

# A Sermon

---

*Given by*

GEORGE W. BUSH

*at*

*Second Baptist Church*

Houston, Texas
March 6, 1999

# Faith Can Change Lives

---

*We're all bound by the power of faith. . . .*
*Faith can help change a culture that desperately needs changing.*

—George W. Bush

I AM HONORED TO BE HERE TODAY, but I must confess that back in the early '60s, I think it was about 1961 or '62—I never dreamed I'd be here.

My first exposure to Second Baptist Church came after my mother said, "Son, I don't want you driving down Woodway; there's a hurricane coming." That was Hurricane Carlos. So, of course, I got in the car and drove down Woodway. And I saw the roof get blown off this church. I never dreamed I'd be inside of the church then, and I promise you, I never dreamed I'd be coming as your governor.

It's a huge honor to be the governor of Texas, and I want to thank you for welcoming me to this most important church. I oftentimes talk about the bully pulpit. It is a wonderful feeling to be in the real thing, but I'm not going to let it go to my head.

I'm mindful of the time a mother and her son went to church, and this happened where they had flags around the chapel. And the young man said to his mother, "Mother, what are all the flags for?" And she said, "Well, those are for all the young men who died in service." He said, "Well, which one—the nine o'clock or the eleven o'clock service?"

I'm also honored to be a Methodist among all the Baptists. Watching

205

the baptismal ceremony made me realize we have some differences in our denominations. For example, we sprinkle; you immerse. It's like the time that Baptist preacher got up and said, "I want everybody, everybody who wants their souls washed white as snow, to stand up." People sprung to their feet, except for one fellow.

He [the preacher] said, "Why didn't you stand up?"

He said, "Well, I had my soul washed at the Methodist church."

He [the preacher] said, "No, no, you didn't have your soul washed at the Methodist church. You had your soul dry-cleaned."

Our differences are few compared to the things we have in common. And that's what I'd like to talk to you about today.

You and I are here because we believe that faith can change lives. We know faith can change Texas, and we know faith can help change our culture. Faith is the framework for living. It gives us the spirit and heart that affect everything we do. It gives us hope each day. Faith gives us purpose to right wrongs, to preserve our families, and to teach our children values. Faith gives us conscience to keep us honest, even when nobody else is looking.

And faith can change lives. I know firsthand because faith changed mine. I grew up in the church, but I didn't always walk the walk. There came a point in my life when I felt empty. And so, by chance, or maybe it wasn't chance, I got to spend a weekend with the great Billy Graham, and as a result of our conversations and his inspiration, I searched my heart and recommitted my life to Jesus Christ.

My relationship with God through Christ has given me meaning and direction. My faith has made a big difference in my personal life and my public life as well. I make decisions every day. Some are easy, and some aren't so easy. I have worries just like you do. I worry about my family. I worry about putting them in the fishbowl of politics.

And I pray. I pray for guidance; I pray for patience. My seventeen-year-old twin daughters think I *really* need to pray for patience. And I pray for peace. I firmly believe in the power of intercessory prayer, and I know I could not do my job without it.

I have moments of doubt, moments of pride, and moments of hope. Yet my faith helps a lot, because I have a sense of calm knowing that the Bible's admonition, "Thy will be done," is life's guide. In this hectic world, there is something incredibly reassuring in the belief that there is a divine plan that exceeds all human plans.

I believe in the separation of church and state. The church is *not* the state. And the state is surely *not* the church. Anytime the church enters into the realm of politics, the church runs the risk of losing its mission—teaching the Word of God. Politics is a world of give and take, a world of polls, too many polls of the human vision. The church is built on the absolute principles of the Word of God, not the word of man.

But I want to make this clear: we will welcome, we *should* welcome the presence of people of faith into the political arena. It is essential that believers enter the arena. Just as your faith helps determine how to live your life, your involvement in politics helps determine how well our democracy functions. Democracy is only as good as the people who are willing to participate.

Fortunately, our great state, Texas, is blessed with many people of faith who are willing to get involved and make their voices heard, and as importantly, to help a neighbor in need. You see, as a result of people of faith becoming involved in our society, faith is changing Texas. We learned that government programs cannot solve all our problems. You see, government can hand out money, but what it cannot do is put a hope in our hearts or a sense of purpose in our lives. It cannot fill the spiritual well from which we draw strength every day. Only faith can do that.

So one of my missions as the governor of this state has been to unleash the compassion of Texas with laws and policies that say to churches and synagogues and mosques and people of all faiths, "We want you to love your neighbors as you'd like to be loved yourself. We want you to become involved."

And we're seeing proof of our faith in Texas. There are little armies of compassion transforming Texas—one heart, one soul, one conscience at a time. And we've got some great drill sergeants in that army of compassion, one of whom just introduced me—Ed Young. Or Kirbyjohn Caldwell, or Tony Evans, or a friend of mine, Tilly Bergen, who I call the Mother Teresa of Arlington. I don't call her that; Arlington calls her that.

Our faith-based laws—supported, by the way, by both Republican and Democrats—remove government as a roadblock for people of faith to answer the call. Whether it be second-chance homes or single, teenage mothers, or faith-based drug rehabilitation programs, Texas is one of the leaders in our nation when it comes to faith-based initiatives.

Perhaps the most bold experiment in determining whether faith can change lives in government is the result of turning an entire prison over to Chuck Colson's InnerChange Ministry. This experiment is taking place down the road in Fort Bend County, Texas. Instead of the usual prison rehabilitation programs, which don't work very well, Texas is doing something differently. We're turning to the Bible. We're trying something profound. We're saying, "Why don't we change our hearts first and foremost, and then change the life."

Many volunteers are helping inside the prison. But one of the crucial tests is going to be whether there'll be volunteers to welcome the prisoner on the outside. We have Christian mentors who are willing to help, many of whom are in this church. And one of the reasons I've come this morning is to thank you from the bottom of our collective hearts—people like Linda Liggen and Earl Nichols Sr. and Bob Bell, who coordinates all the mentors. Thanks for what you're doing.

It shouldn't come as a surprise to you that, as a result of this experiment, the prison culture in this unit has changed. Life is more civil. There is more mutual respect, and there's now a sense of hope. One inmate, named James Peterson, was so upset to hear that he's going to be released before he's finished the ministry that he actually wrote the parole board and asked them to keep him behind bars. In his letter he said there is nothing he'd like more than to be back in the outside world, with his daughter, but he knew, and his family knew, he'd benefit from staying with the ministry.

He wrote, "This is God's program. He's really moving in the prisons, and He's got me right in the middle of it. I feel it an honor to stay here and to complete the commitment I made when I signed up."

Well, after the parole board recovered from its shock, they granted his request, and a week ago James Petersen walked out of prison a free man, a changed man, a man with a job, a man with a new attitude, and a man with a Christian mentor, saying, "Brother James, how can we help?"

My hope is that this program will show, for all to see, that the way to reduce recidivism, the way to change Texas, is to first change hearts.

Oftentimes in our society, we see the need around us. Oftentimes we hear a call, but we fail to do something about it. I think the most vivid example of what I'm trying to describe to you came when a preacher was up talking—preaching, not just talking. And a guy popped up in the middle of the sermon. He said, "Use me, Lord, use me." The preacher ignored him.

Next time he came around, he was giving a sermon again. Same fellow pops up, right about out there, and he said, "Use me, Lord, use me." After the service was over, the preacher came down out of the pulpit. He said, "Fellow, the Lord has heard your call. He would like you to scrape and paint all the pews this week before next Sunday."

Next Sunday the preacher was up giving his sermon. The guy pops up and he says, "Use me, Lord, use me. But only in an advisory capacity."

Our society has plenty of *advisors*. What we need are *doers*, like the people in this church who are following the apostle Paul's admonition to "serve one another in the spirit of love." I want to thank the thousands of volunteers who are the lifeblood of the many outreach ministries in this church—ministry that provides shelter and clothing and food and counseling and parenting and literacy training and mentoring and tutoring and Bible studies, and hope for thousands of Texans. You have proved what I know, that the best welfare programs all across the state of Texas don't exist in government bureaucracy, but they exist inside the walls of churches and synagogues, and we thank you for your mission.

Faith is a powerful tool for change, and it's just the tool we need to confront the biggest challenge facing Texas today. That is, how do we change a culture that says, "If it feels good, do it"? And "if you've got a problem, blame somebody else." The warning signs of our failed culture are everywhere. Men and boys father children and walk away saying, "Hey, they're not my problem. They're yours." Nearly a third of new babies will be born out of wedlock in Texas this year. The toughest job in Texas—the toughest job—is for a single woman to raise children.

Drugs are destroying neighborhoods in our state, and alcohol is too tempting for many of our young. And there are still too many people dependent on the welfare system that has sapped the soul and drained the spirit of many of the people of our state. Many in our country, fortunately though, are awakening to the need for change. And many are searching for the right course of action.

I mentioned Tony Evans from Dallas a little earlier. I heard him give a speech in Greenville, Texas, when we were there to lament the fact that churches had been burned. He said the problem we face in society today is much like the problem he had when a crack appeared in his bedroom wall. He called in a painter, and the guy painted over it. It looked okay for about a week or two. And then zigzags appeared back in the wall. The cracks came back.

So Tony decided to get a new painter. This fellow was an honest man, though. He said, "Sir, I've surveyed the damage. The problem isn't the crack in your wall. It's the fact that you've got a shifting foundation. What you need to do is fix the foundation first, and the cracks will take care of themselves."

And that's what we need to do in our society. We need to fix the foundation first, and faith can help.

My dream is to usher in what I call the "responsibility era"—an era in which each and every Texan understands that we're responsible for the decisions we make in life; that each of us is responsible for making sure our families come first; that we're responsible for loving our neighbors as we'd like to be loved ourselves; and that we're responsible for the communities in which we live.

Government can help. Government can help usher in the responsibility era. After all, we can pass laws. We can pass laws that say, as we did in the Juvenile Justice Code, "If you break the law, there will be a consequence." The Juvenile Justice Code clearly says, "You'll be held responsible for the decisions you've made." That's a conservative approach. By the way, it's a compassionate approach to say to our young that discipline and love go hand in hand.

But here's what government cannot do—what seems to be the false hope of the last thirty years—government can't make people love one another. I wish we could. I'd sign that law. Or if someone could tell me how much money it takes to cause people to love one another, we'd pass that budget—the love budget. But the truth of the matter is, love comes not from government. It comes from the hearts and souls of decent Texans.

Cultures change . . . one act of compassion at a time. That's how cultures change. And each of us must participate. We must promote good values in our homes and in our public institutions. We must not be afraid to teach our children right from wrong. We must say to our children, "Aim high, stay in school, don't use drugs, don't use alcohol, and remember there is honor—not shame—in abstaining from sex until you're married."

We must teach our children bedrock values—not the values of one religious denomination over another, but Judeo-Christian values that have stood the test of time. The importance of family. There are obligations to love your neighbor, give an honest day's work for an honest day's wages. Don't lie, do not cheat, do not steal. Respect others. Respect their opinions, and remember, it's you who is responsible for the decisions you make in life.

Now I know I painted a pretty tough picture about Texas and some of the culture problems we have, but I warn you, I'm an incurable optimist. You see, I've seen a culture change once in my lifetime, so I know it can change again to a better day for all. And I know, I know faith can lead the way, because faith transcends all boundaries. It is the journey of the heart and soul which transcends race, ethnicity, and creed for all God's children. And faith supplies what we need to treat each other in a decent and civilized way.

A point was driven home to me recently when Laura and I went to Israel. If you've never been to Israel, I strongly urge you to go. It was a fantastic experience!

First, the history was interesting. Imagine choppering around the West Bank with Ariel Sharon. He pointed and said, "When I was nineteen, I fought here. When I was twenty-three years old, here's where we had the battle." From the helicopter view, it struck me how small Israel is, especially compared to a few of the counties here in the state of Texas.

The politics were interesting, but the most important part of the journey was the religious experience we all had. I was in a delegation made up of four governors—two Catholics, a Mormon, and a Methodist. There was one other Gentile, and the rest were Jewish friends of mine.

We all went to the Sea of Galilee, where Jesus delivered the famous Sermon on the Mount. And we stood on the very spot where He delivered the Sermon on the Mount. We looked out over the Sea of Galilee as the sun was setting, and a person in our delegation said, "Why don't the governors read Scripture?" So three governors went first. And, that finally finished, I decided *not* to read Scripture. I decided to read "Amazing Grace," which is my favorite hymn.

Afterward, we got on a helicopter and went back to Tel Aviv, and we were fixing to leave for the airport. But we had a series of toasts.

Unbeknownst to us, at the Sea of Galilee, one of the Jewish guys and one of the Gentiles went down and kneeled together in prayer, and joined hands, and put their hands together in the Sea of Galilee. As we were toasting, the Christian fellow stood up and said, "I want to share an experience that I've had with this friend Lou." Then he described the scene of Jew and Gentile on bended knee. And out of his mouth came the words of a hymn that he had known as a young boy—a hymn that he said he hadn't sung in a long time, but a hymn that he got word for word exactly correct. And I want to read that hymn to you:

Now it is a time approaching by prophets long foretold,
When all share well together one Shepherd and one fold.

Now Jew and Gentile meeting from many a distant shore,
Around an altar kneeling one common Lord adore.

We're all God's children. We're all bound by the power of faith. Faith can change lives. Faith can change Texas. And faith can help change a culture that desperately needs changing.

Thank you for having me here. And God bless you all.[1]

----

# Appendices

- *Photo Credits*
- *Endnotes*
- *Index*

# Photograph Credits

1.  George W. Bush talks to reporters at Arlington Stadium in Texas on April 18, 1989, after both the American and National League owners approved the sale of the Texas Rangers to a group headed by Bush and Edward M. Rose III. (AP Photo).

2.  Young George Bush with parents, George Bush Senior and Barbara Bush. (REUTERS/Photo by Larry Downing.)

3.  George W. Bush and family pose at Kennebunkport family home. George W. Bush, wife Laura, daughters Barbara and Jenna pose for family portrait in Kennebunkport in this undated file photo. (CM/SV CAMPAIGN BUSH WASHINGTON Photo by HO).

4.  President Bush speaks during a tribute to the life and legacy of slain civil rights leader Martin Luther King Jr. at the First Baptist Church of Glenarden in Landover, Md., near Washington, Monday, January 20, 2003. Bush was invited to the altar by Pastor John K. Jenkins Sr., right. Martin Luther King Jr. successfully led blacks in opposing segregation using nonviolent resistance tactics until he was assassinated in 1968. A Federal holiday in his name was first celebrated in 1986. (AP Photo/J. Scott Applewhite).

5.  Texas Governor George W. Bush and his wife Laura ride in the inaugural parade with the Capitol in the background Tuesday, January 19, 1999, in Austin, Texas. Governor Bush was sworn in for his second term of office earlier in the day. (AP Photo/Harry Cabluck).

6.  Republican presidential hopefuls, from left, Steve Forbes; Alan Keyes; Texas Governor George W. Bush; Senator Orrin Hatch of Utah; Senator John McCain of Arizona; and Gary Bauer line up on the stage prior to the GOP debate, Monday, December 13, 1999 in Des Moines, Iowa. (AP Photo/John Gaps).

7.  President Bush and the first lady on tour of Hermitage. While Russian President Vladimir Putin speaks to the media, President George W. Bush steals

away for a moment with first lady Laura Bush while touring the Hermitage in St. Petersburg May 25, 2002. Russian President Vladimir Putin and his wife Lyudmilla escorted the couple on the tour. (REUTERS/Kevin Lamarque).

8. President Bush prays during church service at the National Cathedral. President George W. Bush prays with his wife Laura and vice president Dick Cheney (2nd R) and his wife Lynne (R) during a morning church service at the National Cathedral in Washington January 21, 2001. Behind Bush L-R are his father, former president George Bush, his mother Barbara, his daughters Jenna and Barbara, and his mother-in-law Jenna Welch. Bush will host an open house at the White House later in the day. (GMH/JP BUSH WASHINGTON Photo by RICK WILKING).

9. President Bush meets with Israeli Prime Minister Sharon in Washington. President George W. Bush laughs along with Israeli Prime Minister Ariel Sharon (L) after Sharon momentarily lost track of his remarks during a news conference in the Rose Garden, July 29, 2003. Sharon said Israel would press ahead with the construction of a West Bank security fence that Bush has called an obstacle to peace in the Middle East. (REUTERS/Photo by MIKE THEILER).

10. President Bush, right, is greeted by British Prime Minister Tony Blair at Hillsborough Castle Monday, April 7, 2003, in Hillsborough, Northern Ireland. Bush and Blair are grappling with three of the world's toughest conflicts in Bush's 19-hour visit to Northern Ireland discussing war and rebuilding in Iraq while trying to revive peace efforts in Northern Ireland and the Middle East. (AP Photo/Susan Walsh).

11. U.S. President George W. Bush carries a platter of turkey and fixings as he visits U.S. troops for Thanksgiving in Baghdad, Thursday, 27 November 2003. United States President George W. Bush paid a surprise visit to troops stationed in Iraq for the U.S. Thanksgiving holiday on Thursday. His two-hour stay in the Iraqi capital of Baghdad was kept secret for security reasons, and media were not informed of the visit until Bush was airborne and on his way back to the U.S. (EPA/ANJA NIEDRINGHAUS).

12. Bush asks for a moment of silence for victims in tower disaster. U.S. President George W. Bush asks for a moment of silence after the World Trade Center in New York was struck by two different aircraft, September 11, 2001. A fire also is said to be blazing at the Pentagon in Washington. (REUTERS/Win McNamee).

# ENDNOTES

## Chapter 2

1. Letter from Bob Landreth and others (3/6/2002) and reply from President Bush (3/25/2002), kindly made available by signatory Jim Sale.

2. Quoted in Mickey Herskowitz, *Duty, Honor, Country: The Life and Legacy of Prescott Bush* (Nashville: Rutledge Hill Press, 2003).

3. Ibid., p. 18.

4. Robert Green Ingersoll. Source: http://www.infidels.org/library/historical/robert_ingersoll/on_new_religion.html

5. The International Metaphysical League. Source: http://website.lineone.net/~newthought/ahotntm9.html

6. James Smith Bush, *More Words about the Bible* (New York: John W. Lovell Company, 1883) p. 44.

7. Herskowitz, op. cit., pp. 22–23

8. Ibid., p. 25

9. Ibid., p. 36

10. Bill Minutaglio, *First Son: George W. Bush and the Bush Family Dynasty* (New York: Three Rivers Press, 1999), p. 21.

11. Herskowitz, op. cit., p. 49

12. Doug Wead, *George Bush: Man of Integrity* (Eugene, OR: Harvest House Publishers, 1988), p. 132.

13. John Stott, *Focus on Christ: An Enquiry into the Theology of Prepositions* (London & Cleveland, Collins, 1979). Reissued as *Understanding Christ* (Grand Rapids, MI, Zondervan, 1981). Revised and illustrated edition released as *Life in Christ* (Eastbourne, Kingsway, 1991 and Wheaton, Tyndale House, 1991).

14. Ibid., p. 145.

15. Wead, op. cit., p. 134.

16. Ibid., p. 53.

17. Ibid., pp. 58–59.

18. Ibid., p. 62.

19. Ibid., p. 65.

20. It was Harriman's fearsome image that terrified the mail clerk in the movie *Butch Cassidy and the Sundance Kid* into not opening a safe on the train when ordered to do so by the bandit character played by Paul Newman.

21. From Philip Kunhardt Jr., et. al., *The American President* (New York: Riverhead Books, 1999), pp. 336–345.

22. At the risk of approaching immodesty, perhaps the title for "*most* beautiful" ought to go to Stowe School, Bucks, England, set on 700 acres of the former estate of the Dukes of Buckingham; the author's own *alma mater*.

23. Minutaglio, op. cit., p. 61.

24. Herskowitz, op. cit., p. 76.

25. Doug Wead, op. cit., pp. 8–9.

26. Ibid., p. 135.

27. Herskowitz, op. cit, p. 78.

28. George Bush: *All the Best: My Life in Letters and Other Writings* (New York: Touchstone, 1999), p. 64.

29. Ibid., p. 70.

30. Barbara Bush, *Barbara Bush: A Memoir* (New York: St. Martin's Paperbacks, 1995), p. 48.

31. Quoted in Pamela Killian, *Barbara Bush: Matriarch of a Dynasty* (New York: St. Martin's Press, 2002), p. 43.

32. Wead, op. cit., p. 47.

33. George W. Bush, *A Charge to Keep* (New York, 1999: William Morrow and Company Inc), p. 14.

34. *Barbara Bush: A Memoir*, p. 50

35. Ibid.

36. Minutaglio, op. cit., p. 57

37. Ibid.

38. George W. Bush, *A Charge to Keep*, p. 19.

39. Ibid.

40. Quoted in Minutaglion, p. 73.

41. Bush, *A Charge to Keep*, p. 21.

42. Ibid., pp. 20–21.

43. Ibid., p. 22.

44. Minutaglio, op. cit., p. 72.

45. George W. Bush, *A Charge to Keep*, p. 7.

46. Ibid., pp. 6–7.

**Chapter 3**

1. Bush, *A Charge to Keep*, p. 133.

2. Bill Minutaglio, *First Son: George W. Bush and the Bush Family Dynasty* (New York: Three Rivers Press, 1999), p. 159.

3. Pamela Kilian, *Barbara Bush: Matriarch of a Dynasty* (New York: St. Martin's Press, 2002).

4. Alexandra Robbins, *Secrets of the Tomb: Skull and Bones, The Ivy League and the Hidden Paths of Power* (New York: Little, Brown and Company, 2002), p. 175.

5. Ibid., p. 175.

6. Strobe Talbott. Conversation with the author, October 20, 2003.

7. Barbara Bush. Conversation with the author, November 15, 2003.

8. Ibid.

9.  Helen Thorpe, "Go East, Young Man," *Texas Monthly*, June 1999. From website: www.texasmonthly.com/mag/1999/jun/east.2.php.
10.  Minutaglio, op. cit., p. 92.
11.  Terry Johnson. Minutaglio, op. cit.
12.  Robert McCallum, Minutaglio, op. cit.
13.  Bush, *A Charge to Keep*, p. 47.
14.  William F. Buckley, *God and Man at Yale* (Washington, D.C.: Regnery Publishing, 1978).
15.  Robbins, op. cit., p. 175.
16.  Helen Thorpe, op. cit.
17.  Minutaglio, op. cit., p. 106.
18.  Mickey Herskowitz, Conversation with the author, November 2003.
19.  Robbins, op. cit., p. 21.
20.  Minutaglio, op. cit., p. 101.
21.  Bush, *A Charge to Keep*, p. 49.
22.  Ibid., p. 50.
23.  Minutaglio, op. cit., p. 121.
24.  Ibid., p. 120.
25.  Bush, *A Charge to Keep*.
26.  Minutaglio, op. cit., p. 126.
27.  Ibid., p. 146.
28.  Ibid., p. 148.
29.  Remarks of Rev. Kirbyjon Caldwell, as recorded by the author at Tenth Anniversary of the Power Center, Houston, Texas, September 12, 2003.
30.  Bush, *A Charge to Keep*, p. 58.
31.  Bush *A Charge to Keep*, p. 50.
32.  Ibid., p. 59.
33.  George Bush [Sr.] *All the Best: My Life in Letters and Other Writings* (New York: Simon and Schuster, 1999) p. 182.
34.  Ibid., p. 184.
35.  Ibid., p. 202.
36.  Conversation of Rev. Kan Xueqing with Charlene Fu, Beijing, August 2003.
37.  Bush, *A Charge to Keep*, p. 61.
38.  Minutaglio, op. cit. p. 170.
39.  Bush, *A Charge to Keep*, p. 80.
40.  Patricia Kilday Hart, "The Bush Report," *Texas Monthly*, September 1999.
41.  Minutaglio, op. cit., p. 193.
42.  Ibid., p. 197.
43.  Don Poage. Conversation with the author, December 2003.

**Chapter 4**

1.  From Midland's official Internet website, www.ci.midland.tx.us/gwb.htm
2.  Karl Rove, Conversation with author, December 2003.
3.  George Neumayr, "Midland Ministers to the World, *The American Spectator*,

January, 2004.

4.   Source: Quoted on website http://democracyunbound.com/shrubgrows.html

5.   Don Evans, Secretary of Commerce. Conversation with the author, October 2003.

6.   Source: Arthur Blessitt website, www.arthurblessitt.com/bush.html

7.   Ibid.

8.   Arthur Blessitt. The other verses Blessitt used in his conversation with Bush were:  Romans 5:8 ("God demonstrates His love toward us, in that while we were yet sinners, Christ died for us."), Romans 10:13 ("For whoever calls upon the name of the Lord shall be saved."), John 14:6 ("Jesus said, 'I am the way, the truth, and the life. No one comes to the Father except through Me!'"), John 1:43 ("Follow me."), Mark 8:34 ("Whoever desires to come after Me, let him deny himself, and take up his cross and follow Me."), Matthew 11:28 ("Come to Me, all you who labor and are heavy laden, and I will give you rest."), John 14:27 ("Peace I leave with you, My peace I give to you;  not as the world gives do I give you.  Let not your heart be troubled, neither let it be afraid.").

9.   The full text of the prayer Blessitt says he prayed with George W. is found in the same location on the Blessitt website.  It begins, "Dear God, I believe in you and need you in my life.  Have mercy on me a sinner.  Jesus, as best I know how, I want to follow you.  Cleanse me from my sins and come into my life as my Savior and Lord. . . . Thank you, God, for hearing my prayer.  In Jesus name I pray."

10.   Arthur Blessitt. Conversation with the author, September 2003.

11.   Don Poage. Conversation with the author, December 2003.

12.   Barbara Bush. Conversation with the author, November 2003.

13.   Bush, A Charge to Keep, p. 136.

14.   Ibid., p. 136.

15.   Karl Rove. Conversation with the author, December 2003.

16.   Bush, A Charge to Keep, p. 136.

17.   Don Evans, Secretary of Commerce. Conversation with the author, October 2003.

18.   Karen Hughes. Conversation with the author, November 2003.

19.   The One Year Bible (Wheaton, IL:  Tyndale House, 1986).

20.   Don Poage. Conversation with the author, December 2003.

21.   Ibid.

22.   Don Evans. Conversation with the author, October 2003.

23.   Bush, A Charge to Keep, p. 137.

24.   Don Evans. Conversation with the author, October 2003.

25.   Bush, A Charge to Keep, pp. 132–133.

26.   Ibid., pp. 135–136.

27.   Source: website for transcript:
       http://www.pbs.org/wgbh/pages/frontline/shows/choice2000/bush/wead.html

28.   Ibid.

29.   Bush, A Charge to Keep, p. 184.

30.   Doug Wead, All the Presidents' Children: Triumph and Tragedy in the Lives of

*America's First Families* (New York: Simon and Schuster, 2003).
31.  George [H. W.] Bush, *All the Best*, p. 409.

## Chapter 5

1.  Karen Brandon, "George W. Bush: The Son also rises," in *Orlando Sentinel*, January 18, 2000.
2.  Joe Nick Patoski, "Team Player," *Texas Monthly*, June 1999. From website: www.texasmonthly.com/mag/1999/jun/team.2.php
3.  Ibid.
4.  Molly Ivins and Lou Dubose, *Shrub: The Short but Happy Political Life of George W. Bush* (New York: Random House, 1999) p. 36.
5.  *Meriam-Webster Dictionary*.
6.  "Wesley Family," in *Encyclopedia Britannica*, (Chicago: Encyclopedia Britannica, Inc., 1977), Macropaedia Volume 19, p. 760.
7.  Source: website http://rylibweb.man.ac.uk/data1/dg/methodist/poor/
8.  Mark Tooley, Director of the United Methodist Committee at the International Religion and Democracy, conversation with T. Diane Bryhn, researcher, January 13, 2004.
9.  Rev. Mark Craig. Conversation with the author, September 2003.
10.  Mercer Reynolds. Conversation with the author, December 2003.
11.  Bill Minutaglio, *First Son: George W. Bush and the Bush Family Dynasty* (New York: Three Rivers Press, 1999), p. 264.
12.  Ibid., p. 229.
13.  Karl Rove. Conversation with the author, December 2003.
14.  Ibid.
15.  Bush, *A Charge to Keep*, p. 25.
16.  Ibid., p. 44.
17.  Ibid., end-papers.
18.  Ibid., p. 43.
19.  Minutaglio, op. cit., p. 300.
20.  A Google search on the Internet has dozens of entries, ranging from the assertion by San Francisco radio host Michael Savage that he invented the term in 1994 to a funny anagram website that concocts out of "compassionate conservative" the phrase "conspire to save a vast income" (www.anagramgenius.com/archive/compas.html).
21.  Bush, *A Charge to Keep*, pp. 234–235.
22.  "Faith and Power Profile: Marvin Olasky," United Press International, March 29, 2001.
23.  Minutalgio, op. cit., pp. 313-314.
24.  Marvin Olasky, *The Tragedy of American Compassion* (Washington, D.C.: Regnery Publishing, 1995).
25.  Bush, *A Charge to Keep*, p. 213.
26.  Bush, *A Charge to Keep*, p. 215.
27.  Mark A. R. Kleiman, "Hey, Wait a Minute," *Slate Magazine*, August 5, 2003.

28. Karen Brandon, Joseph T. Hallinan and Bob Kemper, "The Son Also Rises," *Orlando Sentinel*, January 18, 2000.
29. Minutaglio, op. cit., p. 315.
30. Bush, *A Charge to Keep*, p. 146.
31. Ibid.
32. Source: http://www.geocities.com/RainForest/Canopy/2525/karlamain.html
33. Tucker Carlson. Conversation with the author, January 2004.
34. Bush, *A Charge to Keep*, p. 150.
35. Source: http://www.tylwythteg.com/enemies/Bush/bush.24.html
36. Jim Mayfield. Conversation with the author, September 2003.
37. Ibid.
38. Jim Mayfield. Conversation with the author, October 2003.
39. Bush, *A Charge to Keep*, p. 2.
40. Ibid., p. 9.
41. Ibid.

## Chapter 6

1. Karl Rove. Conversation with the author, December 2003.
2. Tony Evans. Conversation with the author, January 2004.
3. Kirbyjon Caldwell, *The Gospel Of Good Success: A Roadmap to Spiritual, Emotional, and Financial Wholeness* (New York: Simon and Schuster, 2000). Excerpt available on website http://aalbc.com/books/the2.htm
4. *Christianity Today* online, October 5, 2001, http://www.christianitytoday.com/ct/2001/012/7.60.html
5. Karl Rove. Conversation with the author, December 2003
6. Video of sermon, courtesy of Second Baptist Church, 6400 Woodway, Houston, Texas 77057. The White House has given permission for the printing of the transcript.
7. Ibid.
8. Ibid.
9. Uri Dan. Conversation with the author, October 2003.
10. Sam Howe Verhovek, "Is there room on the Republican ticket for another Bush?" *New York Times*, September 13, 1998.
11. The Associated Press, December 4, 1998.
12. Abraham Fox. Anti-Defamation League, December 8, 1998.
13. Jane Borthwick, "Now Is the Time Approaching," *Thoughtful Hours*, 1859.
14. Bush interview with the Baptist Press, August 31, 2000.
15. Adair Margo. Conversation with author, September 2003.
16. Don Evans. Conversation with the author, October 2003.
17. Karen Hughes. Conversation with the author, November 2003.
18. Conversation with the author, January 2004.
19. Ibid.

**Chapter 7**

1. Barbara Walters, "Interview with Governor George W. Bush," *NBC 20/20*, July 28, 2000.
2. Bush, *A Charge to Keep*, p. 6.
3. David Barton, "A Praying President"
http://www.christianity.com/partner/Article_Display_Page/0,,PTID320166/CHID6 34376/CIID1690700,00,html
4. President George W. Bush, inaugural speech, January 20, 2001, source www.cnn.com
5. Ibid.
6. David Frum, *The Right Man: The Surprising Presidency of George W. Bush* (New York: Random House, 2003) p. 4.
7. Ibid., p. 18.
8. "Remarks by the president at National Prayer Breakfast," Washington Hilton Hotel, Washington, D.C., February 1, 2001, www.whitehouse.gov
9. Quoted in Martin B. Copehaver, "Formed and Reformed." (The Making of a Postliberal: Two Stories), *The Christian Century*, October 14, 1998.
10. "Remarks by the president at the Radio-Television Correspondents Association 57th Annual Dinner, Washington Hilton Hotel, Washington, D.C., March 29, 2001.
11. John J. Diiulio Jr., "Compassion In Truth and Action—How Sacred and Secular Places Serve Civic Purposes, and What Washington Should—And Should Not—Do to Help," March 7, 2001. Source: www.whitehouse.gov
12. Gary McMullen, "Increased Need, Smaller Resources," *The Ledger*, (Lakeland, Florida) July 12, 2003.
13. Joseph L. Conn, "Historic Battle: Bush administration approves public funds for repair of historic churches, as faith-based initiative attempts 'revolutionary march' through government," Americans United for Separation of Church and State, July 1, 2003.
14. President Bush, "Remarks by the president to the American Jewish Committee," May 3, 2001. Source: www.whitehouse.gov
15. Source: www.whitehouse.gov
16. Rabbi Jonathan Ginsburg, "My Visit with the President," (email distributed by William C. Daroff).
17. Deputy Executive Director, Republican Jewish Coalition October 1, 2003.
18. Israeli citizens. Conversations with the author, Jerusalem, October 2003.
19. Michael Horowitz. Conversation with the author, November 2003.
20. Tony Stothard, *Thirty Days: Tony Blair and the Test of History* (London: HarperCollins, 2003) p. 39.
21. "Remarks by the President and Prime Minister Blair in Joint Press Conference," Camp David, Maryland, February 23, 2001. Source: www.whitehouse.gov
22. Cited in David Frum, *The Right Man: The Surprising Presidency of George W. Bush* (New York: Random House, 2003) p. 88.

## Chapter 8

1. David Frum, *The Right Man: The Surprising Presidency of George W. Bush* (New York: Random House, 2003), p. 91.

2. Frum, op. cit., p. 81.

3. Judy Keen, *USA Today*, May 17, 2001. Source: http://www.USATODAY.com/News/Washington/2001-05-18-Faith.html

4. Britt Hume, "Interview with President George W. Bush, Fox News Television, September 22, 2003.

5. Remarks by the president at National Prayer Breakfast, Washington Hilton Hotel, February 1, 2001. Source: www.whitehouse.gov

6. Remarks by the president at National Hispanic Prayer Breakfast, Capital Hilton, Washington, D.C., May 16, 2002. Source: www.whitehouse.gov

7. Justin Webb, reporting on the British Broadcasting Company.

8. Oswald Chambers, *My Utmost for His Highest* (a book of 365 daily devotional meditations that has been published in many different formats and constantly in print for the past several decades. Chambers was a chaplain in the British army who died in Egypt in 1917. The devotional *My Utmost for His Highest* was compiled after his death from his widow, based on the many messages he had written for the soldiers under his care).

9. Cited by David Barton, "A Praying President" (no date) on website: http://www.Christianity.com/partner/Article_Display_Page/0,, PTID320166/CHID6343776/CIID1690700,00.html

10. Rich Lowry, "George Bush Keeps His Distance," in *The Pittsburgh Post-Gazette*, August 17, 2003.

11. Frum, op. cit., p. 110.

12. Ibid., p. 128.

13. Ibid., pp. 136–137.

14. President's remarks at National Day of Prayer and Remembrance, Washington National Cathedral, Washington, D.C., September 14, 2001. Source: www.white-house.gov

15. Frum, op. cit., pp. 138–139.

16. Ibid., p. 140.

17. Remarks by the president at Islamic Center of Washington, D.C., September 17, 2001. Source: www.whitehouse.gov

18. Khaled Saffurin. Conversation with the author, January 2004.

19. Remarks by the president at Houston Power Center, August 2003. Source: www.whitehouse.gov

20. President's Remarks at National Prayer Breakfast, February 7, 2002. Source: www.whitehouse.gov

21. Frum, op. cit., p. 239.

22. Press Conference of President Bush and Prime Minister Tony Blair, London, November 14, 2003. Source: www.whitehouse.gov

23. William McKenzie, "Words reveal much about Bush—Religious language puts him in duty-obligation camp," *Dallas Morning News,* July 22, 2003.

24. Peggy Noonan, Interview with George W. Bush, *Ladies Home Journal.*

25. Remarks by the president at Royal Banqueting House, Whitehall, London, England, November 2003. Source: www.whitehouse.gov

26. Ibid.

27. Interview of the president by Trevor Kavanagh of *The Sun,* The Oval Office, White House, Washington, D.C., November 14, 2003. Source: www.whitehouse.gov

28. Ibid.

## Chapter 9

1. Peter Berger. Source www.acton.org

2. Alexis de Tocqueville. Cited in Tim Lahaye and S. Nobel, *Mind Siege* (Nashville: Word Publishing, 2000), p. 93.

3. Archille Murat. Citied in Os Guinness and others, *The Great Experiment* (McLean, VA: The Trinity Forum, 2001), p. xvi.

4. Noah Webster. Cited in Michael Novak, *On Two Wings: Humble Faith and Common Sense and the American Founding* (San Francisco: Frontier Books, 2001), p. 37.

5. Ibid.

6. Novak, op. cit., p. 15.

7. Ibid.

8. Ibid.

9. Ibid.

10. Ibid., p.19.

11. Thomas Jefferson. Cited in John McCollister, *So Help Me God: The Faith of America's Presidents* (Louisville, KY: Westminster/John Knox Press, 1991).

12. Novak, op. cit., p. 18.

13. McCollister, op. cit.

14. Novak, op. cit., p. 30.

15. Novak, op. cit., p. 31. (Punctuation has been changed slightly to render the account in direct speech.)

16. McCollister, op.cit., p. 34.

17. Kathy Baker, Project Editor, *The Presidential Prayer Team: Devotional* (Nashville: Thomas Nelson, 2003), p. 35.

18. McCollister, op. cit., p. 21.

19. Source: http://www.patriotist.com/lgarch/20031124.htm

20. Cited in Ann Schraff, *The Faith of the Presidents* (St. Louis, MO: Concordia, 1978), p. 29.

21. McCollister, op. cit., p. 47.

22. Ibid., p. 82.

23. Ibid., p. 87.

24. Ibid., p. 87.

25. Ibid., p. 88

26. Lincoln's words in the Second Inaugural are cited in almost every well-packed reference book of the United States. These were taken from the Internet after a search in www.google.com

27. McCollister, p. 89.

28. Source http://acgray.tripod.com/ontolondon.html

29. Ibid.

30. McCollister, op. cit. p. 123

31. Ibid., p. 127.

32. Ibid., p. 131.

33. Ibid., p. 136.

34. Ibid., p. 153.

35. Ibid., p. 161.

36. Ibid., p. 194.

37. Ibid., p. 200.

38. Presidential Prayer Team, p. 81.

39. White House observer. Conversation with the author, September 2003.

40. Karen Hughes. Conversation with the author, November 2003.

41. Source: http://www.progressive.org/feb03/comm0203.html.

42. Deal Hudson. Conversation with the author, September 2003.

43. Michael W. Smith. Conversation with the author, November 2003.

44. James Robison. Conversation with the author, December 2003.

### A Sermon Given by George W. Bush

1. George W. Bush. A sermon delivered at the Second Baptist Church, Houston, Texas, March 6, 1999. Used by special permission of the White House.

# Index

## Index

### —U/V—
United Methodist Church, 88–89, 91
University of Texas (Austin), 36, 52
Urban Alternative, The, 114
Verhovek, Sam Howe, 127

### —W—
*Walden: Or, Life in the Woods,* 20
Walker, Dorothy, 22. *See also* Bush, Dorothy Walker
Walker, Elsie, 48
Walker, George Herbert "Bert", 22
Wallis, Jim, 145
Walters, Barbara, 135
Washington, George, faith views, 181–83
Washington National Cathedral, 137, 162
Watergate, 54–55, 194
Wead, Doug, 27, 81, 82, 83, 84, 93, 105
Webb, Justin, 158
Webster, Noah, 178
Weizman, Ezer, 122
Welch, Laura, 8, 58. *See also* Bush, Laura
Wen Jiabao, 156
Wesley, John, 89–90

Wesley–Rankin Community Center, 91
Whitefield, George, 181
Wilkerson, Dave, 101
Wilson, Woodrow, 191–92
Windsor Village United Methodist Church (Houston), 54, 116
Winthrop, John, 196
Witherspoon, John, 179–80, 188
Wolfman, Cathryn, 43–44
World Trade Center, 163–64. *See also* September 11, 2001

### —X/Y/Z—
Xueqing, Kan, 57
Yale College, 17. *See also* Yale University
Yale University
  George H.W., 29
  George W., 36, 40–49
  Prescott Bush, 21.
  *See also* Skull and Bones (Yale)
Yarborough, Ralph, 42
Young, Ed, ix, 120, 208
Zapata Petroleum Corporation, 33–34

237